Poor Relief in Ireland, 1851–1914

Poor Relief in Ireland, 1851–1914

Mel Cousins

PETER LANG
Oxford • Bern • Berlin • Bruxelles • Frankfurt am Main • New York • Wien

Bibliographic information published by Die Deutsche Nationalbibliothek
Die Deutsche Nationalbibliothek lists this publication in the Deutsche Nationalbibliografie; detailed bibliographic data is available on the Internet at http://dnb.d-nb.de.

A catalogue record for this book is available from the British Library.

Library of Congress Cataloging-in-Publication Data:

Cousins, Mel.
Poor relief in Ireland, 1851-1914 / Mel Cousins.
p. cm.
Includes bibliographical references and index.
ISBN 978-3-0343-0737-6 (alk. paper)
1. Public welfare--Ireland--History--19th century. 2. Public welfare--Ireland--History--20th century. 3. Poor laws--Ireland--History--19th century. 4. Poor laws--Ireland--History--20th century. 5. Poor--Government policy--Ireland--History. 6. Poverty--Government policy--Ireland--History. I. Title.
HV250.3.C69 2011
362.5'560941509034--dc23
2011022255

Cover image: *Inside Portumna Workhouse* © Paul Oakes

ISBN 978-3-0343-0737-6

Hochfeldstrasse 32, CH-3012 Bern, Switzerland
info@peterlang.com, www.peterlang.com, www.peterlang.net

Printed in Germany

To my father and my mother

Contents

Acknowledgements

I would like to acknowledge the assistance of a large number of people in the completion of this book. First, I must thank Professor John Stewart, who supervised the thesis on which this book is based, for his courteous and comprehensive advice and guidance over the period of this study. His knowledge of poor law (and related issues) was only matched by his ability tactfully to deflect my wilder inclinations to go off on tangents. I would also like particularly to thank Inga Brandes, originally of the University of Trier and now of FernUniversität in Hagen. Inga was a constant and generous source of information (based on her own extensive studies of the Irish poor law) and critical comment over my period of study. During my period at Oxford Brookes University, Professor Steve King (now of the University of Leicester), Dr Virginia Crossman and Dr Elizabeth Hurren provided much assistance and support. I would also wish to thank Dr Ina Scherder (originally of Trier, now at Oxford Brookes) who generously provided information on her own research on the Galway poor law union and Anna Schüle of Trier who provided me with a copy of her Masters dissertation on outdoor relief in Milford. Finally I would like to acknowledge the very helpful comments of Dr Caitriona MacDonald and Dr Larry Geary.

The research has drawn on a wide range of archival and library research in both the United Kingdom and Ireland and I would like to thank all the staff involved (too numerous to name here) for their assistance and advice. I would, in particular, like to thank the many county archivists who facilitated my searches in the (underutilised) local poor law archives.

List of Illustrations

Tables

Figures

Maps

Introduction

This book examines poor relief in Ireland from the immediate aftermath of the Great Famine (about 1851) to the onset of the Great War (1914), by which time the poor law had been subverted by a range of other policy measures such as the old age pension and national insurance. The aims of the study are:

i) to establish the empirical basis of the provision of poor relief in the period, analysing over time the provision of indoor and outdoor relief and expenditure levels;
ii) to chart regional variations in the provision of poor relief and examine the reasons for those variations;
iii) to examine particular issues which highlight political and social class struggles in relation to the provision of poor relief; and
iv) to consider the broader role of the poor law and the boards of guardians in local politics and community.

Why study the poor law?

There are, for the purposes of this study, two basic reasons why the poor law was important. First, because of the scope and importance of the services which were provided. Starting initially in 1838 it provided the main form of poor relief in nineteenth-century Ireland – a country which was, in overall terms, considerably 'poorer' than England with national income per capita only about 40 per cent of the United Kingdom level.[1] This role

1 See generally C. Ó Gráda, *Ireland: A New Economic History*, Oxford University Press, Oxford, 1994; K.A. Kennedy, 'Irish National Accounts for the Nineteenth and Twentieth Century', ESRI memorandum series 197, Dublin, 1994.

was subsequently expanded by the addition of a range of other responsibilities including dispensary medical care,[2] public health, labourers' cottages,[3] and others. The focus of this study is, however, primarily on the poor relief aspects of the poor law.

A second reason to study the poor law is because of its importance – particularly outside large cities – as a form of local democracy and for its role in the creation and politicisation (or *politisation*) of local communities.[4] I use the term 'politicisation' in the sense that the politicisation of a group or a society is the socio-historic action by which political issues penetrate the daily lives of the members of that group or society. In early nineteenth century Ireland, the main form of local government was the elite, undemocratic and inefficient grand jury.[5] The poor law boards of guardians, which were – at least partially – democratically elected, thus played a very important role in the later nineteenth century not only for their formal role but as an expression of local democracy and community. Until local government reform in 1898, the boards were, in many areas,[6] the only form of local democracy and, even where other forms existed, the boards often appear to have been considered the most important. In addition to their role in the administration of the poor law, the boards had an important symbolic function in local communities (in terms of their status in the community) and contributed in an important way to their politicisation. Clearly the administrative and symbolic – but no less real – roles of the boards are interrelated.

2 R.D. Cassell, *Medical Charities, Medical Politics: The Irish Dispensary System and the Poor Law, 1836–72*, Royal Historical Society, Woodbridge, 1997.

3 From the introduction of the relevant legislation in 1883 until these responsibilities were taken over by the rural district councils in 1899.

4 There is an extensive literature on the concept of politicisation of local communities in Continental Europe. See *La Politisation des Campagnes au XIXe Siecle*, École Française de Rome Editions, Rome, 2000. See the interesting discussion of the concept in L. Le Gall, 'Des Processus de Politisation dans les Campagnes Françaises (1830–1914): Esquisse pour un État des Lieux', in J.-C. Caron, F. Chauvaud (eds), *Les Campagnes dans les Sociétés Européennes (1830–1930)*, PUR, Reims, 2005.

5 See V. Crossman, *Local Government in Nineteenth-Century Ireland*, IIS, Belfast, 1994.

6 Outside the relatively small number of towns with other local government institutions (e.g. town commissioners). See Crossman, *Local Government*.

Historiography and the poor law in post-Famine Ireland

There is a limited historiography on the poor law in post-Famine Ireland. Gray's recent study looks in detail at the establishment of the poor law in 1838 but concludes just before the Famine.[7] Nicholls' contemporary account, by one of the 'founders' of the Irish poor law, remains an essential source for the earlier period but ends as this study begins.[8] Burke provides an account which is heavily reliant on parliamentary papers in the period to 1872.[9] Crossman's recent pamphlet is the only treatment of the poor law over its full life but is of necessity only an outline.[10]

There are only two serious monographs which focus specifically on the poor law in this period.[11] The first is Feingold's excellent study of the 'social transformation of power' in Ireland as Nationalist tenants took over control of the poor law boards of guardians from the landlords in the 1870s and 1880s. Feingold's detailed findings are discussed in more detail below

7 P. Gray, *The Making of the Irish Poor Law, 1815–1843*, Manchester University Press, Manchester, 2009.

8 G. Nicholls, *A History of the Irish Poor Law*, Murray, London, 1856.

9 H. Burke, *The People and the Poor Law in Nineteenth Century Ireland*, WEB, Dublin, 1987. This book – despite its title – purports to focus on the South Dublin union but, in fact, includes material from a wide geographical range.

10 V. Crossman, *The Poor Law in Ireland 1838–1948*, IESHS, Dundalk, 2005. There have been a considerable number of local studies of aspects of the poor law, though most focus on the Famine period. O'Mahony's study of the Cork union is a recent example of a study which extends from the formation of the union to the late nineteenth century focussing largely of the experience of life within the Cork workhouse: C. O'Mahony, *Cork's Poor Law Palace: Workhouse Life 1838–1890*, Rosmathún Press, Cork, 2005. There are a number of recent and ongoing theses being completed by scholars at the University of Trier. Only limited material is yet available in English: see, for example, I. Scherder, 'Galway workhouses in the nineteenth and twentieth centuries: function and strategy,' and I. Brandes, '"Odious, degrading and foreign" institutions? Analysing Irish workhouses in the nineteenth and twentieth centuries', both in A. Gestrich, S. King and L. Raphael (eds), *Being Poor in Modern Europe: Historical Perspectives 1800–1940*, Peter Lang, Bern, 2006, 181–98 and 199–228 respectively.

11 See also Cassell, *Medical Charities* which focuses on the dispensary, which formed an important part of the poor law but falls outside the scope of this study.

and this study develops on his work by looking in more detail at what this 'take over' of power involved and what the new guardians did with the functions they had assumed.

Crossman's recent book examines aspects of the operation of the poor law in the 1880s and 1890s looking in particular at the local administration of the poor law and the relationship between local boards and the central administration.[12] She discusses several interesting episodes in the period including the role which a small number of boards played in supporting (or attempting to support) evicted tenants during the 1880s. Overall, however, the book lacks a clear focus and precise research questions. Perhaps as a result, her conclusions are, to a certain extent, somewhat unsupported by evidence and/or overstated. Crossman concludes, although heavily weighed down with qualifiers, that 'granting relief to evicted tenants enabled poor law guardians to make a substantive contribution to the land campaign by shifting the balance of power in land disputes away from landlords and towards tenants'.[13] However, Crossman arguably understates the extent to which boards which pursued this approach were exceptional and failed to achieve their objectives. This issue is pursued in more detail in chapters 6 and 7. In a similar vein she states that the increasing influence of elected poor law guardians 'encouraged a more populist approach to poor law

12 V. Crossman, *Politics, Pauperism and Power in Late Nineteenth-Century Ireland*, Manchester University Press, Manchester, 2006. See also V. Crossman, 'The New Ross Workhouse Riot', *Past and Present*, (2003), 135–58; '"With the experience of 1846 and 1847 before them": The Politics of Emergency Relief 1879–84', in P. Gray (ed.), *Victoria's Ireland: Irishness and Britishness, 1837–1901*, Four Courts Press, Dublin, 2004, 167–82; 'The Charm of Allowing People to Manage Their Own Affairs: Political Perspectives on Emergency Relief in Late Nineteenth-Century Ireland', in D.G. Boyce and A. O'Day (eds), *Ireland in Transition 1867–1921*, Routledge, London, 2004, 193–208; 'The humanization of the Irish Poor Laws: Reassessing developments in social welfare in post-Famine Ireland', in A. Gestrich, S. King and L. Raphael (eds), *Being Poor in Modern Europe: Historical Perspectives 1800–1940* Peter Lang, Bern, 2006, 229–50; 'Welfare and Nationality: The poor laws in nineteenth-century Ireland', in S. King and J.W.S. Stewart (eds), *Welfare Peripheries: The Development of Welfare States in Nineteenth and Twentieth Century Europe*, Peter Lang, Bern, 2007, 67–96; and 'Cribbed, Contained and Confined? The Care of Children under the Irish Poor Law', *Eire-Ireland*, 44, 1 & 2 (2009), 37–61.

13 *Politics, Pauperism and Power in Late Nineteenth-Century Ireland*, 99.

administration, most evident in the provision of labourers cottages and outdoor relief'.[14] As Crossman does not provide data as to patterns of poor relief one cannot say whether tenant controlled boards were more likely to provide outdoor relief than landlord controlled boards. Again this study draws on statistical data to examine patterns of poor relief and to explain those patterns.[15]

Aims of the book

Firstly, given the absence of work on poor relief to date, this book establishes the empirical basis of the provision of poor relief in the period, analysing over time the level of indoor and outdoor relief and expenditure levels. It draws on both administrative and Census (published and manuscript) data to look at who benefited from the poor law and has matched poor law administrative data for a number of poor law unions with Census manuscripts to identify the type of persons in receipt of outdoor relief and their family structure.

Secondly, given the extent to which poor law policies were determined at a local level and drawing on recent historiography,[16] the book looks at regional variations in the provision of poor relief and examines the reasons for those variations.

14 Ibid., 217.

15 While Crossman does show a difference in policy between Nationalist and Conservative boards in relation to building labourers' cottages, the bulk of labourers' cottages were built where the bulk of labourers lived and the author does not attempt to examine whether the limited number of houses built in Ulster was due to Conservative politics or the more limited number of labourers (as a percentage of the population) in most northern unions.

16 See, in particular, P. Lindert, 'Poor Relief before the Welfare State: Britain versus the Continent, 1780–1880', *European Review of Economic History*, 1998, 101–40 and S.A. King, *Poverty and Welfare in England 1700–1850: A Regional Perspective*, Manchester University Press, Manchester, 2000.

Thirdly, the book examines particular issues which highlight political and social class struggles as to the provision of poor relief including: opposition to union rating in the 1860s; the causes for the rise in outdoor relief from the 1860s onwards; and the extent to which, from the 1880s, Nationalist controlled boards actually adopted different policies to landlord controlled boards.

This aspect of the book is informed by Feingold's study of the nationalisation of the poor law boards of guardians in the period 1872–86.[17] The boards consisted of a mix of elected and ex-officio guardians. Up to the late 1870s, the vast majority of officerships were held by landlords (99 per cent of chairmen were landlords). During the Land War this dominance was challenged and tenant officers increased markedly. Feingold analyses the factors relating to tenant control, distinguishing between 'radical' (i.e. tenant controlled) and 'conservative' (landlord controlled) counties. Radical counties tended to be more Catholic. A finer grained breakdown indicates that larger farmers tended to be more radical while areas dominated by small farms led neither to landlord nor tenant control. A combination of religion and farm size appears to provide a convincing prediction of political composition. Feingold argues that large tenant farmers became the rural social and political elite with shopkeepers filing this role where the large farmer class was weaker. He argues that the change in control had practical effects on the administration of the poor law with a rise in outdoor relief in Munster and Connacht coinciding with a rise in tenant control. This study re-examines these findings and, in particular, questions whether a link can be seen between the take-over of the boards and relief policies.

Fourthly, and related to the above, the book looks at the broader role of the boards in local politics and community. Feingold's work highlighted the role which the struggle for control of the boards played in preparing Nationalists for local government after 1898,[18] but perhaps underempha-

17 W. Feingold, *The Revolt of the Tenantry: the Transformation of Local Government in Ireland 1872–1886*, Northwestern University Press, Boston, 1984.

18 Feingold's thesis is again confirmed in research for this study which shows the extent to which board officeholders went on to become local authority members post 1898 (see chapter 9).

sised the extent to which local boards were already playing an important role in local government.[19] This study discusses this broader symbolic role in some detail.

Structure of the book

In chapter 1, an overview is provided of developments in the Irish poor law from 1851 to 1914, looking in particular at the available statistics on the provision of relief and tracing developments as to how much relief was provided and who was relieved in the period. Chapter 2 examines regional variations in poor relief, identifying three main groupings: northern unions (consisting of most Ulster unions) which were of average wealth but provided rather low relief and generally very little outdoor relief; peripheral western unions (all along the western coastline) which were very poor and where the level of relief provided was constrained by a lack of resources; and southern unions, controlled from the 1880s by Nationalist guardians, which provided higher levels of relief but which had a high level of variations in terms of wealth and relief. Chapter 3 examines the role which the poor law played in supporting households and families.

This is followed by a series of chapters which examine particular issues which highlight political and social class struggles in relation to the provision of poor relief. Chapter 4 looks at the post-Famine decades and, in particular, the opposition to union rating – showing how, in this period, the landlords retained an effective control over poor law policies despite nascent politicisation. Chapter 5 examines the Land War and local politics and considers the impact which the Land War had on the administration of poor relief. Chapter 6 looks at the causes for the rise in outdoor relief from the 1860s onwards and, in particular, during the Land War period.

19 M. Cousins, 'Poor law politics and elections in post-Famine Ireland', *History Studies*, 6, (2005) 34–47, and see Chapter 9.

Chapter 7 looks in detail at the policies adopted by unions during the plan of campaign in the late 1880s. Chapter 8 then looks at the poor law in the period of late-Victorian Conservative hegemony – discussing in particular the impact of the democratisation of local government in 1898 on the poor law. Chapter 9 examines the broader role of the boards in local politics and community. Chapter 10 provides a brief epilogue as to the 'death' of the poor law with the introduction of the range of new Liberal welfare reforms in the period from 1908–11. Finally, a closing chapter will examine the conclusions to be drawn from this study.

CHAPTER 1

Poor Relief in Ireland, 1851–1914

This chapter outlines trends in poor relief over the period, 1851 to 1914 in the context of economic and demographic change in Ireland. The first part of the chapter looks at the historiography concerning the relationship between poor relief and economic and demographic change. In the second part of the chapter, key changes in the socio-economic context are outlined, before examining trends in poor law numbers over the period and looking at the composition of those relieved (drawing on both administrative and Census data).[1] Finally, these trends are examined in their socio-economic context.

Historiography

The question as to the relationship between developments in the poor law and broader economic and demographic trends has been examined in the literature on the development of the British and European poor laws.[2] Firstly, studies have looked at the macro relationship between the poor law and economic and political structures. For example, Solar has argued that 'poor relief played an integral, and to a degree autonomous, part in

1 The family and household status of recipients of poor relief is examined in chapter 3.

2 In general, most studies focus on particular countries (or regions) in particular periods. Obviously, their findings are specific to the time and place and do not necessarily imply that the same outcome would occur in a different time or place. Thus the discussion here focuses on studies which raise suggestive issues as to the Irish case which will be discussed later in this study.

England's economic development'.[3] However, Solar's interesting article is largely based on assertions as to what the impact of poor relief might have been expected to be rather than any quantitative examination of the relationship between poor relief and economic development.[4] One of the more detailed comparative studies of the causes of different levels and structures of poor relief has been carried out by Lindert.[5] He found that, in general, richer countries transferred a higher share of national income to the poor. However, he identified a very considerable fall in expenditure on the poor law as a percentage of national income after 1834 in England. He suggests that the reason for this fall may be that the newly enfranchised classes had stronger reasons to oppose tax-based relief than the elites who controlled Parliament at the start of the century.

Secondly, there are a range of studies which look at the relationship between the poor law and economic and demographic trends. Boyer, for example, examined the relationship between poor law expenditure and the agricultural labour market in southern England.[6] He found that politically dominant farmers made use of the system of poor relief to reduce their wage bill to agricultural labourers. Boyer suggests that, overall, the poor law at worst had little effect on the economy and at best stimulated growth by increasing the profit rates of labour-hiring farmers or the rental income

3 P. Solar, 'Poor Relief and English Economic Development before the Industrial Revolution', *Economic History Review*, xlviii, (1995) 1, 1–22; Id., 'Poor relief and English Economic Development: a renewed Plea for Comparative History', *Economic History Review*, l, (1997) 2, 369–74.

4 King's criticism of Solar focuses largely on what he sees as 'an inadequate appreciation of the diversity and complexity of poor law practice in England': S.A. King, 'Poor Relief and English Economic Development Reappraised', *Economic History Review*, l, (1997) 2, 360–8.

5 P. Lindert, 'Poor Relief before the Welfare State: Britain versus the Continent, 1780–1880', *European Review of Economic History*, 1998, 101–40.

6 G.R. Boyer, 'The Old Poor Law and the Agricultural Labor Market in Southern England: an Empirical Analysis', *Journal of Economic History*, xlvi, (1986) 1, 113–36. See also G.R. Boyer, *An Economic History of the English Poor Law, 1750–1850,* Cambridge University Press, 1990; and L. Kiesling, 'Institutional Choice Matters: The Poor Law and Implicit Labor Contracts in Victorian Lancashire', *Explorations in Economic History, 33, 1,* (1996) 65–85.

of landlords.[7] Clark and Page examined the effect of reductions in poor relief payments after the introduction of the new English poor law on land rents in a large set of rural parishes.[8] They argue that – contrary to the views of both the 1832 Poor Law Commission and Boyer – the pre-1834 poor law mainly involved a transfer of income to the indigent with little wider repercussions on labour performance, investment or labour mobility. They suggest that the beneficiaries from the reform were largely rural landowners in the south-east of England.

A number of studies have examined whether poor relief has had an impact on demographic trends. For example, Mokyr has suggested that the absence of a poor law in Ireland before 1838 may have contributed to marital fertility. He suggests that as Irish people did not have recourse to outdoor relief they may instead have decided to have children to serve as 'insurance policies and pensions' thereby increasing fertility levels.[9] Malthus, of course, suggested that the effect lay in the opposite direction, arguing that the payment of child allowances under the poor law increased the birth rate. A number of studies have examined whether poor relief payments in England had an impact on birth rates while King has recently examined the relationship between poor relief and local mortality rates.[10] However, none of these issues have been examined in any detail in an Irish context. The relationship between the poor relief and family/household structures is discussed in more detail in chapter 3.

7 G.R. Boyer, 'The Poor Law, Migration, and Economic Growth', *Journal of Economic History*, 46, 2, (1986), 419–30.

8 G. Clark and M. Page, 'Is There Profit in Reforming the Poor? The English Poor Law 1830–1842', Department of Economics, UC-Davis, 2000.

9 J. Mokyr, *Why Ireland Starved: a Quantitative and Analytical History of the Irish Economy, 1800–1850*, Harper Collins, London, 1985.

10 On birth rates see G.R. Boyer, 'Malthus was right after all: Poor Relief and Birth Rates in South-Eastern England', *Journal of Political Economy*, 97 (1989), 93–114; J.P. Huzel, 'Malthus, the Poor Law, and Population in Early Nineteenth-Century England', *Economic History Review*, xxii (1969) 430–52; J.P. Huzel, 'The Demographic Impact of the Old Poor Law: More Reflexions on Malthus', *Economic History Review*, xxxiii (1980) 367–81. On mortality see S.A. King, 'Pauvreté et Assistance. La Politique Locale de la Mortalité dans l'Angleterre des XVIIIe et XIXe Siècles', *Annales*, 61(1), (2006), 31–62.

Economic and social trends

In order to understand the operations of the poor law one needs to place these in their broader socio-economic context. Ireland before the Famine was a relatively populous country with a total population of over 8 million people or 30 per cent of the total United Kingdom population. However, per capita income was low in comparative terms so that national income per capita was only about 40 per cent of the United Kingdom level.[11] Unfortunately there is no consistent series of estimated GDP for nineteenth-century Ireland. In general, the estimates which have been made indicate an overall rise in GDP from about £80–100 million per annum just before the Famine to about £135–150 million just before the First World War. One of the most recent estimates by O'Rourke is set out below.[12] The basic picture in post-Famine Ireland was of a dramatic fall in the population combined with an increase in gross domestic product. At an individual level this led to some catch-up, with Ireland's per capita GDP rising from perhaps 56 per cent of the United Kingdom total in 1861 to 66 per cent by 1911.[13] However, this still saw a fall in Ireland's total GDP from about 11 per cent of the United Kingdom total in 1861 to only 6 per cent in 1911. These general trends do not, of course, take account of specific economic crises such as those in 1859–63 and again in the late 1870s and early 1880s.

11 K.A. Kennedy, 'Irish National Accounts for the Nineteenth and Twentieth Century' ESRI memorandum series 197, Dublin, 1994.

12 K.H. O'Rourke, 'Monetary Data and Proxy GDP Estimates: Ireland 1840–1921,' *Irish Economic and Social History* 25 (1998), 22–51.

13 F. Geary and T. Stark, 'Examining Ireland's Post-Famine Economic Performance: the Distribution of Gross Domestic Product between the Countries of the United Kingdom, 1861–1911' ESRI working paper 71, Dublin 1996.

	Per capita (£)	Total (£M)
1864	12.50	72.5
1870s	20	108
1914	32.5	143

Table 1.1 Irish GDP, 1864–1914
Source: K.H. O'Rourke, 'Monetary Data and Proxy GDP Estimates: Ireland 1840–1921,' *Irish Economic and Social History* 25 (1998), 22–51.

There is an absence of reliable wage figures for the period. Most of the figures which are available are once-off or applied to very limited occupations. The data for agricultural labourers are perhaps the most relevant as these constitute a large number of workers and as many recipients of poor relief were former agricultural or general labourers. Fitzpatrick states that wages for agricultural labourers rose from 84*d.* per week in 1860 to 113*d.* in 1893 and 129*d.* by 1911, although the extent to which these are fully comparable over time is unclear.[14] Turner provides an alternative estimate based of a small number of sample farms indicating that wages rose (on a sample of 10 farms) from 5.9*s.* per week in 1850–5 to 10.4*s.* by 1896–1903 or (on a sample of 22 farms) from 7.6*s.* in 1866–75 to 9.5*s.* by 1896–1903.[15] As can be seen, although all sources agreed that wages rose over the period there are some differences between the figures. However, Turner's sample of 10 farms indicates an increase of about 60 per cent between 1856 and 1903 while Fitzpatrick's figures show a similar increase of about 50 per cent in the period from 1860 to 1911. These figures are for the actual wages paid and the question arises as to trends in real wages over the period. O'Rourke and Williamson report estimates that real agricultural wages rose, in terms of an index, from about 60 in 1850 to 110 by 1910

14 D. Fitzpatrick, 'The Disappearance of the Irish Agricultural Labourer, 1841–1912,' *Irish Economic and Social History* 7 (1980), 66–92.

15 M. Turner, *After the Famine: Irish Agriculture 1850–1914*, Cambridge University Press, Cambridge, 1996.

(1900 = 100).[16] O'Rourke and Williamson also estimate that Irish urban wages increased from about 60 per cent of the United Kingdom level in 1850 to 90 per cent by 1910.[17] However, comparing the wages data with Geary and Stark's estimates of GDP per capita, agricultural wages would appear to have fallen compared to per capita GDP (from about 150 per cent in 1860 to 90 per cent in 1914).

Of course, in looking at wage rates account must be taken of the cost-of-living. In a recent study, Kennedy has developed estimates for the cost of living from the late seventeenth century.[18] Over the period from the 1850s to 1913, the cost of living first increased considerably to the mid-1870s (from about 75–90 (urban-rural) in 1850 to about 130–5 in 1873) before falling to about 80 in the late 1890s (1890–1900=100). The index then rose again to about 110 in 1913, increasing dramatically to over 250 at the end of the First World War.

Despite the significant population change, Ireland remained a predominantly agricultural country and there was relatively little change in the overall employment structure over the period in question.[19] Agricultural employment constituted almost half the total workforce both in 1861 and 1911 (dramatically higher than the English case) while industrial employment fell back slightly over the period from 26 per cent in 1861 to 22 per cent in 1911. Conversely, service employment rose in Ireland from 24 per cent to 31 per cent by 1911. In contrast in England, industrial employment was the largest category making up about half the total workforce and agricultural employment fell from 18 per cent in 1861 to only 7 per cent by 1911. However, within these overall sectors, there were considerable declines in particular

16 K.H. O'Rourke and J.G. Williamson, *Globalization and History: the Evolution of a Nineteenth-Century Atlantic Economy*, MIT Press, Boston, 1999, 149.

17 Ibid.

18 L. Kennedy, 'The Cost of Living in Ireland, 1698–1998' in D. Dickson and C. Ó Gráda, (eds), *Refiguring Ireland: Essays in Honour of L.M. Cullen*, Lilliput Press, Dublin, 2003, 249–76.

19 F. Geary and T. Stark, 'Examining Ireland's Post-Famine Economic Performance: the Distribution of Gross Domestic Product between the Countries of the United Kingdom, 1861–1911' ESRI working paper 71, Dublin, 1996, table 2.

employments in Ireland such as, for example, agricultural labourers.[20] There were also important regional variations with many parts of Ulster being considerably more industrialised than the southern provinces. In 1871, for example, Armagh, Antrim and Down were three of the four counties with the highest level of male employment in manufacturing. Similarly, six of the Ulster counties had at least 40 per cent of occupied women employed in manufacturing – a level matched by no southern county but comparable with developments in certain parts of Britain.[21]

The large agricultural sector obviously includes a range of different social classes from the small number of very large landlords to landless agricultural labourers. It is clear that there was a reallocation of land holdings over the period in question, with small farms (1–5 acres) becoming steadily less common and larger farms more common.[22] However, this change was not very dramatic over the period. Legislation in 1870 and 1882 increased tenants' rights although the practical implications of this in terms of land tenure remained somewhat unclear.[23] From the mid-1880s on tenants gradually began to purchase their holdings and this increased dramatically after the 1903 Wyndham Land Act. There is a lack of clarity as to the social class implications of changes in the agricultural sector over this period. Clark has argued that in the pre-Famine period there was relatively little distinction between the large group of small farmers and agricultural labourers – both whose interests tended to be opposed to those of larger farmers.[24] However, he argues that after the Famine labourers were proletarianised, i.e. reduced to pure wage labour, with the smaller land holding farmers becoming more generally aligned with larger farmers. Fitzpatrick, however, has suggested that, to the contrary, Irish labourers

20 D. Fitzpatrick, 'The Disappearance of the Irish Agricultural Labourer, 1841–1912'.

21 L. Kennedy, P.S. Ell, E.M. Crawford and L.A. Clarkson, *Mapping the Great Irish Famine*, Four Courts, Dublin, 1999, 156–7.

22 T. Guinnane, *The Vanishing Irish: Households, Migration and the Rural Economy in Ireland, 1850–1914*, Princeton University Press, New Jersey, 1997, 42–3.

23 See generally, P. Bull, *Land, Politics and Nationalism: a Study of the Irish Land Question*, Gill and Macmillan, Dublin, 1996.

24 S. Clark, *Social Origins of the Irish Land War*, Princeton University Press, New Jersey, 1979.

as a class became less rather than more distinct from Irish farmers in the post-Famine period.[25] While the issue cannot be addressed in detail here, I would tend to agree with Clark's view. Fitzpatrick, largely for data reasons, counts together non-landholding agricultural labourers and the 'assisting relatives' of farmers, including persons who would subsequently inherit a farm. While this is valid in terms of his main objective which is to measure the size of the non-farmer agricultural labour force, it would seem to be mistaken from a social class perspective to conflate these two groups. While, at the margins, it might be difficult to distinguish between a landless labourer and a farmer with a very small holding, this does not affect the point of principle that the class positions are distinct.

Demographic trends

The key issue in terms of demography in the period was the very considerable fall in the population, from 8.2 million in 1841 to 4.4 million by 1911. Emigration continued throughout the period though falling from a post-Famine peak of 152,100 in 1851 to (still very significant) 30,600 by 1911.[26] While the main fall in the population occurred during and immediately after the Famine period, population continued to decline over the whole period. This was driven primarily by emigration. In total, in the period from 1851 official statistics indicate that over 4 million people emigrated from Ireland. Econometric studies have suggested that the level of emigration can largely be explained by the difference between the wages in Ireland and the destination countries. Hatton and Williamson have argued that most of the fall in the Irish emigration rate after the Famine can be explained by the declining wage

25 D. Fitzpatrick, 'Disappearance'. See also the discussion in K.T. Hoppen, *Elections, Politics and Society in Ireland, 1832–1885*, Clarendon, Oxford, 1984 at 102–5; and A.W. Orridge, 'Who Supported the Land War?: An Aggregate-Data Analysis of Irish Agrarian Discontent, 1879–1882', *Economic and Social Review*, 12 (1981) 203–33.

26 W.E. Vaughan and A.J. Fitzpatrick, *Irish Historical Statistics: Population*, Royal Irish Academy, Dublin, 1978, tables 3 and 54.

gap between home and abroad and other measures of relative labour market performance including living standards and poverty indicators.[27] Ó Gráda has argued that emigration was highest in areas of low wages and poor housing conditions.[28] The poor law did, of course, provide some level of support to emigration but this was very minor in the overall scheme of things.[29]

Guinnane shows the extent of regional population change.[30] For the period from 1851 up to 1881, population loss is highest in a band of counties running from the south-west of Ireland (Limerick and Clare) over to the southeast and up through the midlands to Co Meath. This is also more or less the area of the highest level of poor relief in the period. For the period from 1881 up to 1911, a different pattern is apparent with population loss being highest generally in the midlands and west. In contrast, the two main cities (Dublin and Belfast) were the only areas of population gain in the period 1851–1911. In addition to more or less permanent emigration, there was also a high level of seasonal emigration particularly from western counties. Although such migration was concentrated in a small number of generally poor and generally low outdoor relief unions, no consistent relationship between poor relief and migration can be identified.

The population loss in rural areas increased the level of urbanisation. Compared to Ireland's closest neighbour Great Britain, Ireland had a relatively low level of urbanisation in the nineteenth century.[31] Nonetheless the six largest cities made up about one-quarter of the total population and Ireland's level of urbanisation was similar to that of France or Belgium and higher than in countries such as the Nordic countries, Austria-Hungary and Spain.[32] The most rapid growth was in Belfast which trebled in size between 1851 and 1901.

27 T.J. Hatton and J.G. Williamson, 'After the Famine: emigration from Ireland 1850–1913', *Journal of Economic History*, 53 (1993), 575–600.

28 C. Ó Gráda, *Ireland: a New Economic History*, 233.

29 See G. Moran, *Sending out Ireland's Poor: Assisted Emigration to North America in the Nineteenth Century*, Four Courts, Dublin, 2004.

30 T. Guinnane, *The Vanishing Irish: Households, Migration and the Rural Economy in Ireland, 1850–1914*, Princeton University Press, New Jersey, 1997, 90–1.

31 T. Guinnane, *Vanishing Irish*, 121–2.

32 S. Halperin, *War and Social Change in Modern Europe*, Cambridge University Press, 2004, table 3.8.

In terms of household structures, very little information is available for the nineteenth century. The published Census did not report details of household structures and manuscript census returns have generally not survived for the nineteenth century. There is little indication that household size fell considerably over the period.[33] While households became somewhat smaller the main impact of the falling population was a significant fall in the *number* of households. There was a considerable decline in marriage in the period.[34] The percentage of people never married (at age 45–54) rose from 25 per cent in 1851 to a staggering 47 per cent by 1911. It has been argued that there may be a relationship between relief for the aged poor and non-marriage in that one of the reasons for marriage was, in effect, provision of insurance for old age. In so far as particular unions provided – or failed to provide – adequate relief for old age, this might have some impact on marriage trends. These issues are discussed in more detail in chapter 3.

Trends in poor relief

Firstly, the daily numbers on poor relief per 100 of the population are outlined in comparison to those in England and Wales. As can be seen there was relatively little variation in the numbers on indoor relief as a percentage of the population over the period. In contrast, there was a significant rise in the proportion of the population on outdoor relief up to the mid-1880s and these numbers stabilised thereafter. In comparison, the numbers on indoor relief in England and Wales were always somewhat lower. However, outdoor relief was originally considerably higher in England and Wales than in Ireland and it is only towards the end of the period, following the

33 Guinnane, *Vanishing Irish*, 162.

34 Guinnane, *Vanishing Irish*, chapter 7.

English 'crusade against outdoor relief',[35] that a convergence towards the Irish level can be seen. Lindert indicates that Continental countries were generally more likely to rely on outdoor relief than England which means that the Irish system was, in comparative terms, particularly reliant on indoor relief for most of its history.[36]

	Ireland		England and Wales	
	Indoor relief	Outdoor relief	Indoor relief	Outdoor relief
1861	0.78	0.06	0.54	3.56
1871	0.86	0.40	0.62	3.75
1881	1.04	1.18	0.63	2.18
1891	0.89	1.33	0.57	1.79
1901	0.93	1.30	0.58	1.52

Table 1.2 Daily numbers on poor relief in Ireland and England and Wales (per 100 population), 1861–1901
Source: T. Guinnane, 'The Poor Law and Pensions in Ireland', *Journal of Interdisciplinary History* xxiv (1993), 271–91.

Figure 1.1 shows trends in relation to the average daily *numbers* on poor relief over the period in question.[37] The general trend was for a slight decline in the numbers in receipt of indoor relief. However, having regard to the significant decline in the population over the period which fell from 5.8 million in 1861 to 4.4 million in 1911, this indicates a slight rise in the number of people in receipt of indoor relief per head of population. In contrast, there is a considerable increase in the number of people on outdoor relief in the period up to the 1880s and this declines somewhat thereafter. Again,

35 See E. Hurren, *Protesting about Pauperism: Poverty, Politics and Poor Relief in Late-Victorian England, 1870–1900*, Royal Historical Society, Woodbridge, 2007.
36 P. Lindert, 'Poor Relief before the Welfare State', op cit., at 120 and table 3.
37 In general, data are given in this section for the Census years. However, the data concludes in 1908 to avoid the impact of the Old Age Pensions Act introduced in that year.

given the change in the overall population this translates into a rise in the proportion of the population on outdoor relief up to the 1880s and a stabilisation thereafter. Important increases occurred during, for example, the agricultural depression of 1859–64 and – as can be seen in figure 1.1 – in the Land War period of the 1880s.

Figure 1.1 Numbers in receipt of indoor and outdoor relief, 1861–1908
Source: Database of poor law statistics.[38]

The composition of persons in receipt of indoor relief changed considerably over that period and the age and gender breakdown of the workhouse inmates changed over time. In 1859, when the lowest numbers of people were in receipt of indoor relief, 30 per cent of those in the workhouses were children, 43 per cent adult women and only 27 per cent adult men.[39] The

38 For the purposes of this research, the author compiled a database of poor-law-related statistics drawing on the annual reports of the Poor Law Commission and Local Government Board and on special returns for the 1906 Viceregal Commision and 1909 Royal Commision on the poor laws (see Appendix 2).

39 Twelfth annual report of the Commissioners for Administering the Laws for Relief of the Poor in Ireland, HC 1859 Session 2 [2546] xi, 317.

proportion of children in the workhouse population fell steadily over time to about 13 per cent by 1905.[40] Interestingly, however, the proportion of men and women in the workhouse also changed. The proportion of men rose significantly so that by 1905 they made up 44 per cent of the adult workhouse population compared to 43 per cent for women. The Census provides information on the age of those on indoor relief. In 1881, 28.3 per cent of inmates were under 15 while almost one-third (31.3 per cent) were over 60.[41] Over time, there was an 'ageing' of the workhouse population with a fall in the proportion of children and a rise in the older age group. In 1906, one in five of all those in workhouses were under 16, over one-third (37.1 per cent) were aged between 16 and 60 while 42.5 per cent were 60 or over. By 1911, following the introduction of the old age pension (see chapter 10), there had been a fall in the proportion of older people to 38.5 per cent of the total and the number of working age inmates rose to 41.5 per cent.

While data are available as to the composition of the workhouse population based on the poor law categorisation, it seems likely that too much weight should not be attached to these categorisations. The term 'able-bodied', for example, referred not to persons who were able-bodied in any meaningful sense of the term but simply to those who were not on a special medical diet (at least by 1909). Having regard to these concerns, those categorised as 'able-bodied' men made up 5 per cent of the population in 1859. By 1905, able-bodied men (including casuals and vagrants) still made up 6 per cent of the total workhouse population. Able-bodied women made up about 16 per cent of the workhouse population in 1859. This proportion fell to about 4 per cent by 1905. Children made up about 30 per cent of the population in 1859. As has been seen, this fell to about 13 per cent by 1905. In contrast the numbers in hospital, having increased dramatically from 14 per cent in 1851, remained at about one-third of the workhouse population over the period. Finally, a residual category of other persons not in hospital increased from about 10 per cent of the population

40 Report of the Vice-Regal Commission on Poor Law Reform in Ireland. Volume I, 1906 [Cd. 3202], li, 349, 16.

41 Census of Ireland, 1881. Part II. General report, 1882 [C.3365], lxxvi, 1, table 130.

in 1859 to 45 per cent of the total population by 1905. This grouping in 1859 included persons disabled and permanently disabled from labour but not requiring hospital treatment. By 1905 a more detailed breakdown is available showing that the group consisted mainly of the aged and infirm (32 per cent),[42] the 'insane' (7 per cent) and unmarried mothers (5 per cent).

More detailed analysis at 1859, 1877, 1891 and 1907

In the section above, the overall national data as to the operation of the poor law have been set out. However, it must be recalled that there was significant variation between poor law unions. The availability of detailed data as to the numbers relieved, the valuation[43] and the rates for individual unions allows us to examine the relationship between these factors. For example, if one looks at welfare state spending today, richer countries in Europe spend more (as a percentage of gross domestic product) on their welfare systems than do poorer countries. Can a similar tendency be seen in relation to poor law unions in the nineteenth century? In order to examine this issue, data as to indoor and outdoor relief, expenditure, rates and the valuation for each of the 160–3 unions in 1859, 1877, 1891 and 1907 have been examined. The dates chosen reflect key points in the development of the poor law in Ireland. 1859 was the point when poor relief was at its lowest, 1877 represents the poor law before the Land War while 1891 shows how poor relief changed over the 1880s. Finally 1907 represents the poor law immediately before the introduction of the old age pension in 1908. Some key data as to the average levels of rates, indoor and outdoor relief, expenditure and valuation are set out in table 1.3.

42 Many bedridden or ailing and feeble.

43 The rateable valuation of land was intended to represent the value of land occupied by an individual and was used as a basis for assessing rates payable.

	1859	1877	1891	1907	Increase %
IR/100 population	0.64	0.81	0.84	0.89	39
OR/100 population	0.03	0.60	1.39	1.43	5442
Cost of IR maintenance (*d.*)*	24.00	36.25	35.75	43.75	82
Average cost of OR/person (*d.*)	10.35	14.93	15.83	16.00	55
Expenditure/100 population (£)	6.90	14.60	19.27	24.44	258
Valuation/population (£)	2.04	2.52	3.13	3.69	81
Rates (*d.*)	8.77	14.70	15.93	17.99	105

Table 1.3 Key poor law data, 1859–1907
Source: Database of poor law statistics.
* This is the average weekly cost of provisions and necessaries only, excluding clothing.

As can be seen in the above table, the number of persons receiving indoor relief relative to the overall union population rose by almost 40 per cent. It should be recalled that this rise – which is higher than that shown in table 1.2 – is due to the starting point in 1859 which is the year when the Irish poor law population was at its (post-Famine) lowest. In fact, as has been seen, the total number in receipt of indoor relief did not rise significantly but the overall population fell thereby affecting the ratio. The cost of indoor relief rose with the basic cost of maintenance rising by 80 per cent in the period. Studies of workhouse diets indicate that there was some improvement in the nutritional standard in the period which presumably contributed, in part, to this increase.[44] Outdoor relief was paid only to a very limited extent in 1859 but by 1907 there were, on average, 1.43 persons in receipt of outdoor relief for every hundred persons living in the union. The average out relief payment per week was much less than the cost of indoor relief and it rose more slowly than did indoor maintenance costs. Expenditure (per 100 population) increased much more dramatically by

44 L.A. Clarkson and E.M. Crawford, *Feast and Famine: A History of Food and Nutrition in Ireland 1500–1920*, Oxford University Press, Oxford, 2001.

over 250 per cent. The valuation per head of population increased much more slowly from about £2 in 1859 to £3.69 in 1907 – a rise of 81 per cent. As will be seen this rise was not uniform across the country. A combination of the increasing expenditure and a smaller increase in valuations meant that average rates increased by the over 100 per cent in the period from just under nine *d.* in 1859 to almost 18 *d.* by 1907.

Looking first at the relationship between the level of indoor relief[45] and valuation[46] there is a reasonably strong correlation between the two (0.45 and 0.49 in 1859 and 1907 respectively). Thus there is a tendency for the level of indoor relief to rise as the valuation rises. However, when the picture is examined in more detail, a more nuanced account is found (figures 1.2 and 1.3). Here, in both years, there is a somewhat inverted U-shaped trend in relation to relief and valuation. Unions with a low valuation tend to have lower numbers on indoor relief, suggesting that expenditure is constrained by the lack of resources in these unions. Expenditure tends to rise as valuation rises and the highest spending unions (or those with the highest number on indoor relief) are unions with somewhat above-average levels of valuation – somewhat under £3 per head of population in 1859 and somewhat over £4 in 1907. However the wealthiest unions are not amongst the highest spending. This may be because the overall wealth of these unions resulted in lower numbers of poor people or perhaps because wealthy landowners provided higher levels of private benefits to those who would otherwise rely on the poor law.

45 The level of indoor relief was measured both in terms of the numbers of persons relieved per 100 population in the union and in terms of the expenditure per 100 population. Both measurements are, however, highly correlated.

46 Valuation is the total valuation of the union per head of population. There are, of course, a number of difficulties in using valuation as a measure of wealth. The relationship of valuation to, for example, the rent of land varied both over time and space. However, it would seem to provide the best available indicator of wealth.

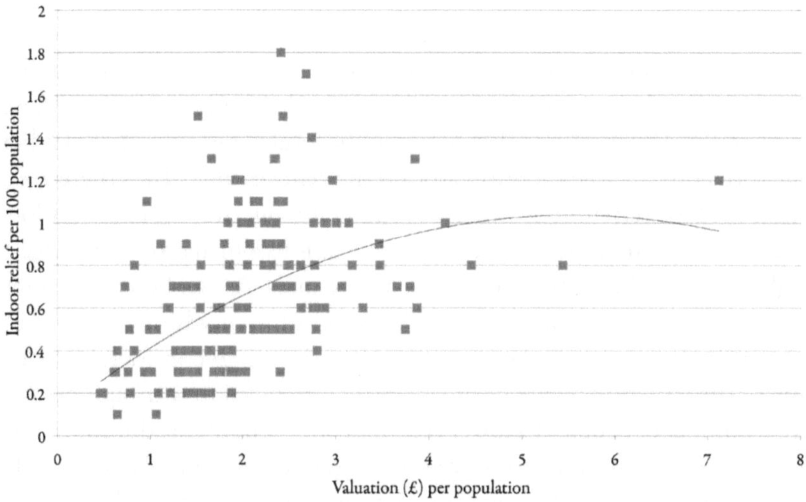

Figure 1.2 Indoor relief and valuation by union, 1859
Source: Database of poor law statistics

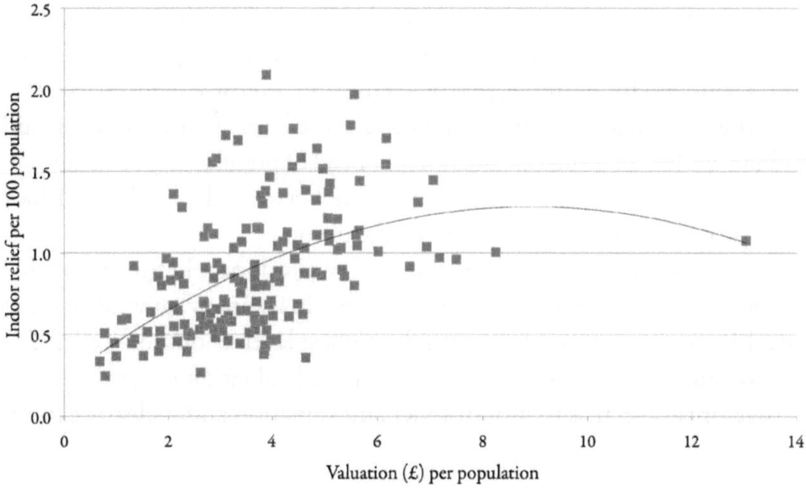

Figure 1.3 Indoor relief and valuation by union, 1907
Source: Database of poor law statistics

Turning to the relationship between the rates paid by a union and the amount of indoor relief provided, again there is a reasonably strong correlation between the two (0.47 and 0.56 respectively in 1859 and 1907). There is generally a linear relationship between the level of rates and that of relief but with considerable variation around the central line.[47] Thus there are a number of western unions which pay high rates but provide relatively low levels of indoor relief. Conversely, there are unions which provide relatively high levels of relief at the same costs on the rates. As can be seen, unions with rates at about 2*s.* in the £ provide support to anything from 0.4 to 1.9 persons per 100 population.[48] This variation is, in considerable part, due to the structure of the poor law system: rich unions can support the same number of people at a lower rate than poor unions. In addition, some unions are small and have lower administrative costs than large (usually western) unions. Controlling for variations in the valuation, the correlation between rates and the level of indoor relief rises considerably (0.76). However, some part of the variation may also be due to (i) inefficiency in the provision of relief in unions, and/or (ii) to the provision of somewhat more generous standards of accommodation, clothing and food, and/or (iii) to the fact that particular unions have a higher proportion of more costly paupers (for example, persons requiring intensive medical care).

There is a weaker relationship between the level of outdoor relief paid and the wealth (in terms of valuation per head of population) of the union. In fact, in 1907 there is a correlation of 0.36 between the level of outdoor relief provided[49] and the valuation of the union.

There is a general trend for the level of outdoor relief to rise with a rise in the valuation. However, this relationship is somewhat weak and the wealthiest unions are *not* those with the highest levels of outdoor relief. The relationship between outdoor relief levels and valuation is not dissimilar to that already seen as to indoor relief and valuation and it clearly cannot

47 The outlyer here is the peripheral Belmullet union with very high rates but low relief.

48 Leaving aside the exceptional case of Ballyvaughan, which supported no less than 2.8 persons per 100.

49 That is the number of persons supported by way of outdoor relief per 100 population.

fully explain the separate patterns in relation to payment of outdoor relief (a matter discussed in chapter 6).[50]

The poor law in its economic and social context

Amongst the issues to be examined in this study is the relationship between poor relief and economic and demographic change. This section discusses the relationship between these trends and developments in the poor law. Table 1.4 indicates that poor relief *per se* made up less than 1 per cent of Irish gross domestic product in the period and grew only slowly over time.[51] Unfortunately, the absence of an annual series of GDP data means that it is not possible to track the impact in times of depression but clearly this percentage would have risen as poor relief spending rose in depressions while GDP would have fallen. This would be particularly the case in the period 1879–82. Nonetheless, there is little indication that the significant change in Irish economic, demographic and political structures between 1860 and 1911 had any impact on the level (if not the composition) of poor relief expenditure itself.

	Poor relief	Poor relief, dispensary services, industrial schools and lunatic asylums
1860	0.6	0.85
1877	0.7	1.1
1908	0.75	1.4

Table 1.4 Poor relief as percentage of GDP, 1860–1908
Source: Database of poor law statistics; GDP from Geary and Stark, op. cit.

50 Controlling for the level of indoor relief somewhat strenghtens the relationship between outdoor relief and valuation (0.42).

51 Given the uncertainties of the GDP figures it is possible that no growth took place.

However, if one takes a broader measure and looks at related expenditure one sees a somewhat different picture. Including spending on the poor law dispensary service, industrial schools, and lunatic asylums, one gets both a somewhat higher figure for expenditure but – more importantly – a clearly rising trend (an increase of about two-thirds compared to an increase of only 25 per cent for poor relief itself).[52] If one included other poor law-related services such as labourers' cottages (introduced in the 1880s) the increase would be even greater. This highlights the fact that the system of poor relief itself gradually became less important in the overall social services provided by the state.

One can also look at the expenditure on indoor and outdoor relief compared to the average wage of the Irish agricultural labourer and as to GDP per capita (subject to the caveats as to this data discussed above).

	Indoor relief		Outdoor relief	
	Wages	GDP	Wages	GDP
1860	29	42	12	18
1870s	–	39	–	15
1893	32	–	12	–
1910	34	29	12	11

Table 1.5 Indoor and outdoor relief as a percentage of agricultural wages and GDP per capita, 1860–1910
Source: Database of poor law statistics; wages from Fitzpatrick, op. cit.; GDP from Geary and Stark, op. cit.

Indooor relief (excluding clothing) remained at about 30 per cent of agricultural wages – perhaps rising somewhat over the period. However, given the more rapid increase in GDP per capita, indoor relief fell back compared to

52 The role of industrial schools and lunatic asylums in relation to the poor law is discussed in Chapter 10. It would appear that these played a supplementary and, to some extent, substitutive role with regard to the poor law. The main drivers of the increase are the lunatic asylums.

per capita GDP from over 40 per cent in 1860 to about 30 per cent by 1910. As a percentage of agricultural labourers' wages, average outdoor relief payments appear to have remained surprisingly stable over the period at about 12 per cent of the average wage. However, again reflecting the fact that the agricultural wage fell back compared to GDP per capita (although growing in real terms), this represents a fall compared to GDP per capita.

Conclusion

The finding that expenditure on poor relief itself did not increase significantly (as a percentage of GDP) over the period, and despite the considerable economic, demographic and political changes, is itself significant. It shows, firstly, that despite its importance as the main support for the destitute, poor relief constituted only a small proportion of Ireland's national income in the nineteenth and early twentieth centuries. Expenditure on poor relief would be dwarfed by expenditure on the old age pension introduced in 1908. This would suggest that poor relief *per se* played a rather limited role in Ireland's economic development – contrary to Solar's thesis as to the 'old' poor law in England. While further econometric study is obviously required, the scale of the Irish poor law would tend to suggest an outcome more similar to that proposed by Boyer of at worst having little effect and at best stimulating growth by increasing the profit rates of labour-hiring farmers. Secondly, the stability in spending over time – despite the dramatic changes in political control – raises questions, which will be discussed in subsequent chapters, about the extent to which changes in the political composition of the boards of guardians led to changes in poor relief policy. While there was considerable stability in terms of expenditure, there was a significant shift towards outdoor relief and the reasons for this are discussed in more detail in chapter 6. This, inter alia, looks at the link between employment patterns and poor relief, drawing on the work of authors such as Boyer.

In general it can be seen that poor relief expenditure was related to the wealth of a union (echoing Lindert's findings at a national level).[53] However, this link was not particularly strong in statistical terms. The regional variations in poor relief will be outlined in chapter 2 and the causes for these regional patterns analysed. Finally, issues concerning the relationship between poor relief and family and household structures will be discussed in chapter 3.

53 P. Lindert, 'Poor Relief before the Welfare State: Britain versus the Continent, 1780–1880', *European Review of Economic History*, 1998, 101–40.

CHAPTER 2

Regional Trends in the Poor Law

In this chapter, regional trends as to the poor law are analysed. The first part of the chapter looks at the extent to which different regional groupings of unions can be identified, before turning to the distinctive characteristics of the six large urban areas which account for about a quarter of all poor law expenditure. The chapter concludes with analysis of the issues arising from these regional variations and the factors underlying them.

Why categorise?

Given the growing literature on typologies of poor law systems,[1] a question which has received only very limited attention is that of the precise role and value of typologies.[2] As Arts and Gelissen point out, a key question is whether typologies based on ideal-types have theoretical and empirical value.[3] They argue that ideal-types have no value insofar as they are goals in themselves but only if they are the means to an end. Max Weber has stated that 'sociology seeks to formulate type concepts and generalized

1 See S.A. King, *Poverty and Welfare in England 1700–1850: A Regional Perspective*, Manchester University Press, Manchester, 2000.

2 See the discussion in S.A. King and J.W. Stewart (eds), *Welfare Peripheries: the Development of Welfare States in Nineteenth and Twentieth Century Europe*, Peter Lang, Bern, 2007.

3 W. Arts and J. Gelissen, 'Welfare States, Solidarity and Justice Principles: Does the Type Really Matter?', *Acta Sociologica*, 44 (4), 2001, 283–99.

uniformities of empirical process' in distinction to history which focuses on the causal analysis and explanation of individual actions, structures and personalities. He argues that 'an important consideration in the formulation of sociological concepts and generalizations is the contribution that sociology can make towards the causal explanation of some historically and culturally important phenomenon'. In this regard 'sociological analysis both abstracts from reality and at the same time helps us to understand it, in that it shows us with what degree of approximation a concrete historical phenomenon can be subsumed' under theoretical concepts which are adequate on the level of meaning.

Weber argues that in order to give meaning to these terms 'it is necessary for the sociologist to formulate pure ideal types of the corresponding forms of action which in each case involve the highest possible degree of logical integration by virtue of their complete adequacy on the level of meaning'. However, precisely because of this fact, Weber accepts that it is seldom if ever that a real phenomenon can be found which corresponds exactly to one of the ideal types. He goes on to add that it is often convenient for the sociologist 'to employ average types of an empirical statistical character, concepts which do not require methodological discussion'. It is important to distinguish between these two forms of ideal type or typology: firstly, a typology which seeks to explain a concrete historical phenomenon in terms of theoretical concepts, and, secondly, typologies of a statistical nature.

The approach adopted in this chapter aims to retain a theoretical underpinning but without seeking to adopt rigid 'ideal types'.[4] While this approach is underpinned by theory, it is not an ideal type in the Weberian sense falling somewhere mid-way between the strict theoretical construction of an ideal type and the theoretical statistical grouping. It may be that a flexible approach, which, while analysing the theories of power

4 For a related debate as to modern welfare states, see G. Esping Andersen, *Three Worlds of Welfare Capitalism*, Princeton University Press, New Jersey, 1990 and the subsequent debates discussed in M. Cousins, *European Welfare States: Comparative Perspectives*, Sage, London, 2005, chapter 6.

and social systems of production underlying poor law patterns also recognises contingent factors in the development of patterns of poor relief, may be a more reliable instrument for classifying poor law systems and thus may compensate in validity and reliability for what it loses in economy of explanation.

Regional trends

Overall patterns of relief and rates

In relation to valuation (measured as valuation per head of population), in 1859 there is a clear north-south and west-east gradient. The unions with the lowest valuation are in the north, northwest, west and southwest of the country (see map 2.1). The richer unions, in contrast, are generally in a band from north Munster running over to Leinster, across to Wicklow and up into Meath and Louth. The richest unions are in Co. Meath.

The trends as to valuation did not change markedly in the period to 1907 (map 2.2) although the valuation per head of the Ulster and Leinster unions rose more rapidly than the average, as can be seen by the larger number of Ulster unions which now fall into the 'high' grouping. The richest unions are clustered in an area of north Leinster while almost all of Leinster, eastern Munster, east and south Ulster, and much of eastern Connacht have above-average valuations. In contrast, the peripheral western unions have seen little rise in their valuation and their situation has, in relative terms, got worse.

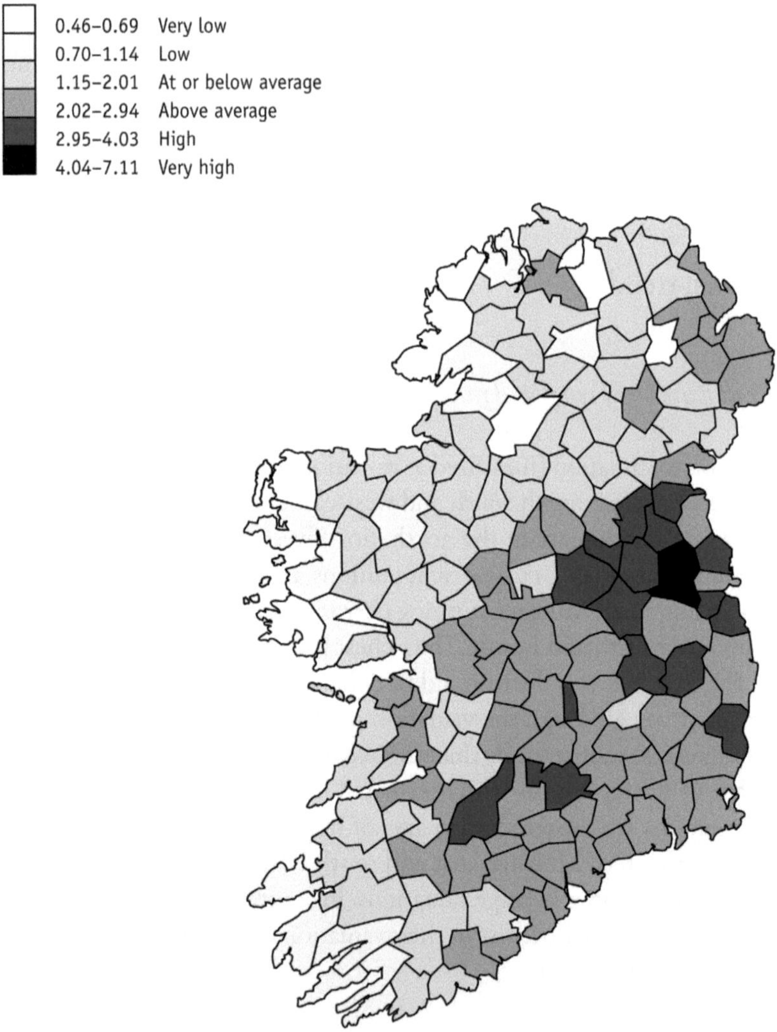

Map 2.1 Valuation by union (£/100 population), 1859

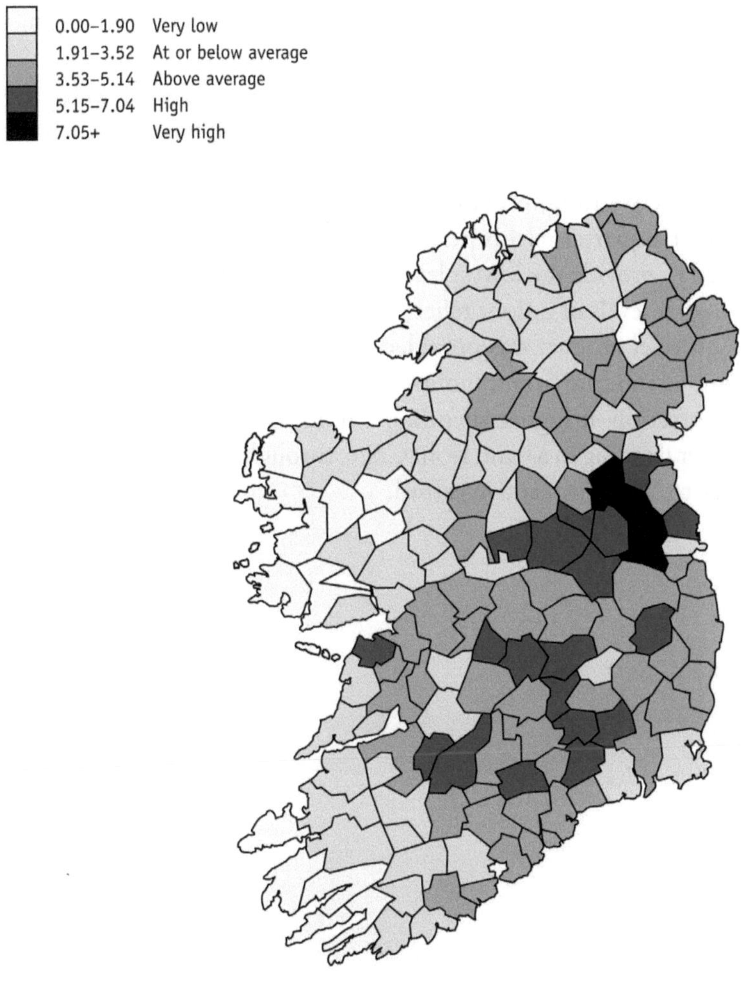

Map 2.2 Valuation by union (£/100 population), 1907

Turning to the levels of indoor relief, in 1859 there is a broadly north-south and east-west division (see map 2.3). The unions providing the lowest level of indoor relief are in the north and west (including a number of unions in west Cork and Kerry). Only five northern unions provide above-average levels of relief, and none a high level.[5] The unions providing the highest level of relief are in the south of the country clustered around Limerick, Cork and Waterford, and Dublin.

This pattern had changed somewhat by 1907 although a clear north-south difference remains (map 2.4). Firstly, in most unions there had been a considerable rise in the level of relief provided per head of population. As was seen above, the level of indoor relief per 100 of the population increased by about a quarter in this period. The northern and western unions still tended to provide the lowest level of indoor relief. All the unions providing higher levels of indoor relief were in the southern half of the country. A high level of relief was provided by the Dublin unions and by a band of unions running from Dublin into the Midlands. However the biggest concentration of higher-spending unions was in Munster and southern Leinster running in a band from Clare, through Limerick, Cork and Tipperary to Waterford and Wexford.

5 Antrim, Belfast, Cavan, Clogher and Lisburn.

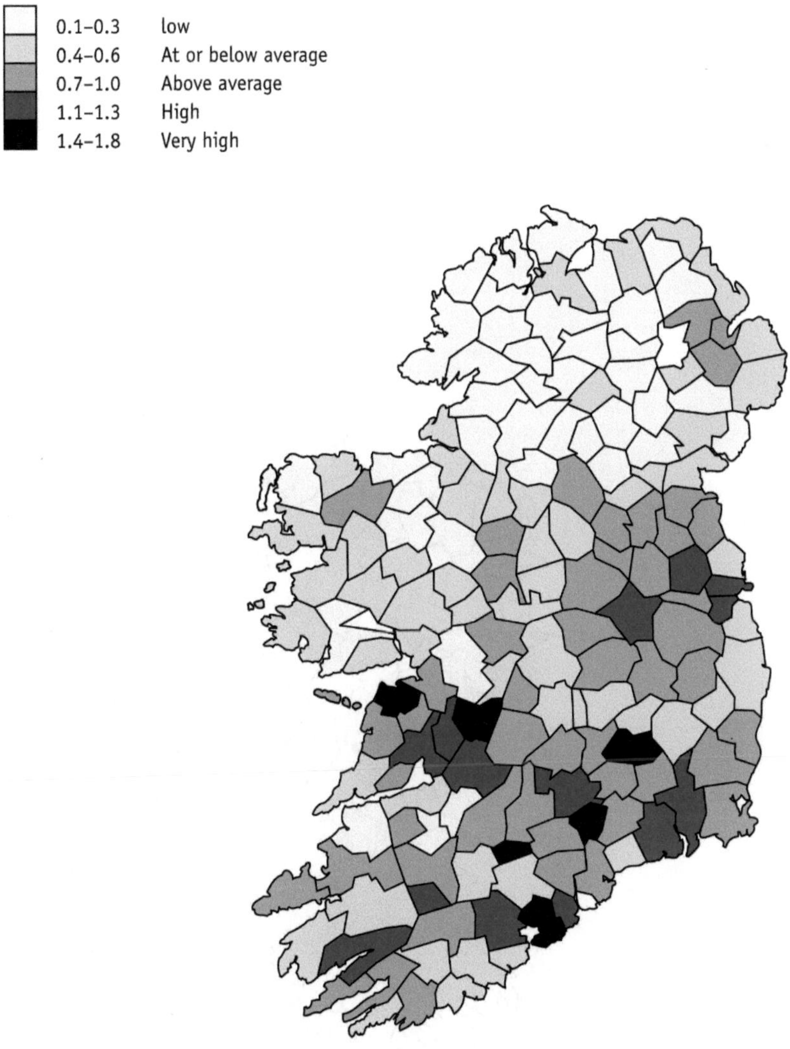

Map 2.3 Indoor relief by union (numbers relieved/100 population), 1859

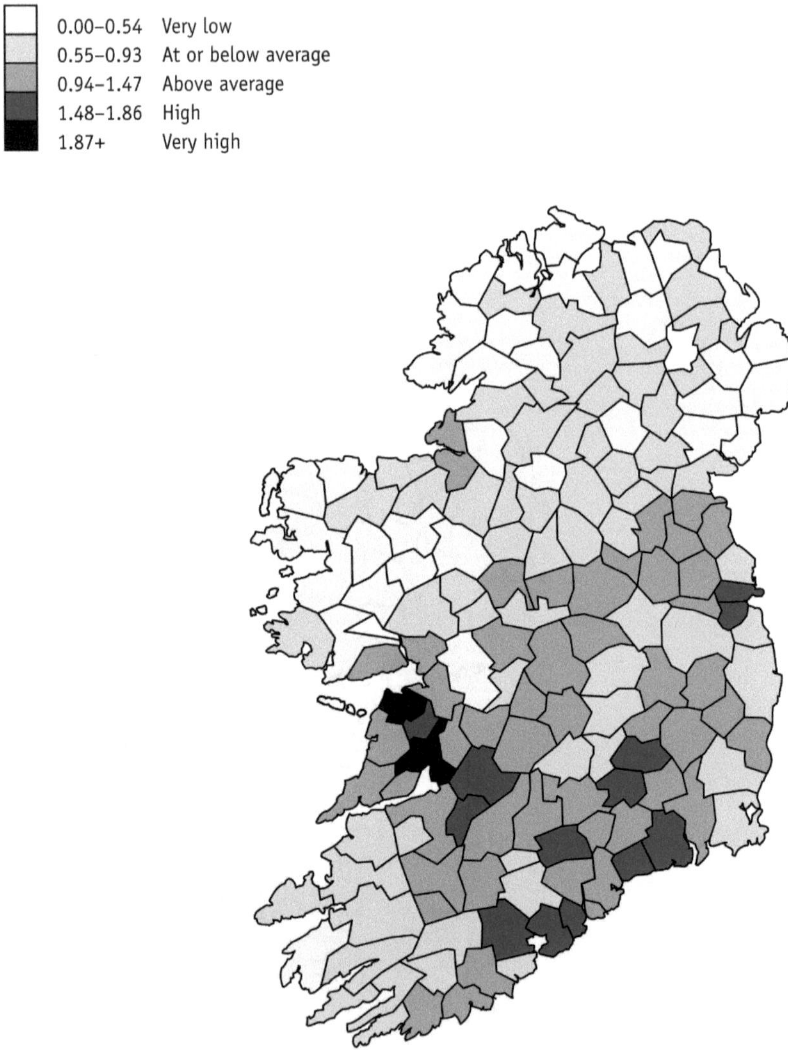

Map 2.4 Indoor relief by union (numbers relieved/100 population), 1907

Looking at the regional provision of outdoor relief, in 1859 a considerable part of the country – particularly in the north and west – provided no (or almost no) outdoor relief.[6] Outdoor relief was strongly concentrated in Leinster and, to a lesser extent, some of the Munster unions. The highest spending unions when it came to outdoor relief tended to be concentrated in north Leinster, running from Louth to Mullingar, and in south Leinster. By 1877, outdoor relief had become more widespread although many northern and some southern unions still provided no out relief. The heaviest levels of relief were concentrated in Leinster (and particularly south Leinster) and north Munster. It is noteworthy that the three big urban unions (Belfast, and north and south Dublin) provided no or very low levels of outdoor relief although the smaller – and more rural – unions of Cork, Limerick and Waterford provided above-average or high levels.

By 1907, there had been some changes in out relief patterns although a clear north-south pattern remains (map 2.6). First, it should be noted that the overall level of out relief had increased considerably over the period. Out relief was now payable in almost all unions although many northern unions paid very low levels of relief. Western unions were now also more likely to use outdoor relief and some poor western unions paid quite high levels of relief. However the highest levels of out relief remained in the Munster and Leinster unions. The northern cities continued to pay low levels of relief, the two Dublin unions were about average, while the smaller southern cities paid above-average or high levels of relief.

6 Given that much of the 1859 map would be blank, map 2.5 relates to 1877, by which time outdoor relief had become more widespread.

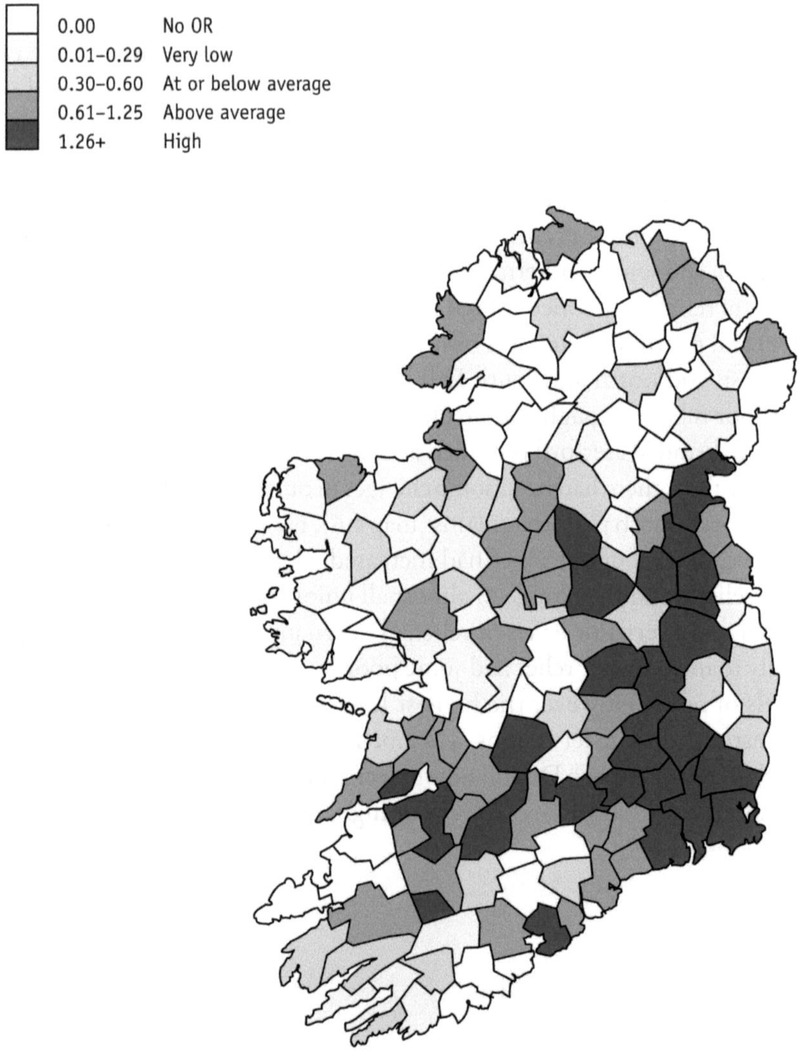

Map 2.5 Outdoor relief by union (numbers relieved/100 population), 1877

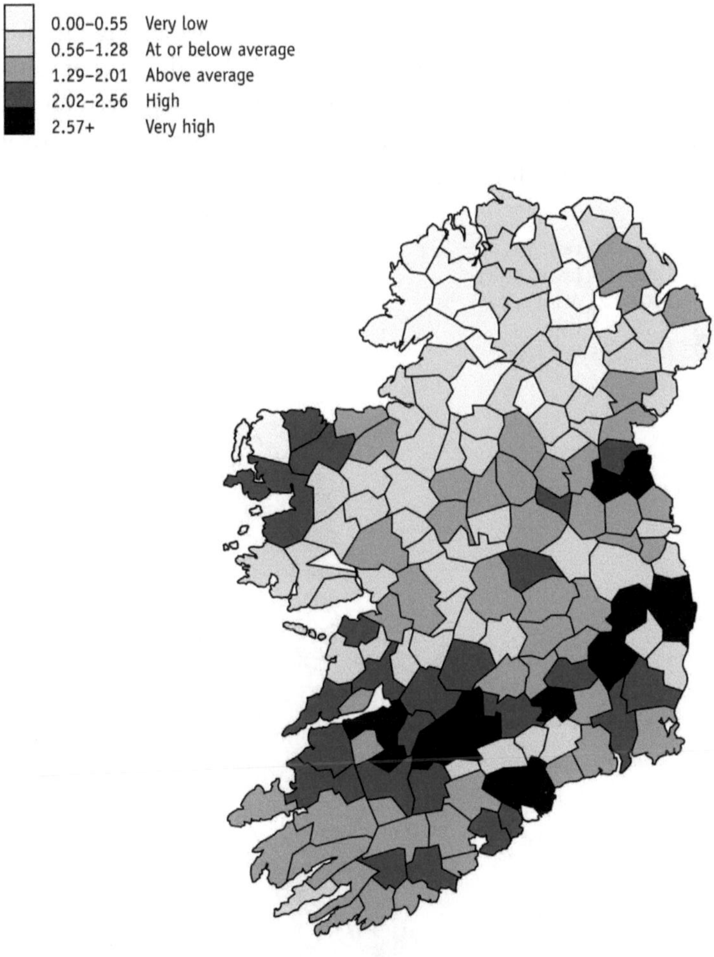

Map 2.6 Outdoor relief by union (numbers relieved/100 population), 1907

Finally, maps 2.7 and 2.8 outline the regional incidence of rates. Here the regional pattern is broadly similar in both 1859 and 1907, although rates have increased considerably over that period. The pattern as to rates is quite different from that seen in relation to valuation and the provision of relief. Again Ulster tends to have a low overall level of rates. However, the peripheral western unions, which had a low valuation per head and generally provided lower levels of indoor and outdoor relief, have amongst the highest levels of rates in the country. In both 1859 and 1877, the level of valuation and the rates payable in individual unions are weakly negatively correlated. In other words, there is a slight tendency for the richer unions to pay lower rates and, conversely, for the poorer unions to pay higher rates.

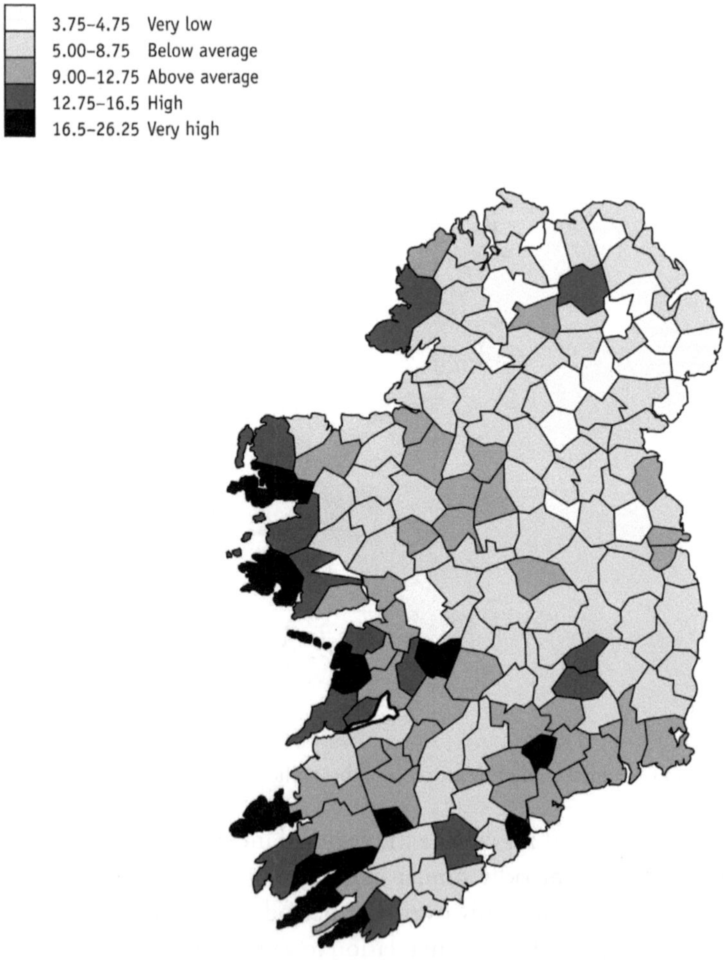

Map 2.7 Rates by union (d.), 1859

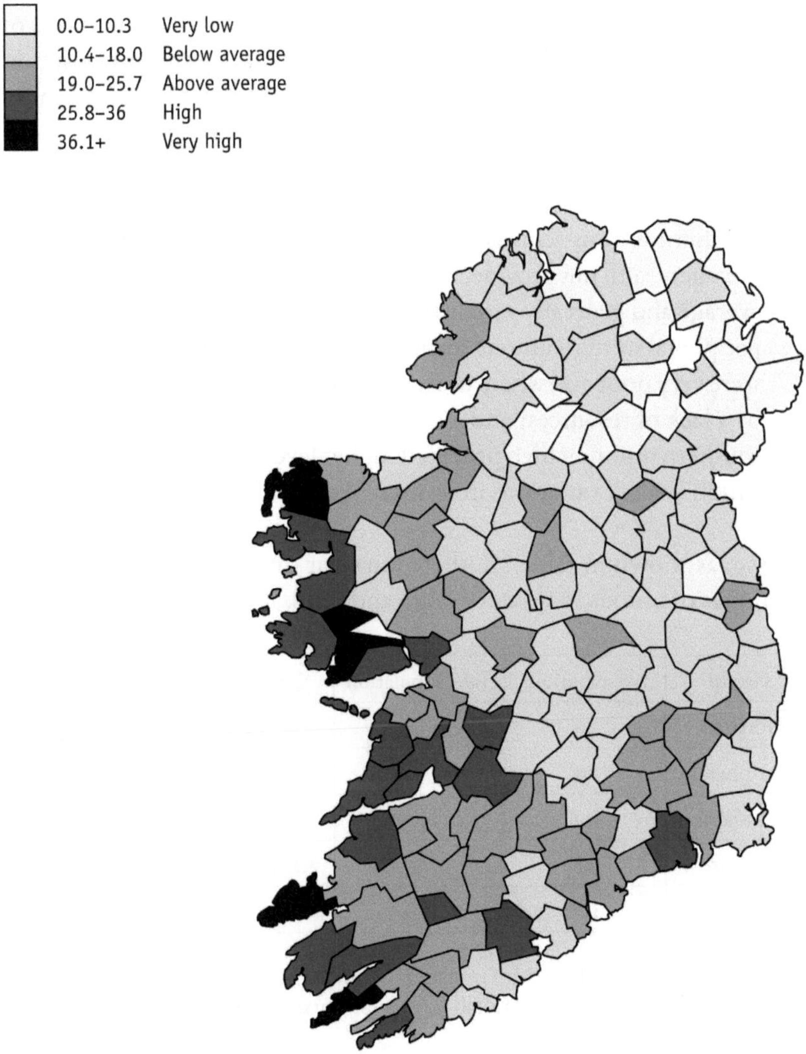

Map 2.8 Rates by union (d.), 1907

Poor law groupings

Looking at the maps above, one can see some clear patterns in terms of regional groupings (although there was, of course, significant variation within regions). Based on similarity in patterns of relief, rates, and wealth, in terms of valuation per population, three clear groupings of unions can be identified over the period from the 1850s to the 1900s. These are:

1) northern unions (consisting of most Ulster unions) which were of average wealth but provided rather low relief compared to the national average and generally very little outdoor relief;
2) peripheral western unions (mainly along the western coastline) which were very poor and where the level of relief provided was constrained by a lack of resources;[7] and
3) southern unions which provided higher levels of relief but which had a high level of variations in terms of wealth and relief.[8]

In 1859, as shown in table 2.1, there are clear differences between these groupings of unions in terms of relief and rates.

Group	No. of unions	Val./population	Rate *d.*	IR/100 population
Northern	36	1.77 (0.35)	5.73 (1.32)	0.40 (0.21)
Peripheral	19	0.79 (0.20)	13.56 (5.50)	0.44 (0.28)
Southern	108	2.35 (0.89)	9.03 (3.15)	0.76 (0.32)
Mid-western	*21*	*1.58 (0.24)*	*8.18 (1.76)*	*0.45 (0.13)*
All	163	2.04	8.77	0.64

Table 2.1 Groupings of unions in 1859[9]
Source: Database of poor law statistics

7 Because of their poverty (i.e. low levels of rateable valuation) these unions had the highest levels of rates despite supporting relatively low numbers of paupers.

8 The term 'southern' refers to all the unions outside Ulster with the exception of those falling into the peripheral western group.

9 All data are group averages with standard deviation in brackets.

As can be seen, the thirty-six northern unions (all the unions in the province of Ulster with the exception of those in the peripheral group (see below)) have below-average valuation, the lowest average rates and the lowest average level of relief. In 1859, none of the northern unions provide any significant level of outdoor relief.

The nineteen peripheral unions, mainly along the western seaboard from Donegal, through Galway to west Cork and Kerry, were the poorest in the country.[10] Similar to the northern unions they provide low levels of relief and no union in 1859 provided any significant outdoor relief. However, in stark contrast to the northern unions, their rates are the highest in the country. In 1859, this group includes eight northern unions whose rates are below the group average. The southern Kenmare union has the highest rates in the country (2 *s.* 2¼ *d.*).

Finally there is a group of over 100 southern unions. The valuation for these unions is above average, their rates are about average and their level of relief is above average. This is the only grouping in which any considerable level of outdoor relief is paid, although even here this is very limited. Given the size of this grouping there are considerable variations within it from relatively poor western unions to the very rich Meath unions such as Navan and Kells. However, the only consistent sub-group within the south is a group of about twenty poorer mid-western unions, running from Sligo and north Mayo down to Longford and Athlone, which is poorer than the national average and provides low levels of relief. However, in contrast to the northern unions, it has average levels of rates. There are also some non-contiguous unions[11] which show a similar pattern and it is arguable that these unions should be seen as a poorer variant of the southern group rather than as a distinctive group in itself. While, as can be seen from maps 2.1–2.8 above, one can also see clusters of similarity as to certain aspects of poor law policy, it is difficult to identify any other solid groupings within the southern group.

10 The group is composed of all unions whose valuation per population falls one standard deviation or more below the national average.

11 For example, Clonakilty and Mitchelstown.

Turning to 1907, there is a striking similarity in patterns. Not only are there still three clear groups but there has been little change in the membership of those groups.

Group	No. of unions	Val./ population	Rate *d.*	IR/100 population	OR/100 population
Northern	37	3.47 (0.59)	10.30 (2.20)	0.57 (0.13)	0.68 (0.42)
Peripheral	19	1.39 (0.42)	27.45 (10.16)	0.55 (0.2)	1.04 (0.65)
Southern	103	4.19 (1.61)	19.01 (5.66)	1.06 (0.37)	1.77 (0.59)
Mid-western	*17*	*2.70 (0.44)*	*17.38 (2.99)*	*0.62 (0.19)*	*1.29 (0.44)*
All	159	3.69	17.99	0.89	1.43

Table 2.2 Groupings of unions in 1907
Source: Database of poor law statistics

Again there is a group of nearly forty northern unions. Despite the fact that Ulster has no clear (southern) geographic boundaries and is religiously quite heterogeneous,[12] only one northern union (Bailieborough, which is on the border with Leinster) had changed its policy sufficiently to be reclassified as a 'southern' union. As can be seen from tables 2.1 and 2.2, the northern unions increased in wealth more rapidly than the overall average for the country (growing by 96 per cent in terms of valuation per head of population compared to a national average of 81 per cent) and are now close to the national average. As part of this overall trend two more central Ulster unions (Enniskillen and Limavady) and Ballyshannon have moved out of the peripheral grouping and are classified here with the northern group. Despite its growing wealth, this group maintained one of the lowest levels of indoor relief (albeit up somewhat on 1859) and the lowest level of outdoor relief. Given that virtually no outdoor relief at all

12 In 1911 Roman Catholics formed a large majority of the population in Donegal and Cavan but a clear minority in Antrim and Down.

was provided in 1859, this still represents an increase in the level of relief provided but if anything the northern unions have become more rather than less distinct over time.[13]

Again 19 unions form a peripheral western group all along the western seaboard. Fourteen of these were also peripheral in 1859. Three northern unions have moved into the northern group proper (one – Gortin – has been amalgamated with the neighbouring Omagh union in 1870) while four additional southern unions (contiguous to the existing group) have moved into full peripherality.[14] The average valuation per population of these unions has increased by less than 50 per cent from 1859 seeing them fall even further behind. The level of indoor relief remains very low although these unions are increasingly relying on outdoor relief (albeit below the national average). Given that relief has increased relatively more rapidly than wealth, rates in these unions have soared to an average of over 2*s.* Only one of the northern peripheral unions (Donegal) maintains a low level of rates while Belmullet now has the unenviable record of the highest rates in the country (at 4*s.* 4*d.* although Cahirciveen, Castletown, Clifden, Dingle and Oughterard are also very high at about 3*s.*).

The block of over 100 southern unions is on average still the wealthiest, and pays the highest indoor and outdoor relief with rates which are just above average. Again there is considerable variation within the group but the only clear sub-group to emerge is again a group of 16 poor mid-western unions.[15] These unions again have a valuation per population well below the national average and relatively low outdoor relief. However, in contrast to the northern unions, they pay at least average levels of outdoor relief and have average rates.

13 Only 5 unions (Antrim, Ballymena, Banbridge, Newry and Newtownards) paid at or about the national average level of outdoor relief in 1907.

14 Again measured as having a valuation per population one standard deviation below the national average. These are Castlebar and Claremorris in Mayo, Galway (in Co. Galway) and Bantry in west Cork.

15 Three poor mid-western unions now fall into the peripheral group (Castlebar, Claremorris and Galway) while Ballymahon is now part of the main body of southern group of unions.

Thus while there is some rise in levels of indoor relief (based on the low point of 1859) and a significant increase in outdoor relief, there is a high level of stability in regional patterns of relief. Before turning to look at the reason for these divisions, we turn first to look at the patterns of relief in six key urban areas.

Urban/rural

Irish urban structure

The existing historiography has, in general, focused much more on the Irish countryside than Irish cities. Compared to some other European countries – in particular Ireland's closest neighbour Great Britain – Ireland had a relatively low level of urbanisation in the nineteenth century. Nonetheless the six largest cities (which were covered by seven poor law unions)[16] made up about one-quarter of the total population. Although 'city' is a legal term in Irish law, the attribution of the term to a conurbation owes more to historical chance than population. There were six cities which were clearly the largest over the period in question – all having at all times a population of over 20,000.[17] These range from the large cities of Dublin and Belfast, to the medium sized (but declining) southern city of Cork to a number of small regional capitals (table 2.3).

As can be seen in table 2.3, which shows the cities in order of population, Dublin was historically the largest city and its population grew moderately in the period.[18] Belfast, in contrast, had grown from a town

16 Only Dublin – divided into North and South unions – had more than one union.

17 There is no other conurbation which had a population of that size in the period while it is difficult to identify any clear cut-off line once one goes below that level. Only Galway and Kilkenny cities had comparable populations in pre-Famine Ireland.

18 The suburbs (which include Pembroke and Rathmines and Rathgar) are an integral part of the city and the separate classification owed more to political factors. For most purposes using the Dublin city and suburbs data will give a more accurate impression of the city.

of under 20,000 in 1801 to the second largest city by 1861 and almost trebled its population in the period to 1901. Similarly, although on a smaller scale, Londonderry almost doubled its population by 1901. By contrast Cork and Limerick experienced population loss although Waterford saw modest growth. Belfast was a predominantly Protestant city though with a significant Catholic minority. In Londonderry city the Catholic population had a small majority but the surrounding area (which was included in the union) had a Protestant majority and urban government was largely in Protestant hands. By contrast all the other cities were mainly Catholic.

Unfortunately for present purposes, the city boundaries do not always match closely with those of the poor law unions. In 1861, in the largest cities (Dublin and Belfast) the urban population made up 73–85 per cent of the union population. However, the smallest cities (Londonderry and Waterford) were dominated by their hinterlands with the urban population making up only about a third of the union.[19] This problem persisted in 1901, albeit to a lesser extent, although the details had changed. By 1901, Belfast city overflowed the poor law union; the Dublin city population made up three-quarters of the unions' total; while the remaining cities constituted between 56–67 per cent of the union. Although the match is far from perfect one would, however, expect that – particularly in 1901 – the city population would have a considerable impact on overall union policy and practice.

	1861	1901	Change
Dublin	246,465	290,638	17.9
Dublin city and suburbs	296,413	355,181	16.5
Belfast	119,393	349,180	192.5
Cork	79,594	76,122	-4.4
Limerick	43,924	38,151	-13.1
Londonderry	20,519	39,892	94.4
Waterford	22,869	26,769	17.1

Table 2.3 Population of 6 main cities, 1861–1901
Source: Vaughan and Fitzpatrick, *Irish Historical Statistics*, table 10.

19 In Cork and Limerick the urban population made up about half the union.

The structure of the poor law in urban Ireland

As set out in tables 2.4 and 2.5, there was considerable variation in poor relief in Irish cities in 1861 and this variation had increased by 1907.

	IR/100 pop.	Rate (*d.*)	Valuation/Pop. (£)
Belfast	0.8	8.25	2.23
Londonderry	0.5	7.50	2.12
Cork	1.2	14.75	1.92
Limerick	1.1	11.50	1.95
Waterford	1.3	12.75	2.35
North Dublin	1.3	12.25	2.34
South Dublin	1.1	10.25	2.44
Average	1.04	11.04	2.19
National Average	0.64	8.77	2.04

Table 2.4 Poor relief in major cities, 1859
Source: Database of poor law statistics

As can be seen, in 1859 there is relatively little variation in terms of the wealth of the six cities, measured as the valuation per head of population.[20] There is more variation in the levels of poor relief measured both as the numbers on poor relief per 100 population[21] or the level of spending per 100 population. Both measures are reasonably closely correlated (0.68) although (for reasons which are unclear) Limerick had about average levels of persons on indoor relief but at a very low cost. As can be seen in 1859, urban unions (except Londonderry) provided above-average levels of relief

20 Although the wealth of the cities was at about the average for the whole of the country, there was significantly more variation in rural areas, from the wealthy eastern farmlands to the very poor peripheral western unions.

21 At that time all unions had no or very low levels of outdoor relief.

and, excluding the northern cities, had above-average rates despite their average levels of wealth. Londonderry and, to a lesser extent, Belfast stand out as having below-average levels of relief on both measures while all the southern cities are above average.

	IR/100	OR/100	Rates (*d.*)	Valuation /pop. (£)
Belfast	0.8	0.1	10	3.83
Londonderry	0.5	0.1	9.5	3.15
Cork	1.6	2.0	28.5	2.92
Limerick	1.7	2.1	31.75	4.29
Waterford	1.7	1.7	27	3.34
North Dublin	1.6	1.1	25	2.85
South Dublin	1.8	1.5	21.5	3.82
Average	1.3	1.0	21.9	3.50
National average	0.89	1.43	17.99	3.69

Table 2.5 Poor relief in major cities, 1907
Source: Database of poor law statistics

By 1907, there is still a relatively small variation amongst the cities in terms of wealth. Most fall around the national average with only North Dublin and Cork noticeably below and only Limerick significantly above. In terms of poor relief, Londonderry and Belfast are now even more distinctive. With the exception of the introduction of a small level of outdoor relief, overall patterns of poor relief have changed hardly at all in Londonderry. While the level of indoor relief has increased slightly in Belfast, levels remain well below average and outdoor relief is marginal. In contrast, there has been an increase of about one-third in indoor relief in the southern cities and a significant shift towards outdoor relief. The north-south divide can also be seen in terms of rates, with the southern cities having rates two to three times those of the northern cities.

Compared to the national average in 1907, the key urban unions, again excluding Londonderry, provided average or above-average levels of indoor relief. However, there is a clear division as regards outdoor relief. The two northern cities provided minimal outdoor relief, well below the average for the northern group, the Dublin unions were at about the average level while the three southern cities which contained, it will be recalled, large rural populations were more in line with the overall southern pattern (see table 2.5).

Overall while the big urban unions are somewhat distinctive in that, except for the three rurally-dominated, southern cities, they are more likely to rely on indoor relief (and less on outdoor) than the average rural union, the urban unions are also clearly affected by the broader regional groupings with a clear, and growing, divergence showing between northern and southern relief patterns. Possible reasons for this will be discussed in part 3.

Explaining regional variation

Southern unions

As has been seen, the southern group forms the main body of Irish unions. Some of the key factors shaping their pattern of relief have already been outlined in chapter 1. In general the level of relief provided in southern unions is related – up to a point – to the wealth of the union. Unions with a valuation per population above average provide more relief than those below average, although the richest unions do not provide the highest levels of relief. This is consistent with Lindert's findings, at a national level, which indicated that richer countries transferred a higher share of national income to the poor.[22] As seen in chapters 1 and 3, demographic factors such as the proportion of older people in the population and the percentage of the older population who never married also appear to have

22 Lindert, 'Poor Relief before the Welfare State', 127.

influenced the level of relief. Lindert argues that a key explanation for the structure and level of poor relief is who had political power and what was in their economic self-interest. One can indeed argue that this goes some way to explaining the patterns of Irish poor relief in the period. The greater reliance on indoor relief (compared to England and Wales) was a deliberate outcome of the design of the original 1838 Act which did not allow any outdoor relief and of the post-Famine policy of the Poor Law Commission which discouraged use of outdoor relief. The reasons behind the subsequent growth in outdoor relief are discussed in more detail in chapter 6 where it is argued that the level of relief provided was influenced by the importance of agricultural labour in the local workforce with unions with higher proportions of agricultural labourers providing higher levels of outdoor relief. Southern and northern boards clearly adopted different approaches to the provision of relief. However, such a division can be seen in 1859 – long before any 'Nationalist' take-over of the boards – and it is argued that the difference in policy is *not* primarily due to any particular 'Nationalist' or 'tenant' policy on poor relief (see below for further discussion of the policy of northern boards).

Peripheral unions

The approach of the peripheral group of unions is explained by their poverty. The peripheral western unions were – at the same time – those likely to have a high demand for relief and those with a very limited capacity to fund such relief. Thus these unions had the highest levels of rates in the country despite rather low levels of relief. It is noteworthy that several peripheral unions had a very low proportion of ratepayers (and persons entitled to vote for the local poor law guardians) indicating both that the cost of poor relief would be borne by a narrow group of persons and that voters in such a restricted franchise did not favour generous relief.[23]

23 In 1874, in Dunfanaghy, Glenties, Clifden, Oughterard and Belmullet only 4–5 per cent of the population was entitled to vote in the poor law elections compared to a national average of 10 per cent. 'Return from each Poor Law Union in Ireland, of the

While it is difficult to determine at this distance in time, some boards may have been less efficient in their management of relief than others and the degree of intolerance for inefficiency was no doubt higher in unions whose finances were always finely balanced. In addition, the poverty of these unions meant that they were hit by frequent subsistence crises in the late nineteenth and early twentieth centuries which had a lesser (if any) effect on other unions.[24] The government response to these crises did not encourage good local management. Although various approaches were adopted, they broadly shared the principle that state support would only be provided as a last resort. Thus the local boards had every incentive to present the situation in the worst light possible, and arguably to allow the situation to worsen, while the Irish government was highly sceptical of local calls for state support. Fundamentally, however, the problem was that, in these unions, local property was insufficient adequately to provide for local poverty.

Northern unions

The different approach adopted by the northern boards raises more difficult questions. To a certain extent, in line with Lindert's approach, factors present in the south were absent, or present to a lesser extent, in the north. Northern unions were on average less wealthy than southern unions and generally had lower proportions of agricultural labourers in their populations. Kennedy et al. show that, at least in the period up to 1871, there was a higher proportion of both men and women employed in manufacturing in parts of Ulster.[25] Perhaps it might be argued that industrial employment was more regular or, overall, better paid and that therefore the more

---

number of Persons entitled to Vote in each such Union for Poor Law Guardians…', HC 1874, (253), lvi, 1.

24 See V. Crossman, *Politics, Pauperism and Power*, chapter 4.

25 L. Kennedy, P.S. Ell, E.M. Crawford and L.A. Clarkson, *Mapping the Great Irish* Famine, Four Courts, Dublin, 1999, 156–7.

industrial areas had less need of the poor law.[26] However, these factors are insufficient to explain fully the differences in approach. The uneven spread of manufacturing employment across Ulster does not seem to be related to levels of relief. In addition there was considerable variation in the type of industrial employment from an emphasis on factory work in the east to outwork in Donegal.

One obvious difference is the religious composition of Ulster.[27] While all the southern counties are overwhelmingly Catholic,[28] the Ulster counties varied from the strongly Catholic Cavan (81 per cent in 1881) and Donegal (77 per cent) to the strongly Protestant Down (30 per cent Catholic) and Antrim (26 per cent). There has been surprisingly little study of the impact of religion on poor relief patterns.[29] While there is an absence of work on the impact of such religious divisions on poor relief, one can draw on work on the impact of racism in the United States on its welfare patterns.[30] Alesina et al. suggest two reasons which – by analogy – might lead to lower poor

26 Although previous research in the USA has suggested the opposite, i.e. that the growth of industrialisation was linked to a rise in poor relief expenditure. See J. Underhill Hannon, 'Poverty in the Antebellum Northeast: the View from New York State's Poor Relief Rolls', *Journal of Economic History*, xliv, 4, (1984), 1007–32. Steinmetz, in a study of German cities, did not find any relationship between spending on poor relief and 'industrialisation' (measured by the number of firms in a city) or 'proletarianisation' (manual wage workers as per cent of the labour force): G. Steinmetz, 'The Local Welfare State: Two Strategies for Social Domination in Urban Imperial Germany', *American Sociological Review*, 55, (1990), 891–911.

27 On the role of religion as regards the development of welfare systems see K. van Kersbergen and P. Manow (eds), *Religion, Class Coalitions, and Welfare States*, Cambridge University Press, Cambridge, 2009.

28 In 1881, Wicklow, with 66 per cent Catholics, was the southern county with the lowest Catholic percentage.

29 See S. Kahl, 'The Religious Roots of Modern Poverty Policy: Catholic, Lutheran, and Reformed Protestant Traditions Compared', *Archives Européennes de Sociologie*, xlvi, (2005), 1.

30 A. Alesina, E. Glaeser and B. Sacerdote, 'Why Doesn't the United States Have a European-Style Welfare State?', *Brookings Papers on Economic Activity*, 32, (2001), 187–278. Alberto Alesina: Harvard University Edward Glaeser: Harvard University Bruce Sacerdote: Dartmouth College.

relief in the north of Ireland.[31] First, it is suggested that where there are strong religious divisions in society, a condition which certainly applied in Ulster in the period, and the poor are disproportionately made up of one religious group, and again there is considerable evidence that Catholics were, in general, poorer than Protestants,[32] there will be opposition from rate payers to paying poor relief. An alternative (or complementary) suggestion is that because of the religious differences, northern Irish boards may have had a different ideological approach to payment of relief and may have adopted a more restrictive approach.[33] Of course, these two arguments are not incompatible and it is possible that the differences in ideological approach might be strengthened by sectarianism.

In order to examine these issues, one might look at (i) whether the Ulster boards were, in fact, predominantly Protestant, (ii) whether Catholics received an equitable level of relief; and (iii) whether one can indentify sectarian views amongst the boards. Boards which were informed by a more restrictive approach to the granting of relief might be expected to provide a lower level of relief more generally while boards which were driven by sectarian considerations might be expected both to provide less relief and to provide relief disproportionately to Protestants. As has been seen Ulster boards certainly do provide lower levels of relief but while there is a negative correlation between levels of relief and the percentage of Catholics in the county population, it would appear that this is related to the wealth of the union, i.e. the poorer unions, which provide lower levels of relief, are more likely to have a larger Catholic population.

As will be discussed in chapter 9, up to at least the 1880s the majority of the officers of Ulster boards were landlords and while it is not possible, in the present state of knowledge, individually to establish their religious

31 While the focus of the authors' work is on the impact of racism, their approach is based on the impact of divisions in society and they explicitly acknowledge that 'religious cleavages (for instance) may be more deeply felt that racial ones' in other parts of the world (227).

32 See below.

33 See Kahl, op. cit. T.P. O'Neill argues for a difference in approach to the relief of poverty between the Irish Catholic and Protestant churches ('The Catholic Church and Relief of the Poor, 1815–45', *Archivium Hibernicum*, 31 (1973), 132–45).

composition, it is perhaps safe to assume that Catholics were in a small minority.[34] By 1911, when one can establish the religion of officers from the Census, Catholics do now appear as officers and in Counties Antrim and Down are represented broadly in line with their representation in the community generally. However, there is still a strongly sectarian division and, for example, of the Belfast board (the largest spending board in the north) only two of 40 identified guardians are Roman Catholics. Turning to the composition of those relieved, a special return in 1861 gives the religious breakdown of those in workhouses. Overall, 52 per cent of those relieved were Catholics which is very close to the percentage of Catholics in the overall Ulster population in 1861 (50.5 per cent). However, given the greater poverty of Catholics one would expect that Catholics would make up a greater proportion of those relieved than their share of the overall population and this would suggest that Protestants were overrepresented amongst those on relief in 1861. By 1911 there is a similar pattern: 48 per cent of those relieved indoors were Catholics compared to 43.7 per cent in the overall population. In contrast over 60 per cent of those relieved in charitable institutions in Ulster (in 1901–11) were Catholics although this may be, in part, a response to perceived sectarianism in that Catholic religious orders established large institutions in Ulster in the post-Famine period.[35] Again this would suggest that Catholics are underrepresented on poor relief given their greater level of poverty. In particular in Antrim and Belfast, the percentage of Catholics amongst those relieved (26 per cent) is only slightly higher than their percentage of the overall population (23 per cent) despite the fact that research indicates that Catholics were, on average, poorer than Protestants. Hepburn shows that Catholics in Belfast in 1901 lived in poorer housing, had higher levels of illiteracy and were overrepresented amongst low-skilled employment. Hepburn also shows that there was extensive discrimination against Catholics in the allocation of

34 See, for example, a study reported in the *Belfast Newsletter* which reported that only two of the twelve elected Belfast guardians were Catholics, 27 October 1857.

35 M. Cousins, 'Charity, Philanthropy and Poverty in Ireland, 1850–1914', in I. Brandes and K. Marx-Jaskulski (eds), *Poor relief and charity: rural societies in Europe, 1850–1930*, Peter Lang, Bern, 2008.

employment in nineteenth- and twentieth-century Belfast. Cohen reports similar patterns in part of County Down.[36]

Unfortunately, no published data are available as to the religious composition of those on outdoor relief. However, research (reported in more detail in chapter 3) indicates that of those claiming outdoor relief in Newtownards in the first six months of 1911 only three of the thirty-eight claimants were Roman Catholic.[37] While this is similar to their proportion of the overall union population, given that Catholics were likely to be poorer this would suggest they were underrepresented amongst recipients of relief. However, similar research in Banbridge – where Catholics made up about one-quarter of the population – shows a much higher percentage of Catholics amongst both total claimants and those granted relief (45 per cent.).[38]

The literature on sectarianism and discrimination in Ulster is lengthy and it would be surprising if the pervading sectarianism did not also permeate the boards of guardians.[39] As boards would not have been allowed to

36 A.C. Hepburn, *A Past Apart: Studies in the History of Catholic Belfast, 1850–1950*, UHF, Belfast, 1996: M. Cohen, 'Religion and Inequality in Ireland', *Journal of Interdisciplinary History*, xxv(1), (1994), 1–21.

37 Newtownards and Banbridge were two of the only five northern unions with about average levels of outdoor relief at this time. Roman Catholics made up 7 per cent of the population in the Newtownards union while in Banbridge the proportion was 25 per cent. Census of Ireland, 1911. General report, 1912–13 [Cd. 6663], CXVIII.1, table 122.

38 As outlined in more detail in chapter 3, the study matched the names of claimants reported in the local newspapers with the 1911 Census data, thereby allowing identification of the person's religion (which is not recorded in the poor relief administrative records as regards outdoor relief).

39 See, for example. A.C. Hepburn, *A Past Apart: Studies in the History of Catholic Belfast, 1850–1950*, UHF, Belfast, 1996; I. Budge and C. O'Leary, *Belfast: Approach to Crisis – a Study of Belfast Politics, 1613–1970*, Macmillan, London, 1973; P. Gibbon, *The Origins of Ulster Unionism*, Manchester University Press, Manchester, 1975; A. Jackson, 'Unionist Politics and Protestant Society in Edwardian Ireland', *Historical Journal*, 33(4), (1990), 839–66; M. Cohen, 'Religion and Inequality in Ireland', *Journal of Interdisciplinary History*, xxv, 1 (1994), 1–21. For studies which deal more closely with poverty and the poor law see C. Kinealy and G. MacAtasney, *Hidden*

discriminate on religious grounds in the provision of relief, it is unsurprising that there is not much direct evidence of explicitly sectarian policies, e.g. boards would not have been allowed explicitly to exclude Catholics from relief. However, as will be seen in later chapters, the sectarian tensions in the wider Ulster society are also to be seen in abundance in the operation of the boards.[40]

It is *not* argued that the difference between the patterns of boards north and south can be explained solely by religious differences in the composition of boards and of those relieved.[41] However, it is suggested that an important contributory factor to those differences, albeit one which is impossible to quantify precisely, is (i) an ethos in the Ulster boards which was conducive to the granting of lower levels of relief and to more emphasis on self-sufficiency; (ii) the sectarian tensions which ran throughout Ulster society and which arguably informed the ethos of self-sufficiency, and (iii) in the case of the two large cities, and perhaps smaller urban centres, a desire not to attract unwanted in-migration.

Famine: Hunger, Poverty and Sectarianism in Belfast, 1840–1850, Pluto, London, 2000; A. Jordan, *Who Cared?: Charity In Victorian And Edwardian Belfast*, IIS, 1993; P. Devlin, *Yes we have no bananas: Outdoor Relief in Belfast, 1920–39*, Blackstaff Press, Belfast, 1981. For sectarianism in town governance in the period see G.A. Hall, *Ulster Liberalism, 1778–1876: The Middle Path*, Four Courts, Dublin, 2010, pp. 231–9.

40 There are two rather descriptive studies of the Belfast and Londonderry unions. While both mention the low level of outdoor relief and occasional sectarianism, neither explores these issues in any depth. They are: P. Durnin, 'Aspects of Poor Law Administration and the Workhouse in Derry 1838–1948', in G. O'Brien, *Derry and Londonderry: History and Society*, Geography Press, Dublin, 1991 (summarising the author's *Derry and the Irish Poor Law: a History of the Derry Workhouse*, Waterside Community Local History Group, Derry, 1991); and M. Farrell, *The Poor Law and the Workhouse in Belfast 1838–1948*, PRONI, Belfast, 1978.

41 See K. van Kersbergen and P. Manow, eds, *Religion, Class Coalitions, and Welfare States*, Cambridge University Press, Cambridge, 2009.

Urban v. rural

Lindert found that the English poor law stood out sharply from Continental models in giving more relief in the countryside whereas Continental relief – which was generally organised more on a regional than national basis – favoured towns and cities. He identified an English urban pattern of (1) lower poor rates; (2) lower shares of the population on relief; (3) greater emphasis on indoor relief; and (4) frequent denial of relief to immigrants. If one looks at the data for Ireland (tables 2.4 and 2.5), only the northern cities followed this 'English model'. The southern cities tended to have higher levels of relief than the average, although they generally granted more indoor than outdoor relief. Generally one does not see a distinctive *Irish* urban model and the cities are affected more by the region of which they form part. In the case of the cities of Belfast and Londonderry, it seems likely that an additional factor of concern about in-migration was at play. As has been seen above (table 2.3), these cities (especially Belfast) grew dramatically in the period covered and it is arguable that the guardians may have used control over poor relief as a means of discouraging undesired in-migration.[42]

42 Devlin argues that the provision of inadequate relief was a deliberate policy of the Belfast guardians 'to prevent excessive immigration from the south and west of Ireland and to compel the unemployed to leave Belfast', but without citing evidence in support of this view. The focus of his book is on a somewhat later period. See Devlin, *Yes, we have no bananas*.

CHAPTER 3

Poor Relief and Family Structures

This chapter examines the extent to which poor relief supported families and households. While nuclear and extended families dominated household structures in late nineteenth-century Ireland, at least in rural areas, it is shown that, by 1900, the majority of persons supported in workhouses were single.[1] However, outdoor relief also formed an important part of the Irish poor law system, and data on the household composition of persons supported are not available from official sources. Drawing on a data-matching exercise for a number of poor law unions, it is suggested that the household structure of persons on outdoor relief may have been more complex than the official data would indicate and, in contrast to indoor relief, much more representative of overall household structures.

Poor law and families in Ireland

Unfortunately there is little evidence as to the forms of family and household structure in nineteenth-century Ireland, due to the almost total non-survival of Census manuscripts. However, considerable analysis has been carried out for rural areas for 1901 and 1911.[2] This indicates that extended

1 Household are classified according to the Laslett household classification: P. Laslett and R. Wall, (eds), *Household and Family in Past Time*, Cambridge University Press, Cambridge, 1971.

2 T. Guinnane, *The Vanishing Irish: Households, Migration and the Rural Economy in Ireland, 1850–1914*, Princeton University Press, New Jersey, 1997.

households were common but that simple (or nuclear) families dominated (table 3.1). The data are taken from local studies in five rural areas (including Clare).[3] As can be seen, although there was considerable variation from one area to another, simple and extended families dominated the household structure making up between half and two-thirds; and one-quarter to one-third of all households in each of the areas surveyed.

	Minimum	Maximum
Solitary	2.3	12.6
No family	0.7	7.0
Simple family	51.4	64.3
Extended family	24.3	34.8
Multiple family	0.4	3.3

Table 3.1 Household types in rural Ireland, 1901–11 (per cent of total)
Source: T. Guinnane, *The Vanishing Irish: Households, Migration and the Rural Economy in Ireland, 1850–1914*, Princeton University Press, 1997, table 5.1

There is very little historiography on the role of the poor law in relation to families in Ireland. Demographers such as Guinnane have indeed referred to the possible role which the poor law might have as to issues such as marriage rates but have not explored the issue in detail. Meanwhile, the absence of detailed studies of the poor law itself means that there have been few opportunities to examine the issue. In looking at the poor law the first striking aspect is that, in contrast to the reality of extended families, the poor law and its administrative implementation focused solely on the more immediate family. The data recorded by the poor law authorities focused solely on immediate family relationships (parent-spouse-child) and, in general, no data appear to have been recorded as to more extended family ties.

3 P. Gibbon and C. Curtin, 'The Stem Family in Ireland', *Comparative Studies in Society and History* 20, (1979), 429–53; D. Fitzpatrick, 'Irish Farming Families before the First World War', *Comparative Studies in Society and History*, 25 (1983), 339–74.

There were a number of specific areas in which the poor law impacted on families. First, the poor law authorities required that all members of the family be admitted to the workhouse and it was not possible, in principle, for the parent(s) to leave their children there while seeking work. Second, the poor law imposed responsibility on family members to reimburse the support provided to their spouses and children. Third the poor law set out rules as to the support of illegitimate children. The Irish rules on the maintenance obligations for the fathers of 'bastards' differed to the English law and this was a matter of some controversy at various stages in the nineteenth and early twentieth centuries. However, there is little if any information as to how the law worked in practice. It is unclear whether these rules were implemented in a consistent manner over time and space and, however implemented, what impact they had on Irish families. The first step remains to establish what actually happened in the administration of poor relief from a family perspective.

Macro trends

The effect of the poor law on families

It is possible to look at a macro level at the extent to which different levels of poor law support may influence family structures. For example, it has been suggested that marriage might act as a form of insurance for old age. Thus, one might expect to see a pattern whereby persons in unions which provided high levels of support to older people would see lower marriage rates. Persons who could expect to receive poor relief in their later years might believe that it was less necessary to get married and have a family to provide them with such support.

A special return in 1892[4] provides detailed information on the age of paupers and this return can be analysed to show the extent to which support was given to older people (over 65) in that year both in indoor and out door relief.[5] It is not possible, however, to calculate how much relief was given nor, more intangibly, how salubrious was the workhouse accommodation. There are high variations in levels of support per 100 population and while unions which provided more indoor relief also tended to support more people outdoors the relationship is quite weak.[6] These figures can be compared to the level of non-marriage in 1901, to allow some time for the practice of generosity or lack thereof to have an effect. However, no relationship whatsoever between the two variables is apparent.[7] If one reverses the question to look at the impact of the proportion of persons not married on the level of relief, then somewhat clearer patterns can be seen, a picture supported by the data presented below as to individual unions. The number of older people who are married is quite strongly negatively related to the proportion of the population over sixty on indoor relief (-0.5).

4 Return showing '... the number of persons of each sex of 65 years and upwards...', HC 1892 [360] lxviii, 995.

5 For data reasons, this study is confined to unions which are located within the boundary of a single county, but there is nothing to suggest that they are not broadly representative.

6 North Dublin union, for example, has a very high level of indoor relief and low outdoor relief; Cork has high outdoor relief and a much lower (though above-average) level of indoor relief.

7 The comparison is confined to simple correlations. It may be, of course, that if other factors were taken into account some relationship might emerge, but none whatsoever is apparent from the raw data.

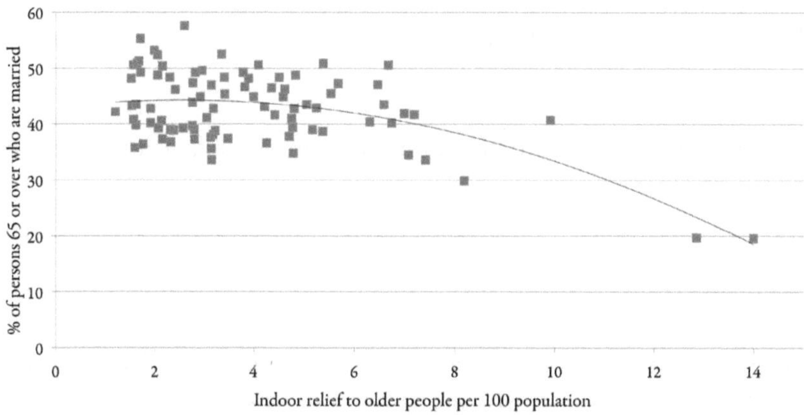

Figure 3.1 Marriage rates and indoor relief for older people, 1906–1911
Source: Database of poor law statistics; Census 1911

Dublin, with a low marriage rate, has one of the highest levels of reliance on indoor relief while western rural unions with high marriage rates have below-average usage of poor relief. However, there is also an interaction between the wealth of a union and use of relief. Controlling for the wealth (measured as the poor law valuation per population) reduces the correlation between marriage and indoor relief (to -0.36) and indicates that there is no correlation between marriage and outdoor relief. These data do suggest indoor relief played a role primarily where family support had broken down but that outdoor relief was payable to a wider range of household types.

Somewhat counterintuitively, the percentage of older people in the population is also strongly negatively correlated with the level of poor relief, i.e. the higher the proportion of older people in the overall population, the lower the proportion of older people on relief. This would appear to be related to the fact that the unions with the highest proportion of older people are mainly northern (Ulster) and western unions which generally provide lower levels of relief while the 'youngest' unions include the Cork and Dublin unions which provide high levels of relief.

Poor relief and households

We turn now to an examination of more micro-level data at the level of individual unions.

Published data

The published reports of the Poor Law Commissioners, subsequently the Local Government Board, are of very little assistance in this regard. Although the annual reports do give data for the numbers of individuals, married couples and children relieved this is not on any one day but over a six-month period. Thus the total number of, say, married couples relieved will count one married couple a number of different times if they are relieved a number of times over that period. Given that it may be assumed that the number of repeat claims varied by family type and over time, these data are of very little use in analysing how the poor law supported families, other than to give some general indication of relative usage. In addition, the type of local administrative data relied on by Levine-Clark in England or Blaikie in Scotland are simply unavailable in an Irish context.[8]

One of the few useful sources of published data is the report of the Viceregal Commission on the Poor Law (1906) which included data which expanded on the categories usually provided by the poor law authorities and included data on marital status at a point in time.[9] As can be seen in table 3.2, which outlines the data provided insofar as it relates to family status, only a tiny minority of Irish workhouses inmates were married cou-

8 M. Levine-Clark, 'The Gendered Economy of Family Liability: Intergenerational Relationships and Poor Law Relief in England's Black Country, 1871–1911,' *Journal of British Studies*, 45, (2006), 72–89; A. Blaikie, 'Nuclear Hardship or Variant Dependency? Households and the Scottish Poor Law', *Continuity and Change*, 17 (2002), 253–80.

9 Appendix to the Report of the Vice-Regal Commission on Poor Law Reform in Ireland. Volume II, 1906 [Cd. 3203] li, 441.

ples (2 per cent) while a further 2 per cent were married women without a husband, mainly of 'indifferent character' if one accepts the categorisation of the workhouse masters. In contrast, unmarried mothers made up 5 per cent of the workhouse population.

	Number	Per cent of inmates
Married couples	375	1.7
Married women	744	1.7*
Widows with one child	60	0.1
Mothers of illegitimate children	2150	4.8
Legitimate children in workhouse	3136	6.9
Illegitimate and deserted children	2764	6.1
Children boarded out	2119	–
Total inmates (excluding boarded out)	45,195	

Table 3.2 Families and the poor law in Ireland, 1905
Source: Viceregal Commission, *Report*, 1906, Vol. I, 16; Vol. II, table 4.
* Although the report does not make it clear, it would appear that these are married women without a husband in the workhouse (i.e. they do not include the 375 wives of the married couples).

Outdoor relief was noticeably more likely to be paid to married couples and almost 20 per cent of such relief went to husbands who were sick or permanently disabled (due to age or incapacity) and their spouses. This increases to over one-quarter of all recipients when the children of such claimants are taken into account.[10] In contrast, one-fifth (21 per cent) of recipients are widows and their children, while about one in twenty (4–5 per cent) are adult women and their children. The largest group (about 46 per cent) consists of single women and men who are permanently disabled. Unfortunately both published and unpublished data on outdoor relief provide

10 This assumes that almost all children of adult males are of adult males with wives, which may overstate this figure slightly.

very limited information as to the family/household status of recipients. First, although the published data indicate where the 'head of household' was in receipt of relief for both him or herself and other family members, the data do not indicate whether apparently 'solitary' persons were in fact living alone or whether they lived with other non-dependent persons, such as, for example, siblings. Second, very few of the outdoor relief registers outside what is now Northern Ireland have survived and even here the registers do not indicate the household status of non-heads.

The only detailed study of an outdoor relief register to date found that in Milford union in the period 1859 to 1922 relief was given to 'single' people – repeating the caveat that it is not known whether such persons lived alone or with others – in 45 per cent of all cases, to widows and widowers in one-third of cases, and to persons classified as married in less than one-fifth (17 per cent) of cases (the remainder are unspecified (4 per cent) or orphans (1 per cent)).[11] This research also indicated that out relief was given predominantly to older people (68 per cent of cases were over 66). In order to gain a better perspective on this issue, the present study matched outdoor relief data from a number of unions for 1901–11 with the manuscript Census data.

The 1906 report of the Viceregal Commission provides limited 'household' data for each of the 160 workhouses so that it is possible to identify regional variations – albeit only for 1905. There was quite a variation amongst the six largest cities (and even between the two Dublin unions). Married couples made up a very small proportion of the population in all workhouses but 'mothers of illegitimate children' ranged from less than 1 per cent (South Dublin Union) to over 6 per cent (Waterford) of the workhouse population while illegitimate and deserted children varied from 1.8 per cent (Cork) to almost 9 per cent (again Waterford). The reasons behind these variations including economic and social factors, varying alternative provision, e.g. religious penitentiaries and orphanages, and boarding out, and union policy remain to be explored further.

11 A. Schüle, 'Outdoor Relief in Milford Union, County Donegal, Ireland from 1859 to 1922' MA Thesis, University of Trier, 2006.

Patterns also varied in rural areas. For example, in the south-western county of Clare married couples made up a small proportion of the population, while mothers of illegitimate children and illegitimate and deserted children were present in all workhouses and made up a numerically small but proportionally large population. In contrast to most urban workhouses, illegitimate children were generally more numerous than legitimate children in Clare. The striking feature is the difference between the types of family which were supported and the breakdown of family types in the Clare region (table 3.1). As has been seen, simple and extended families dominated (at least in rural areas), making up 80–90 per cent of all households, while single people or those living in a household with no family members generally made up less than 10 per cent. In contrast, it is clear that the large majority of those in workhouses were single. For example, data from the Census manuscripts for Galway workhouse show that two-thirds of inmates were single (65 per cent) while one-quarter were widowed (24.5 per cent) and only 10.5 per cent married. The Ennis workhouse shows a very similar breakdown: 65 per cent single, 23 per cent widowed and 12 per cent married.

Survey evidence

Indoor Relief

Given the limitations of the published data, it is necessary to turn to research which has looked specifically at family composition through analysis of surviving poor law records. Burke's analysis of admissions to the South Dublin workhouse in 1861, in the middle of a period of depression, indicates that the majority were adults admitted alone (68 per cent). Single adults admitted with children constituted one-quarter of admissions indicating that, even at this early stage in the poor law, the admission of whole families was uncommon.[12] Only 3 per cent of admissions consisted of two adults and children. While one come across frequent references in more general literature to the rule that whole families had to be admitted to the workhouse, this was a rule of practice rather than a legal requirement and Burke's analysis would suggest that even in 1861 admission of whole families was the exception.[13] However, in comparison to the later period it is worth noting that, in this time of crisis, close to one-third of admissions did relate to families with children or children alone. Of the single adults admitted Burke found that they were a 'young, mobile group'.[14] Over half of all single adults admitted were between the ages of sixteen and thirty and 38 per cent remained for less than two weeks in the workhouse.[15]

The analysis of the indoor relief records for the midland Mullingar union in 1879, also a year of economic crisis, again indicates that – at least in such times – the poor law may have played an important role in supporting families. One of the difficulties of using admission registers is that admissions could last for one day or for months (or even years) and it would be necessary to track different admissions over a considerable period. Unusually, a weekly relief list and abstract for the half year ending March 1879 survives for the Mullingar union. This gives sufficient information to identify the family structure and also shows the number of days relieved in the half year. This allows us to construct a picture of the average composition of the Mullingar workhouse in the period. Mullingar was a union of above-average wealth in the period which paid above-average levels of indoor and outdoor relief.[16]

12 H. Burke, *The People and the Poor Law in Nineteenth Century Ireland*, WEB, 1987, 188.

13 It is not, however, clear that this finding means that, as Burke claims (Ibid., 188), 'the family test for admission… was never strictly implemented', since it is not clear (except in one case study which she cites) that the families admitted had other members who stayed out.

14 Ibid., 190.

15 Ibid., 190 and 348.

16 The weekly register shows all those in the workhouse during the period (both those already there in September 1879 and those admitted during the six months). The records indicate the age and poor law classification (e.g. an able-bodied male member

Family unit	Percentage of people
Married couple only	2.4
Married couple with children	3.6
Parent with children*	14.5
Unmarried mother with children	4.8
Extended families	3.0
Multiple children without parents	2.4
Child alone	12.1
Solitary adult	57.2

Table 3.3 Membership of family units in Mullingar workhouse, 1878–9
Source: Mullingar weekly relief list and abstract for half-year ending 25 March 1879.
* These appear to be parents of legitimate children but the register does not indicate whether they are widowed or currently married.

As can be seen in table 3.3, solitary adults do make up the bulk of those relieved in the workhouse. However, almost one-third are members of extant family units of one form or other – mainly single parents with children. Members of married couples, with and without children, make up 6 per cent of those in the workhouse – a much higher figure than for the later period. In this period, single children without parents constitute one-eighth of those receiving relief. In addition, it is important to note that the admission of single adults to the workhouse does not necessarily mean that the poor law was not playing a role in supporting families outside the workhouse.

of a married couple is coded 1, etc.). Families admitted at the same time appear to be recorded together so that one can identify the family structure. In total the register contains over 1,200 persons in the period and a systematic random sample of 10 per cent was taken.

Category	Number	Age	Average days in workhouse
Able-bodied men	44	31.7	9.1
Able-bodied women	14	27.5	52.8
Not able-bodied men	10	65.9	118.8
Not able-bodied women	7	55.9	140.6
Lunatics, insane persons and idiots	6	33.7	130.6

Table 3.4 Single persons in Mullingar workhouse, 1878–9
Source: Mullingar weekly relief list and abstract for half-year ending 25 March 1879.

In total, eighty-one of the sample were single adults, constituting over half the total person days spent in the workhouse in the period. Of these over half were young able-bodied men admitted for short periods of time and a further 17 per cent were young able-bodied women, although this group stayed somewhat longer. There are also smaller groups of older men and women and of younger persons categorised as 'lunatics, insane persons and idiots' who remained on average much longer in the workhouse.[17] By definition most of the younger people were admitted and discharged during the six month period showing that indoor relief was playing a role in supporting unemployment during the crisis period. It is unfortunately impossible to identify further the former family status of these persons but it would seem very possible that many of the young men and women must have been living as part of broader households prior to admission to the workhouse.

For 1901, it is possible to gather some evidence from the Census manuscripts. While it is difficult to identify family relationship from the Census manuscripts because only initials are given for workhouse inmates,[18] it is clear that family units, including married couples, widows or single mothers and their children, made up a relatively small percentage of 'units' in the

17 In the period the maximum stay was 177 days and fourteen of the twenty-two were in the workhouse for the whole period.

18 It is interesting to note that the Census procedures deprived workhouse inmates of the two most central components of identity: one's name and family status.

workhouse (counting single persons, and related family members as one unit). It is possible to make some attempt to assess this issue by analysing the Census manuscripts for Ennis union (Co. Clare) in 1901 although this is by no means straightforward.[19] Attaching due caution to the nature of this analysis, it is clear that single people, i.e. those in the workhouse without any obvious family connection, made up the vast majority of inmates (71 per cent of people and 87 per cent of 'units'). As expected married couples – none with children – constituted less than 1 per cent of units and widow(er)s with children also only 1 per cent. Married women with children made up 3 per cent of family units (7.5 per cent of inmates) while unmarried mothers made up 5 per cent (8 per cent of inmates). Perhaps surprisingly, families of children with no apparent parent in the workhouse made up no less than 4 per cent of units (10 per cent of the workhouse population). Thus complete nuclear families (husband and wife) with children were not found in the workhouse *at all* while 'incomplete' families (one parent with children or children without a parent) made up 14 per cent of family units and a considerable 27 per cent of inmates.

	per cent of units	per cent of people
Married couple	0.9	1.5
Widow(er) with children	1.2	1.9
Married woman with children	2.7	7.5
Unmarried mother with children	4.7	8.0
Multiple children without parents	3.8	9.7
Solitary	86.7	71.3

Table 3.5 Family units in Ennis workhouse, 1901
Source: Census manuscripts for Ennis workhouse, 1901.

19 I used the Ennis workhouse as it was the only 1901 (and hence pre-old age pension) Census manuscript online. Ennis was a moderately large workhouse of over 400 people (about 1 per cent of total workhouse inmates). Analysis is problematic because only initials rather than names are given and no family relationships are recorded. However, unlike some other workhouses, whoever completed the manuscript for the Ennis workhouse appears generally to have listed family members together.

In contrast to the picture of a relatively young group of single people seen in Dublin in 1861 and in Mullingar in 1879, the average age of the single adults in the Ennis workhouse was close to sixty (58.6) and only about 13 per cent were aged thirty or under.

Outdoor Relief

If the workhouses provided somewhat limited support to nuclear families, the research on outdoor relief shows a rather different picture. As noted above, the official sources provide limited, and misleading, data on the household status of those relieved. Accordingly, for the purposes of this study a matching exercise on outdoor relief data for the western Ballinrobe and northern Banbridge and Newtownards unions was carried out.

Ballinrobe (Co. Mayo) is a western union with a population of 21,200 in 1901, based around the small town of Ballinrobe. Although it was of below-average wealth (in terms of valuation per head of population), it was not a particularly poor union and the valuation per head was £2.86 compared to a national average of £3.48. Levels of relief were somewhat below the national average but Ballinrobe provided a comparatively high proportion of relief outside the workhouse. Ballinrobe supported 0.5 (per 100 population) in the workhouse and 1.0 outside compared to a national average of 0.83 and 1.34. The minutes of the board do not appear to be extant but there is detailed coverage of the meetings in the local *Ballinrobe Chronicle*. This study looked at all claims for outdoor relief in the period October 1900 to September 1901, i.e. the 6 months either side of the 1901 Census, which took place on 31 March 1901.[20] It proved possible to match almost two-thirds of the claims made. There was only one repeat claim in the period. As noted above, Schüle's study in Milford indicated that, drawing on the administrative data alone, relief was paid to single persons and widows in over three-quarters of all cases. Indeed, the administrative

20 Ballinrobe outdoor relief register, 1900–1, Mayo County Archive.

data from Ballinrobe indicated a rather similar picture. Of the seventy-six claims made in the period, almost two-thirds (48) were made by single persons or widows not recorded as having any children. Only just over a third of claims were made by married persons or widows with families. The seventy-six claims represented 162 people, which corresponds with the official figures for the number of new claims in the year and about 40 per cent of the total numbers on outdoor relief in the union.

However, when the administrative data are matched to the Census manuscripts a strikingly different picture appears.[21] Of the fifty-six households where it has been possible to match the two sources of data, it is now seen that no fewer than twenty-five are nuclear (simple) families while a further ten are either extended (9) or multiple (1) households. In addition, there are a further four non-nuclear households, e.g. widows living with a grandson or niece. Only seventeen cases were actually solitary (and even a number of these were, in fact, living with other persons as a visitor or boarder). As one might expect, in a considerable number of cases, the nuclear households in receipt of relief were either older (the claimant being shown as sixty or over in either the Census or administrative data) (15)[22] and/or 'incomplete' (9). In a further three cases there was an inconsistency between the Census and administrative data as to whether the household was incomplete which might suggest the absence or imminent departure of one spouse due to death, search for work or some other reason. Nonetheless in two cases relief was paid to complete nuclear households[23] and in other cases relief was paid to a young man living with his nuclear family.[24]

21 It is highly likely that in some cases, household structures have changed somewhat between the period of the relief claim and that on the Census. However, there appears to be a high level of residential stability.

22 One interesting side issue is that the ages recorded in the outdoor relief registers are, on average, significantly older than the Census ages, so that the claimants, the relieving officer or both overstated the age to increase the 'deserving' nature of the claim.

23 In one case the husband – Henry C. – had a broken arm, *Ballinrobe Chronicle*, 13 September 1900.

24 For example, in December 1900, relief was granted to twenty-six-year-old Patrick M., shown in the Census as living with his mother and three siblings. Similarly, in

In other cases, relief was paid to an adult living with an older parent or relative.[25] It is not clear if the parent/relative was also in receipt of relief. Thus the households revealed by the data-matching exercise are much more complex than the administrative data would suggest.

	Ballinrobe	Newtownards	Banbridge	
Household Type	Awarded	Awarded	Awarded	Refused
Solitary	17	7	16	2
Nuclear	25	20	13	4
Extended	9	6	2	2
Multiple	1	1	0	0
Non-nuclear	4	4	13	2
In workhouse	0	0	0	1
Total	56	38	44	11

Table 3.6 Outdoor relief in Ballinrobe, Newtownards and Banbridge unions by household structure, 1901–11
Source: Ballinrobe outdoor relief register, 1900–1; *Newtownards Spectator*, 1911; *Banbridge Chronicle* 1911; Census 1901 and 1911.

As a result the number of persons in the household and the average household size were much greater than would be indicated by the administrative data. Looking only at identified cases, the administrative records indicated a total of 121 people involved (an average of 2.2 per claim). This is close to the average for all claims of 2.1. In contrast the Census data indicate that the households in which a person was relieved included no less than 194 people (an average of 3.5 persons per household). The household structures of those relieved (table 3.6) are much closer to the general household

April 1901 Thomas L. (in his twenties) was paid relief although he is shown as living with his parents, two siblings and cousin.

25 For example, forty-year-old Mary M. (or thirty-four, if you prefer the Census data), living with her eighty-two-year-old father, was paid relief.

structures in rural Ireland (table 3.1) in contrast to the marked disparity with those relieved in the workhouse. It would appear that, at least in the case of Ballinrobe union, the guardians were using the poor law to support family structures and not only as a response to the break-up of the family.

In Newtownards, all claims granted in the first six months of 1911 were examined and matched to the 1911 Census data.[26] Newtownards was then the second largest town in Co. Down and its principal industry was muslin weaving. In total there were fifty-nine persons who had been newly awarded outdoor relief or whose awards had been increased. However, several of these were duplicates where, for example, an award for a short period was subsequently continued. In total there were forty-six separate persons who were awarded relief in the period. Of these, it proved possible to identify thirty-eight (78 per cent).[27] As in the case of Ballinrobe, many of the claimants were members of nuclear or extended households.[28] Only seven were solitary and in most cases even they were living with or as boarders. Over half those receiving relief were members of nuclear families at the time of the Census and four out of five were members of some form of family. The Census data indicate that the households in which a person was relieved included no less than 172 people excluding boarders (an average of 4.5 persons per household).

Finally, all claims for outdoor relief in the Banbridge union were examined again in the period January–June 1911.[29] Banbridge union is also mainly in County Down. In total there were over seventy separate claims for outdoor relief in the period. However, a small number were from members of the same families and as the focus of this study was on the family unit,

26 Unusually, the names and addresses of those to whom outdoor relief was granted are recorded in the *Newtownards Spectator*.

27 A partial identification in one case, as the claimant is not in the Census but what appears to be his family is.

28 It is, of course, possible that in some cases household structure had changed between the time of the grant of relief and the holding of the Census.

29 The *Banbridge Chronicle* recorded details of all claims (successful and unsuccessful) and gives details of the discussions as to whether or not relief should be granted – thus providing a very interesting source of information.

and as the guardians insisted that claims – even from separated persons – be considered together, these have been treated as single claims. This gave a total of seventy claims for relief. Of these, fifteen were refused and the rest were successful in at least one instance.[30] It has been possible to identify fifty-five of these seventy units (79 per cent). In Banbridge, particularly amongst those granted relief, there was a higher proportion of solitaries and non-nuclear families, though many of these involved siblings living together. However, nuclear and extended families still made up over one-third of those granted relief.[31] The Census data indicates that the households in which a person was relieved included 131 people excluding boarders and unrelated persons (an average of 2.4 persons per household).

The gender of claimants can be identified from the outdoor relief records examined above.[32] There was no clear pattern in the three unions. In Ballinrobe, claimants were more or less evenly split between men and women. In contrast, the majority of claimants in both northern unions were women (56 per cent in Newtownards and 65 per cent in Banbridge). However, the records indicate that men were more likely to claim in respect of a dependent wife so that it can be assumed that in all three unions women made up the majority of the adults supported by outdoor relief.

Conclusion

The available evidence indicates that the Irish poor law was always more likely to provide indoor relief to single persons and to 'incomplete' families. It is clear that single persons made up the vast majority of those supported

30 One claim for an increase was deferred and no outcome is recorded, but as the person was already in receipt of relief it is included here with the successful claims.

31 Although the number of cases is small, the Banbridge data indicate that larger families were more likely to be refused relief in that union.

32 Other than in a small number of cases where names are illegible or only an initial given. Unfortunately the published data is subject to the same qualifications as outlined above in that it is over a six-month period.

in Irish workhouses by the end of the nineteenth century. However, while caution must be exercised given that the data comes from only a small number of unions, there is evidence that at least some Irish unions used outdoor relief to support family structures. However, it must be recalled that outdoor relief was non-existent or very limited in Ireland (with the exception of the Great Famine period) up to the 1860s and that even as late as 1900 many northern unions paid very low rates of out relief while some poor peripheral western unions also had very low levels of outdoor relief. In many cases, Irish poor relief policy focused on providing support only where families had broken down.

The evidence indicates that, first, the institutional poor law and administrative procedures did not reflect the type of family which actually existed in Ireland. It is clear from the Census evidence that extended families were widespread. However, the poor laws – and administrative procedures – were based on the narrower concept of the immediate (nuclear) family. Legal responsibility to maintain was confined to the nuclear family and, presumably as a result, the poor law records are solely interested in marital and parental relationship.

In 1861 and 1879, the evidence suggests that, at least in time of crisis, the poor law played an important role in supporting families and in providing short-term support for unemployed single men and women. However, by the early 1900s, there was a substantial divergence between the type of family unit supported in the Irish workhouse and the family structure which existed in the broader community. While, as has been seen, extended families were common in rural Ireland, the majority of people in the workhouse around 1900 were single and very few married couples were to be found in workhouses. The type of family to be found is dominated by lone parent and 'no parent' family groupings. Such family units are to be found in all the Clare workhouses examined but appear to make up a higher proportion of the population of the urban Ennis workhouse. This would suggest that, to a significant extent, family units only entered the workhouse where they had been unable to form a two-parent unit or where the two-parent unit had broken up due to death, desertion or some other reason. It is not possible, of course, to say that many such units did not exist outside the workhouse. Nor is it clear whether the breakup of a family unit led to economic distress and from there to the workhouse or whether economic distress led to the breakup of family unit, with, for example, a husband going to England to look for work, and thence to the workhouse. It is clear that at least some local unions were much more likely to provide support to nuclear and extended families outside the workhouse, but further local studies would be essential to establish how widespread this pattern was.

CHAPTER 4

The Poor Law in the Post-Famine Decades, 1851–1878

This chapter examines issues which highlight political and social class struggles in relation to the provision of poor relief in the period from 1851 to just before the Land War (the late 1870s). It outlines developments in the period (both general and those specific to the poor law) before going on to look at a number of key poor law issues including, first, the complex governance of the poor law. Secondly the appointment of a Select Committee on the poor law is examined, as well as the subsequent passage of amending legislation in 1862 which legalised the broadening of the poor law system to provide hospital services to a wider public. The chapter concludes by looking at debates concerning union rating, showing how landlords retained an effective control over poor law policies despite nascent *politicisation*. One of the bitterest debates in the 1860s and 1870s was about proposals to move from a system of rating by electoral divisions to one of union rating. The system of rating by electoral divisions had been introduced as a part of a compromise with the Duke of Wellington in the House of Lords in 1838. The effect was, in general, to increase the level of rates paid by one or two electoral divisions, usually the main town(s), to the benefit of rural electoral divisions and, obviously, their rate payers.

Political, economic and demographic change

The 1850s was a period of relative quiet in Irish politics. Agitation in relation to land tenure in the early 1850s led to the establishment of an Independent Irish Party in Parliament, but this party was ultimately short-lived.[1] The following two decades saw considerably more activity. The 1860s saw the growth of the Fenian movement which led to an abortive rising in 1867.[2] Ongoing land agitation led to important land reform in 1870.[3] The early 1870s saw the establishment of a strong Home Rule party which was to play a very important part in the future development of Irish politics.[4] Following the decline of the Independent Irish party, support for Conservative candidates grew so that, by 1859, the Conservative party secured a majority of Irish seats.[5] However, by 1865 the Liberals had regained the majority and the Conservative party had begun its long-term decline in Ireland. In Ireland, however, support for the Liberal party was always inflated by the adhesion of members who would otherwise support a more independent position and the establishment of a coherent Home Rule party before the 1874 elections saw that party win no less than sixty seats, while the Liberal party declined dramatically to only ten seats and the Conservatives continued their decline to thirty-three seats.

1 J.H. Whyte, *The Independent Irish Party, 1850–9*, Oxford University Press, Oxford, 1958.

2 See R.V. Comerford, *The Fenians in Context: Irish Politics and Society 1848–82*, Wolfhound Press, Dublin, 1985 for a detailed but partial account. J. Newsinger, *Fenianism in Mid-Victorian Britain*, Pluto, London, 1994, provides a useful (if short) corrective.

3 E.D. Steele, *Irish Land and British Politics: Tenant-Right and Nationality 1865–1870*, Cambridge University Press, Cambridge, 1974.

4 D. Thornley, *Isaac Butt and Home Rule*, Macgibbon and Kee, London, 1964.

5 B.M. Walker, *Parliamentary election results in Ireland, 1801–1922*, Royal Irish Academy, Dublin, 1978. See K.T. Hoppen, *Elections, Politics and Society in Ireland, 1832–1885*, Clarendon, Oxford, 1984; A. Shields, *Irish Conservative Party, 1852–1868: Land, Politics and Religion*, Irish Academic Press, Dublin, 2007.

The demographic position changed dramatically in the period. The population in 1851 was about 6.5 million, having fallen by about 2 million during the Famine period. The population declined further over the period to 5,400,000 by 1871 and 5,200,000 by 1881. The structure of the population also changed with, in particular, a rise in the proportion of persons never married, from 10 per cent in 1841 to 17 per cent in 1881. Economically, the country saw a steady growth in its national income in the period. Geary and Stark estimated that gross domestic product grew from £96 million (in 1900 terms) in 1861 to £124 million by 1881, a rise of 29 per cent.[6] Because of the declining population, per capita GDP grew more rapidly from £17 (1900 values) in 1861 to £24 in 1881 – a rise of 41 per cent. This meant that per capita GDP rose from about 56 per cent of the United Kingdom average to 66 per cent by 1881. There is an absence of data as to the living standards of the population. Wages certainly rose significantly in nominal terms and life expectancy increased from under forty years before the Famine to about fifty by the early 1870s.[7] Ó Gráda's careful review of the evidence concludes that there was a rise in living standards in the period and this finding is supported by the overall decline in the numbers on poor relief in the period and by the contemporary comments by the poor law inspectors and others. For example, the Poor Law Commission stated that 'visible signs of an improved condition of life are to be found in the appearance of the peasantry in all parts of the country, more particularly in their clothing'.[8] Indicators of housing quality also show a sustained improvement over the period.[9] However, the overall growth and prosperity

6 F. Geary and T. Stark, 'Examining Ireland's Post-Famine Economic Performance: the Distribution of Gross Domestic Product between the Countries of the United Kingdom, 1861–1911', ESRI working paper 71, Dublin, 1996. However, it should be noted that this represented a slight decline in Ireland's GDP as a percentage of the United Kingdom total.

7 C. Ó Gráda, *Ireland: a New Economic History*, 242.

8 Eighth Annual Report of the Commissioners for Administering the Laws for Relief of the Poor in Ireland, HC 1854–5 [1945] xxiv, 523 at 16–17.

9 L. Kennedy et al., *Mapping the Great Irish Famine*, Dublin, Four Courts Press, Dublin, 1999, 76–87.

was broken by an agricultural depression in the period 1859–64. Evictions fell from 4,800 (affecting 25,000 persons) in 1853 to 636 in 1860, before rising again during the agricultural depression.[10] After a peak of almost 2,000 in 1864, evictions fell back to less than 500 in 1877 (affecting 2,200 persons). Similarly, agrarian outrages fell from 469 in 1853 and, after a rise in 1869–70, fell to record lows in the mid-1870s.[11] Overall the period saw a dramatic modernisation of Irish society in terms of, for example, transport and communications. Some key indicators of these factors and of the devotional revolution are set out in table 4.1.

	c.1850	c.1870
Railyways (miles)	400	2000
Postage (letters)	39 million	65 million
Newspapers	100	140
Daily Dublin newspapers	3	8
Illiteracy	71 per cent	33 per cent
Priests (persons per priest)	2100	1300

Table 4.1 Indicators of modernisation, 1850–70
Source: R.V. Comerford, 'Ireland 1850–70: Post-Famine and Mid-Victorian', in *A New History of Ireland*, volume V, chapter 20.

Reflecting the general developments outlined above, as far as the poor law is concerned, there are two distinct periods: (i) a post-Famine period of reductions in numbers and administrative reform to about 1863; and (ii) a (re)politicisation of the poor law with the development of the Home Rule party with specific views on poor law issues.

10 Return of cases of evictions in Ireland…, HC, 1881 [2] lxxvii, 727.

11 Return of outrages reported to the Royal Irish Constabulary…, HC, 1881 [c.2756] lxxvii, 907–9. Agrarian 'outrages' were crimes (such as maiming of cattle, destruction of property, threats and attacks on land agents and landlords) considered to have a broader 'political' implication.

Poor law developments

Recovery and stability, 1851–1863

The main developments in this period included, first, a dramatic reduction in the numbers supported by the poor law in the post-Famine period due to economic and demographic change. Both economic growth and the falling population reduced pressures on the poor law and the numbers in workhouses fell to under 40,000 by the end of the decade, while outdoor relief was almost abolished, with only very small numbers of paupers being relieved in this manner (see chapter 1). A second key feature was administrative expansion of the poor law to include hospital services; while the poor law did provide hospital services this was, in most cases, supposed to be confined to destitute poor persons. However, with the tacit consent of the Poor Law Commission, the local boards admitted 'poor' but non-destitute persons to the workhouse hospital wards and this practice was finally legitimated by Parliament in 1862 (see below).

Emigration remained a topic of debate, although after the immediate post-Famine period the amount of supported emigration was quite low.[12] Conversely removal of paupers (from England and Wales and Scotland) was a constant topic which took up many pages of the annual Poor Law Commission reports and of local minute books.[13] Finally there were ongo-

12 In the period from 1851 to 1877, 31,300 persons were assisted to emigrate under the poor law mainly in the period to 1855. Annual Report of the Local Government Board for Ireland…, HC 1877 [c. 1761] xxxviii, 1.

13 In this period, the number removed from Britain to Ireland significantly exceeded the numbers assisted to emigrate from Ireland by the poor law. However, it is also important to bear in mind the number of Irish-born persons assisted in Britain who were not affected by the law of removal. In 1875, no less than 40,000 persons born in Ireland were in receipt of poor relief in England and Wales. In contrast, the number of persons born in England being relieved in Ireland was 136. (Return of number of persons born in England and Wales receiving relief in Ireland, HC 1876 (206) lxiii, 85. See generally F. Neal, 'The English Poor Law, the Irish Migrant and the Laws of Settlement and Removal, 1819–1879', in D.G. Boyce and R. Swift, (eds), *Problems and*

ing debates about child mortality in workhouses – leading to proposals for boarding out of young children – and illegitimacy and unmarried mothers in workhouses, including discussion on moral classification.

The driving forces behind developments in this period appear to have been (i) the large-scale economic and demographic changes in Ireland and (ii) the administration, in particular the Poor Law Commission. The latter were particularly important in supporting the (initially unlawful) extension of the poor law to provide general hospital services. In contrast there was little political interest in Ireland or England in the poor law.

Religion and the poor law

Religious issues were prominent in this period. These included the appointment and discipline of clergy, payment of clergy, use of Catholic nuns as nurses, provision of appropriate religious facilities and proselytism including the registration of children whose religion was unknown. A related issue was concern expressed by Catholics about the lack of Irishmen and Catholics on the Poor Law Commission. The religious divisions in Ireland are too well-known to require detailed treatment here. Although a substantial majority of the population were Roman Catholic (over three-quarters in the period examined here), the religion of the state was Protestant, the Church of Ireland (whose adherents made up only 12 per cent of the population in 1861).[14] A parliamentary return shows that, in 1861, 87 per cent of workhouse inmates were Catholic overall – and, of course, this percentage would have been higher in many parts of southern Ireland.[15] For example, in Connaught there were only 182 members of the Established Church and one Presbyterian out of 4,893 workhouse inmates, the remainder being exclusively Catholic.

Perspectives in Irish History since 1800, Four Courts, Dublin, 2004. For a local study, see C. O'Mahony, *Cork's Poor Law Palace: Workhouse Life 1838–1890*, Rosmathún Press, Cork, 2005, chapter 3).

14 Obviously not all 'Protestants' were members of the Church of Ireland. However, the term Protestant is used here as reflecting contemporary usage in the texts studied.

15 Report from the Select Committee on Poor Relief (Ireland), HC 1861 (408), x, 1, at 548–53.

There had been a long history of religious tension. Religious tensions continued during the Famine, during which, Christine Kinealy argues, 'widespread hunger was used as a lever for persuading the poor to convert to Protestantism'.[16] These activities left a long folk memory. Religious tensions were further worsened in the 1850s by Lord John Russell's attack on the Catholic religion and the subsequent Ecclesiastical Titles Act arising from the decision by the Pope to establish an English Roman Catholic hierarchy with territorial titles.[17] This led to a strong adverse response among Catholics in Ireland and was an important factor behind the establishment of an independent Irish party and the fall of the Russell government. Tensions were further exacerbated by the decision of Lord Derby's government to enforce the law banning the exercise of the Catholic religion in public and the subsequent Stockport riots.[18]

The 1838 Poor Law Act attempted to take a neutral position as between the different religions in Ireland. Because of religious tensions, and unlike the situation in England and Wales, no clergymen of any denomination were allowed to sit as members of the local boards of guardians. Given the importance of relief in workhouses in the Irish system, the question of the provision of religious services was of particular importance. The Poor Law Act provided that the Poor Law Commissioners were to 'take order for the performance of religious services' in the workhouses and to appoint persons to be chaplains for that purpose, one for the Church of Ireland, another for Protestant dissenters, and another for the Roman Catholic church. The law provided that no inmate of a workhouse was to be compelled to attend any religious service contrary to the religious principles of that person or to which his or her parents or guardians objected. In effect this meant that children were to be registered in the religion desired by the parent or guardian.

16 C. Kinealy, *The Great Irish Famine: Impact, Ideology and Rebellion*, Palgrave, Basingstoke 2002, 156–68. See also I. Whelan, 'The Stigma of Souperism' in C. Póirtéir (ed.), *The Great Irish Famine*, Mercier, Dublin, 1995, 135–54.

17 See J.H. Whyte, *The Independent Irish Party 1850–9*, Oxford University Press, Oxford, 1958, 19–23 and J. Prest, *Lord John Russell*, University of South Carolina Press, Columbia, 1972, 319 et seq.

18 See Whyte, *Independent Irish Party*, 57–61. For a particularly violent local religious struggle, see G. Moran, *A Radical Priest in Mayo: Fr Patrick Lavelle*, Four Courts, Dublin, 1994, ch. 2.

Despite the attempt at religious neutrality, the poor law was not exempt from allegations of proselytism and other forms of religious tensions.[19] The situation was exacerbated when a lacuna in the legislation was identified, in that it did not specifically deal with the situation in which the religion of the person entering the workhouse was not known.[20] It soon became apparent that in a considerable number of cases young abandoned children were admitted to the workhouse in circumstances where little or nothing was known about their parenthood or religion. As early as January 1842, the Poor Law Commissioners referred a case to the Irish Attorney General, Francis Blackburne, for his opinion as to the appropriate response in such circumstances. Blackburne replied that 'the guardians ought… to cause the child to be educated in the religious creed of Protestantism, the religion of the state'. The issue continued to arise before boards of guardians who were clearly reluctant to obey the stark advice of the Attorney General. In some cases, children were brought before the board of guardians and asked to bless themselves as evidence of religion and boards of guardians sometimes voted as to the appropriate religion in which to register the child.[21] In the 1850s the Poor Law Commission sought the legal opinion of the Attorney General on a number of occasions without apparently being able to resolve the issue.

Perhaps surprisingly there is little indication that the Roman Catholic hierarchy, as a body, gave much attention to poor law issues in the 1850s,

19 See, for example, 'Report by Captain Spark relative to charges of proselytism in workhouse of Dingle Union', 1851 (427) xlix, 173. It should be noted that allegations of proselytism were by no means confined to those against Protestants. See, for example, *Daily Express*, 4 May 1860 (report of an enquiry by a poor law inspector into Catholic proselytism in Bantry); *Daily Express*, *Irish Times* and *Dublin Evening Packet*, 4, 11 and 18 October 1860 (complaints of proselytism in the North Dublin union); *Galway Express*, 12 March to 16 April 1870. On religious tensions in the South Dublin workhouse see H. Burke, *The People and the Poor Law*, 87–93. See also J. Robins, *Lost Children: History of the Charity Child in Ireland, 1700–1900*, IPA, Dublin, 1987, 244–57.

20 See M. Cousins, 'Registration of the religion of children under the Irish poor law, 1838–70', *Journal of Ecclesiastical History*, 61(1), (2010), 107–24.

21 For example, in the North Dublin union: *Freeman's Journal*, 2 July 1857.

despite its concerns about proselytism generally.[22] In the late 1850s, it began to pay more attention to this issue. A meeting of the four Irish archbishops in March 1858 drew up a series of resolutions which were forwarded to Rome.[23] These included the resolutions concerning the relations of the Catholic Church and of Catholic chaplains in workhouses which were considered to be 'highly unsatisfactory' the administration of the poor law 'being intrusted almost exclusively to Protestants wholly unacquainted with, or not having respect for the doctrine or discipline of our Church.' The resolution called on the government to 'appoint one or more Catholic Poor-Law Commissioners and a fair proportion of Catholic Inspectors, to set apart in each Work-House an appropriate place to be used exclusively for Catholic worship, to provide a Catholic Education for Catholic Children, and to treat as Catholics all children of Catholic parents or baptized by a Catholic priest.' However, it is not clear whether any specific action was taken on foot of these resolutions. This issue was amongst those addressed by the 1861 Select Committee (see below).

Politicisation and change, 1864–1877

Developments in this period are in striking contrast to the previous decade. There was an increase in political and electoral competition in the 1870s. Conversely, religious issues appeared less important in the period largely reflecting broader developments, in particular disestablishment of the Church of Ireland in 1869.[24]

22 During the 1850s two pastoral letters issued by the Roman Catholic bishops called for a proper classification of the inmates of work houses and objected to the lack of proper provision for religious services and the administration of the poor law by an exclusively Protestant and English board. The 1859 pastoral had also made reference to attempts to convert deserted children to Protestantism. See the evidence to the 1861 Select Committee on the Poor Law Q. 8030 and 8035–6 and *Freeman's Journal*, 1 July 1861.

23 E. Larkin, *The Making of the Roman Catholic Church in Ireland, 1850–1860*, University of North Carolina Press, Chapel Hill, 1980, 400–2.

24 On disestablishment, see, in particular, P.M.H. Bell's excellent study *Disestablishment in Ireland and Wales*, SPCK, London, 1969.

Politics and the poor law

There has been relatively little consideration of the extent to which politics were involved in the poor law in the period from 1851 to just before the beginning of the Land War with the exception, of course, of Feingold's classic study of the transformation of poor law governance which, however, relates primarily to the period after that studied here. In the first part of this period, to the early 1860s, the poor law was relatively rarely an issue in national politics. The one exception to this was perhaps the question of the extension of the powers of the poor law as to the provision of hospital services which is discussed in more detail below. The main impetus for legislative change in this period was the Poor Law Commission and many of the changes which eventually were incorporated into the 1862 Act originated with the Commission. There is little indication that Conservative and Liberals chief secretaries took significantly different approaches to poor law legislation in this period other than on the extension of the role of the poor law concerning hospital services, although Conservative MPs and, to even greater extent, Conservative members of the House of Lords, opposed many of the changes in the 1862 Act. Nor did the Independent Irish Party adopt any distinctive policy on the poor law and to a large extent the views of its members were indistinguishable from those of Conservative members with the exception, of course, of religious issues.[25]

A significant change can be seen in the second half of this period. Even before the establishment of the Home Rule party, some Irish politicians, who would be associated with that party, introduced legislative proposals on union rating and these were continued after the establishment of the party. At least seven bills were proposed on union rating in the period from 1866 to 1876. The Home Rule party also raised the issue of the poor law ballot in a consistent way and bills proposing that poor law elections be

25 Although 'independent' Irish members were usually former or future Liberals, in relation to social issues many independent Irish members in the period from 1830–60 were more conservative than liberal in their approach to the poor law.

conducted by ballot were proposed on an annual basis from 1874 onwards.[26] There are a number of instances of politicisation (in a party sense) of the boards of guardians in the period.[27] It appears that, particularly in Dublin, elections to the boards of guardians were, on occasion, contested on a party political basis.[28] A number of boards of guardians supported political resolutions in favour, for example, of the release of Fenian prisoners, of land reform or an independent Irish Parliament. This suggests a number of conclusions. Firstly, an assumption that the boards of guardians before the 1870s were simply administrative and apolitical in character would be incorrect. There were a number of instances of the involvement of the board of guardians in broader politics in the period from the 1850s to the 1870s, some elections were closely fought, and electioneering sometimes transgressed the boundaries of what was considered legitimate. Overall, however, this research supports Feingold's view that the vast bulk of boards of guardians in the 1870s, before the advent of the Land War, were not greatly politicised in the sense of party or national politics. Relatively few electoral districts were contested and – even where elections did take place – party politics appears to have been involved in an organised way primarily in Dublin.[29] This is all the more striking given the growth of Home Rule in the period and the involvement of Home Rule members in poor law issues. As Feingold shows this position changed dramatically in the

26 The Poor Law Commission opposed ballot elections although Undersecretary T.H. Burke did not agree with this view: NAI CSORP/1878/8595.

27 See M. Cousins, 'Poor law politics and elections in post Famine Ireland', *History Studies*, 6, (2005) 34–47.

28 In Dublin there appears to have been organised political competition between Conservative and Liberal candidates. In other areas, insofar as party competition exists at all, it tends to be between Conservative and Liberal/National candidates. There is little indication that candidates representing workers interests played any significant part in poor law elections. For example, Lane reports that Irish Labour leader P.F. Johnson sought election in 1870 as a poor law guardian in Kilmallock, but was badly defeated with only 53 votes out of 406 cast. See F. Lane, 'P.F. Johnson, Nationalism and Irish Rural Labourers, 1869–82' *Irish Historical Studies*, xxxiii, 130, 2002, 191–208.

29 It is unclear whether this trend also applied in other cities such as Cork and Belfast.

1880s. Nonetheless, while Feingold sees the nascent political activities of the 1870s as a break with the past and a precursor of what was to come during the Land War, one can perhaps better see these activities rather as a continuation (or renewal) of a longstanding involvement in politics, in a broad sense of the term, by the boards of guardians.

Moving beyond the narrower party-political concept, the boards clearly played an important role in the broader politicisation of their communities. As will be seen, local boards took the initiative in using the poor law to expand hospital services to a broader range of persons than the 'destitute' who were entitled to relief. And, local boards also took the initiative in struggles with the Poor Law Commission concerning religious issues. In northern unions, this sometimes took the form of protecting the Protestant ratepayers from what were perceived to be the unnecessary costs of celebrating Catholic religious rites while in the south, it involved boards in registering foundlings as Catholic where their religion was unknown although – in the legal opinion of the Irish Attorney General – they should have been registered in the religion of the State, i.e. as Protestant.

Poor relief policy

The main poor law issues concerned the expansion of outdoor relief and battles over union rating. As has been seen in chapter 1, out relief grew from about 1,500 persons in 1859 to over 30,000 in 1877. There was surprisingly little opposition to this from the Poor Law Commission but the growth was very diverse. In 1869, the Poor Law Commission estimated that only about half the unions used out relief as a regular means of relief.[30] In fact, in 1872, only about one-third of unions spent more than 10 per cent of total poor law expenditure on out relief with Leinster the only province where a majority of unions did so. This is discussed in more detail in chapter 6. There was a fierce debate about the existing rating by electoral divisions which led to wide inequality amongst the 3,500 electoral divisions in Ireland – generally to the benefit of low rated rural districts. This is discussed in detail below.

30 Twenty-second Annual Report of the Commissioners for Administering the Laws for Relief of the Poor in Ireland, HC 1868–9 [4166] xxviii, 339 at 13.

A Local Government Board was established in 1872 but as Cassell has argued this was largely just a change of name in the Irish context and not one new staff member was taken on as a result of the change.[31] Removal remained a matter of much debate both in Parliament and the reports of the Poor Law Commission and the Board. A Select Committee reported on this issue, to little effect, in 1878.[32] The reports of the Commission/Board, and indeed reports of meetings of local boards of guardians, also indicate a considerable interest in the impact of vagrancy in this period.

The Poor Law Commission (later Local Government Board) appears to have been less influential than in the period to 1862, largely allowing boards to act as they chose concerning outdoor relief and, despite supporting union rating, being unable to convince chief secretaries to introduce such a measure. It is interesting to note that the Fenian rising appears to have had little impact on the operation of the poor law, other than leading to the use of surplus space in the workhouses to billet British Army troops. Immediately after the rising, the Poor Law Commission reported that there was little apparent increase of distress and that rates were 'never more easily collected'.[33]

The governance of the poor law

One of the difficulties in analysing the history of the poor law – and yet also one of the most interesting points – is that the structure of the poor law system was highly dispersed. In nineteenth-century Ireland, there was no one centre of power through which the poor law was (or could be) controlled. Rather the poor law operated on a number of different and interrelated levels. Firstly, the local boards of guardians were responsible for the implementation of the poor law in their local areas. Despite the existence of national legislation and of a strong centralised body (the Poor

31 See Ronald G. Cassell, *Medical charities, medical politics: the Irish dispensary system on the poor law, 1836–1872*, Royal Historical Society, Woodbridge, 1997, 148–9; NAI CSORP/1872/5397; CSORP/1876/2010.

32 Report of the Select Committee on Poor Removal, HC 1878–9 [282] xii, 561.

33 Twenty-first Annual Report of the Commissioners for Administering the Laws for Relief of the Poor in Ireland, HC 1867–8 [4042] xxxiii, 413 at 13.

Law Commission and subsequently the Local Government Board), as has been seen in chapter 2, there were very considerable regional variations in how the poor law operated which depended, in significant part, on how the local board of guardians applied the law. While the Poor Law Commission and its inspectors did have a very detailed knowledge of what was going on at a local level and while they did intervene in what were frequently quite minor matters, in other areas the Commission had quite limited success in trying to make the local boards implement its directives, for example, in relation to religious aspects, and in other areas again the Commission sometimes took a quite hands off approach to the operation of the poor law, for example, on the extent to which local boards relied on outdoor relief. In the area of religion, the Commission was unable to persuade some northern boards to provide what it felt were adequate facilities for the celebration of Roman Catholic ceremonies and its subsequent attempts to enforce its views through the courts were unsuccessful.[34] Similarly, the Commission waged long and often unsuccessful battles to persuade the southern boards to record the religion of foundling children as that of the state.[35]

Equally, while the Commission clearly did have access to and influence on the chief secretary in Dublin Castle, the quite limited archives would suggest that chief secretaries tended to have much more regard to the politics of Westminster in deciding whether or not to proceed with the poor law proposals than they did to the views of the Poor Law Commission. The undersecretaries in Dublin Castle (Thomas Larcom (1853–68) and T.H. Burke (1869–82)) were in close contact with the Poor Law Commission, particularly on the more contentious issues and were familiar with the detailed politics of the poor law.[36] Again, however, the archives would

34 See the Poor Law Commission's (unsuccessful) efforts to require the Newtownards guardians to provide what the Commission saw as appropriate religious facilities for Roman Catholics: *R v. Guardians of the Newtownards union*, 12 Ir. Com. Law Rep. 45.

35 See M. Cousins, 'Religious registration', op cit.

36 There is a danger of bias arising from the survival or non-survival of records as, for example, the extensive records maintained by T.A. Larcom (under-secretary 1853–68) show the extent of his interest in the poor law (and indeed almost every other

suggest that the undersecretaries had more limited influence once policy-making moved to Westminster.

Successive chief secretaries, although nominally members of the Poor Law Commission (and subsequently) the Local Government Board, appear to have played little day-to-day role in the development of poor law policy.[37] They were, however, kept informed of more contentious issues and, as we will see, were directly involved in issues such as union rating.[38] However, there is little indication that any took a particular interest in poor relief policy in itself.

Finally, the United Kingdom Parliament played an important role both as a forum for discussing the issues concerning the poor law and as the legislative forum. As will be seen, issues concerning the operation of the Irish poor law were frequently brought before Parliament and, in addition to a number of more minor pieces of legislation, important acts were passed in Parliament in 1862 and 1876 (on union rating). These are discussed in more detail below.

---

conceivable issue), while the absence of records for his murdered successor T.H. Burke (1869–82) make it much more difficult to assess his level of involvement.

37 A Parliamentary return indicates that chief secretaries attended meetings of the Commission quite regularly up to 1851, irregularly thereafter and effectively never after 1855: Return of Number of Attendances at Board of Coms. for Administering Laws for Relief of Poor in Ireland, 1847–59, HC 1869 [147] lviii, 871. Unfortunately, similar information is not available for the 1860s and 70s but there is little in the archives to indicate that most chief secretaries played an active role in the ongoing work of the Commission/board.

38 There were no less than ten chief secretaries in the period from 1852 to 1878 (and a number of chief secretaries served in the post on more than one occasion in that period). There were eight Lords Lieutenant in the period. While the Lord Lieutenant was nominally the chief secretary's superior, by the post-Famine period the chief secretary was usually the senior political figure. Only Carlisle (1855–8, 1859–64, who as Lord Morpeth had been involved in the introduction of the Irish poor law, see Gray, *Making of the Irish Poor Law*) appears to have taken any significant interest in the poor law in this period.

The 1861 Select Committee and the 1862 legislation

As has been seen, the fall in poor law numbers in the period to 1859 was halted by the onset of an agricultural depression which lasted until 1864. This led to considerable increases in poverty in many parts of Ireland (particularly the west) and to a rise in poor law numbers. However, there is little indication in the historical records that the establishment of a Select Committee in 1861 was linked to the depression nor did the issues arising from that depression feature greatly in the evidence before the Committee.

One of the key issues in this period was the debate about the extension of the role of the workhouses to act as general hospitals for poor persons. While the focus of this work is on the relief aspects of the poor law, this debate is of sufficient importance for the future of the poor law to require some detailed consideration here. There are a number of reasons specific to the Irish poor law context which go some way to explain the growth of such services under the poor law. However, these changes must also be seen in the broader context of the 'medicalisation' of society which took place in the nineteenth century[39] and the fact that in other countries also the role of the poor law expanded in the area of medical services. For example, in England and Wales the poor law also played an important role in the provision of medical services although the 1834 Act had little to say on the topic.[40]

Medical services in Ireland before the Famine consisted of a range of uncoordinated and arguably underfunded services provided in voluntary hospitals, county infirmaries (41 in 1845), fever hospitals and dispensaries.[41] There had already been a range of calls for reform of medical services in

39 See L. Rothfield, 'Medical', in H.F. Tucker (ed.), *A Companion to Victorian Literature and Culture*, Blackwell, London, 1998.

40 M.W. Flynn 'Medical Services under the New Poor Law', in D. Fraser (ed.), *The New Poor Law in the Nineteenth Century*, Macmillan, London, 1976.

41 See L.M. Geary, *Medicine and Charity in Ireland, 1718–1851*, University College Dublin Press, Dublin 2004; R.G. Cassell, *Medical Charities, Medical Politics: the Irish Dispensary System and the Poor Law, 1836–1872*, Royal Historical Society, Woodbridge, 1997.

the period before the Famine and these were intensified by the medical needs arising during the Famine period.[42] The Poor Law Commission had a longstanding interest in the provision of medical services. In its 1841 report the Commission noted that while it was clear that Parliament had intended free medical relief for the sick poor in Ireland to be confined to persons absolutely without capacity to pay, it 'may be impossible always to discriminate between this class and the one immediately above it and in a position to contribute moderately; and under existing circumstances it is perhaps right that the latter class should also be supplied with gratuitous medical relief'.[43] Following a number of abortive attempts during the 1840s, the government introduced a Medical Charities Bill in March 1850. This provided that the dispensaries, fever hospitals and county infirmaries were to come within the jurisdiction of a central board which was to include two of the Poor Law Commissioners, the chief secretary, the undersecretary and two or three distinguished medical men.[44] However, this legislation was not passed due to considerable opposition from the medical profession which opposed the involvement of the Poor Law Commission. A new Bill was published in the following year which proposed that the medical services be brought within the remit of a reorganised Poor Law Commission which was to include a new medical commissioner. However, as a result of the opposition of the medical profession the provisions relating to the county infirmaries and fever hospitals were dropped and the Bill as passed in 1851 only applied to dispensary services. While this was a very important addition to the work of the Poor Law Commission, it left open the question of the provision of hospital services.

As early as 1853, the Poor Law Commission, somewhat prematurely, reported that workhouses were 'assuming, especially in large towns, the character of hospitals for the reception of destitute sick persons' and that the 1851 Medical Charities Act – which applied to 'poor' rather to 'destitute'

42 See Cassell, *Medical Charities*, chapters 2–4.

43 Report of the Poor Law Commissioners, on medical charities, Ireland…, HC 1841 session 1 [324] xi, 1, at 13 quoted in Cassell, *Medical Charities*, at 95.

44 See Cassell, *Medical Charities*, 70 et seq.

persons – was likely to develop further this particular character of the Irish poor law. At this stage the Commission expressed some concern that the admission of destitute persons on grounds of sickness would be a 'most serious departure from the original principle of the Irish poor law'.[45] Nonetheless, it is clear that local boards of guardians continued to admit to the workhouses *as hospitals* a broader range of persons than would have been admitted to the workhouse had they not required hospital care. The Poor Law Commission and its inspectors appear to have turned a blind eye to this if not in fact colluding in this approach.

In its 1854 report, the Poor Law Commission proposed that a Bill be submitted to Parliament providing for the absorption of the county infirmaries and fever hospitals (as originally intended in the 1851 legislation).[46] Legislation was introduced in 1854 by the then chief secretary Sir John Young MP (chief secretary 1853–5 under Aberdeen) but again due to opposition was not proceeded with. In June 1854, Alfred Power, chief Poor Law Commissioner, anticipating the withdrawal of the Hospitals' Bill, submitted an alternative approach to Sir John Young.[47] This legislation proposed to allow the guardians to receive into the hospitals or infirmary of the workhouse any poor person who was a dispensary patient, thereby significantly broadening the class of persons who could (legally) be received. However, this Bill, although published, does not appear to have been proceeded with.

In 1857 the Poor Law Commission drafted a Bill for the then chief secretary H.A. Herbert (1857–8).[48] The two key points of the Bill, in addition to a range of more administrative measures, related to the provision of hospital services and the boarding out of children. Clause 2 of the Bill provided that guardians might assist any poor person requiring medical and surgical aid in hospital while clause six stated that as mortality amongst infants was very large and as workhouses were not well suited in all cases for

45 Sixth Annual Report of the Commissioners for Administering the Laws for Relief of the Poor in Ireland, HC 1852–3 [1645] l, 159 at 5.

46 Second Annual Report of the Commissioners for Administering the Laws for Relief of the Poor in Ireland…, 1854 [1759] xx, 219 at 6–15.

47 Power to Larcom, 26 June 1854, NLI Larcom Ms. 7780.

48 NAI CSORP/1857/6827.

the care of infants, it should be lawful for guardians to provide for relief of orphans or deserted children out of doors or otherwise up to the age of five and thereafter subject to the certification by the guardians of attendance at school. Although the legislation was published, it did not proceed as the government fell. The following year, following the change of government, a revised copy of Herbert's Bill was submitted by the Poor Law Commission to the new Conservative chief secretary Lord Naas (1858–9).[49] However, following communication with Naas, the Bill was revised to omit the hospital clauses, despite Power's objection.[50] This Bill was published but was not proceeded with as the government fell in 1859.

In 1860, Edward Cardwell, the new Liberal chief secretary (1859–61), introduced a Bill which was widely opposed by Irish members for what appear to be a range of conflicting reasons.[51] Cardwell wisely referred the issue to a Select Committee[52] which heard evidence and then recommended more or less what Cardwell had in mind anyway. The timing of the Committee might make one suspect a response to the agricultural depression of the period, but this is not apparent anywhere in the debates. In his evidence to the Committee, Alfred Power discussed the 1860 Bill which included a provision to extend the power of the board of guardians to admit poor persons to hospital. He argued that this would remedy the lack of infirmaries. He accepted the boards currently admitted very widely which was 'not exactly legal, though it may be very desirable'.[53]

Archbishop Cullen's (Roman Catholic Archbishop of Dublin, 1852–78) evidence to the Committee was highly critical of the poor law.[54] His

49 NLI Mayo Ms. 11.030. Naas (later the Earl of Mayo) was probably the most senior Irish Conservative of the period and had also served as chief secretary in 1852 and was again to do so in 1866–8.

50 Power to Naas, 12 June 1858, NLI Mayo Ms. 11.030.

51 See Hansard, 160, 144 et seq., 24 July 1860 and the newspaper coverage in NLI Larcom Ms. 7780.

52 Ibid. 146; and see *Dublin Evening Post*, 10 May 1860.

53 Report from the Select Committee on Poor Relief, HC 1861 (408), x, 1, Q. 355.

54 On Cullen's involvement in this area see E. Norman, *The Catholic Church and Ireland in the Age of Rebellion, 1859–73*, Longmans, London, 1965, 73–7 and V. Crossman,

criticisms related both to the specifically religious aspects of the poor law and, more generally, to the overall approach to poor relief. In relation to religious arrangements he was 'altogether dissatisfied'.[55] He believed that mass was celebrated in a most unbecoming way and that separate chapels should be provided in all workhouses.[56] He also objected to a number of other aspects, including the procedures for the nomination of Roman Catholic chaplains, their salaries, the religious instruction of pauper children and the standard of nursing, as many nurses had no training and were of 'a very low character', including women who had had illegitimate children. In relation to the moral aspects of poor relief, Cullen believed that the system injured morals very much. This arose because the family was broken up and inmates were separated from society but, Cullen believed, 'the greatest evil... arises from want of classification'.[57] Having an illegitimate child, Cullen bemoaned, was not considered sufficient reason to place a woman in a separate ward. Cullen favoured the exclusion of certain classes from the workhouse, including the deaf and dumb, blind, and infants and children, all of whom he believed should be boarded out. He believed that the 'meritorious poor' got very little and that the diet was not what it ought to be.[58] Finally, he believed that there were a lack of Irish men and Roman Catholics on the Poor Law Commission and that ex-officio guardians were too numerous.

In general, the Select Committee supported the status quo. It found that the powers of the poor law guardians were sufficient and that no alteration in these powers was necessary or desirable. Equally it recommended that it was not expedient to give the Poor Law Commission powers to control the discretion of the guardians. While it was unable to carry out a detailed investigation of the Medical Charities Act it was satisfied that

'"Facts Notorious to the Whole Country": The Political Battle over Irish Poor Law Reform in the 1860s', *Transactions Of The RHS*, 20, (2010), 157–69.

55 Report from the Select Committee on Poor Relief, Q. 3933.

56 Cullen had recently visited Bicêtre in Paris which had 'a very fine chapel': Q 3936.

57 Q. 3969.

58 Q. 3991 and 3995, although his evidence on the latter point was somewhat undermined by the fact that he referred to a case arising in 1842.

great benefits had been derived from the operation of the legislation. While several witnesses recommended a change to union rating, the Committee believed that it was not desirable to alter the law. However it did recommend an extension in the period of residence required for chargeability from three to five years which it believed would remove undue pressures from highly rated electoral divisions.

It's more important proposals were that the quarter acre clause which prohibited the payment of relief to persons holding more than one-quarter acre of ground should be repealed; guardians should be allowed to board out children up to the age of twelve; and poor law unions should be allowed to admit poor – rather than destitute – persons to hospital. The Committee also recommended that boards should have the power to recover maintenance from the fathers of illegitimate children; that persons who brought children of unknown religion to the workhouse should be given the legal position of parent as to registering the religion of that child; that a separate place for religious worship be provided; and that moral classification should receive special attention. The Committee set out detailed recommendations on poor law elections in order to avoid abuse and a range of recommendations on more administrative issues such as superannuation for officers. The recommendations adopted were largely those proposed to the Committee by Cardwell. However, the recommendations on the separate place of religious worship and moral classification were proposed by Irish members – in particular William Monsell[59] (Liberal, Limerick) – following discussions with Archbishop Cullen.[60]

59 Monsell served as a junior member in the Aberdeen government and in subsequent Liberal governments. He was also the long-standing chairman of the Limerick board of guardians. See M. Potter, *William Monsell of Tervoe, 1812–1894*, Irish Academic Press, Dublin, 2009.

60 The *Dublin Evening Post*, 25 January 1862, refers to meetings of some Irish MPs presided over by Dr Cullen to agree resolutions to be presented to the Committee. It appears that the resolutions agreed related to moral classification; boarding out up to the age of 15; reducing the poor law franchise of the owner to equal to that of the tenant; reducing the number of ex-officios; providing separate places of worship; and providing a Roman Catholic seat on the Poor Law Commission, *Dublin Evening Mail*, 15 February 1862.

Legislation was quickly drafted, largely based on the recommendations of the Committee. The new chief secretary, Sir Robert Peel (1861–5), introduced the legislation in 1862.[61] He stated that of the fourteen positive resolutions of the Select Committee, five approved measures already set out in the 1860 Bill, seven suggested new points of legislation and two related to matters for the Poor Law Commission (concerning religious worship and classification). Somewhat optimistically, he claimed that the latter two points had 'since been dealt with in conformity with the spirit of the recommendations'.[62] The Bill proposed that the quarter acre clause should be abolished and this was agreed without much opposition. Similarly, despite some opposition from Lord Naas and other Irish Conservatives, the proposal on the admission of poor persons to hospital services was comfortably carried in the House of Commons.[63] Although the Select Committee had recommended that boarding out be allowed up to the age of twelve, the Bill proposed to limit this to the age of five. Although there was heated debate about the appropriate age for boarding out, the general principle was agreed and the clause on the religious registration of children was also adopted after a long discussion.[64]

However, the House of Lords adopted a much more critical approach. A number of members objected to the repeal of the quarter acre clause. Lord Donoughmore proposed that it be limited to outdoor relief and was supported by Lord Derby, who otherwise would have voted for abolition.[65] Donoughmore also opposed the provision of medical aid to poor persons arguing that it would destroy county infirmaries. Donoughmore frankly admitted that his opposition was not unrelated to the fact that county infirmaries were funded by a county rate which was paid entirely by tenants while landlords paid 50 per cent of the poor rate.[66] The clause was

61 Hansard, 165, 339 et seq., 14 February 1862.

62 Given that effectively nothing happened in relation to either recommendation, this seems somewhat unlikely.

63 Hansard, 165, 1975, 14 February 1862.

64 Hansard, 167, 94 et seq. 29 May 1862.

65 Hansard, 168, 416, 17 July 1862.

66 Ibid. at 417–18.

defeated by twenty-nine votes to twenty-seven, with a number of senior Conservatives (including Derby) and several Irish members voting against. Finally the provision on religious registration was amended by twenty-six votes to twenty-four to exclude the provision giving parental rights to the person bringing a child of unknown religion to a workhouse. The House of Commons insisted only on restoring the provision in relation to the provision of medical services.[67] In the House of Lords, although a number of Conservative peers maintained their opposition, Lord Derby appeared anxious for a compromise and moved to make the provision temporary. However, on this occasion, the government carried its proposal by twenty-eight votes to twenty, with a number of the Irish peers who voted against on the first occasion not recording a vote on the second.

Thus of the three important proposals arising from the report of the Select Committee (i) the abolition of the quarter acre clause was confined to its application to indoor relief by the House of Lords; (ii) boarding out was restricted to children up to the age of five by the House of Commons; and (iii) the admission of the poor to hospitals was only maintained over the opposition of the House of Lords. However, the Poor Law Commission appear to have behaved as though the quarter acre clause was largely defunct given the powers of relieving officers to provide emergency outdoor relief, and their Lordships carelessly did not alter a clause providing that baptism of a child was conclusive of religion. The Poor Law Commission suggested in its next report that the provision might lead to a delay in admission to workhouses as children being admitted would be baptized first.[68] The overall outcome of the legislation was largely that things went on as the Poor Law Commission thought they should.

After the initial expansion of the role of the Poor Law Commission into the health area in the Medical Charities Act of 1851 and the legalisation of its role in the provision of hospital services in 1862, there were further advances in the role of the Commission on public health in the

67 Hansard, 168, 781, 24 July 1862.

68 Sixteenth Annual Report of the Commissioners for Administering the Laws for Relief of the Poor in Ireland, HC 1863 [3135] xxii, 341.

1860s and 1870s. Legislation in 1865 gave many boards of guardians a role in the provision of sewerage services. Other relevant legislation included the Compulsory Vaccination Act of 1864, the Sanitary Act of 1866 and the Public Health Act of 1878.

An important question is why the poor law system became involved in the provision of medical care – something which had not been seen as a priority in, for example, George Nicholls' 1837 report. It is clear that key figures in the Poor Law Commission had a long-term interest in medical and public health issues and believed that the Commission had an important role to play in this area. Alfred Power, for example, had a longstanding commitment to state medicine and public health.[69] There were also administrative reasons why the Commission might support the expansion of the poor law into the provision of hospital services. As has been seen, there was considerable surplus capacity in the workhouse system in the 1850s (and after) leading to pressure for the amalgamation of unions. The Commission was strongly opposed to such amalgamations and the use of the workhouse space for hospital services helped to provide a rationale for the maintenance of the existing network of workhouses. Nonetheless, this expansion cannot be explained by reference to administrative rationales only. Clearly much of the initiative for the expansion into the provision of hospital services came from the local boards of guardians but there is very little information as to why this approach was adopted. Although the Commission indicated that the development of poor law hospital services took place particularly in 'large towns', data indicate that persons receiving medical treatment were broadly spread throughout the Irish unions.[70] As noted above, it must also be set in the context of the medicalisation of Victorian society and the expansion of the role of the medical profession into a wide range of areas throughout the nineteenth century.

69 See Cassell, *Medical Politics*, at 82.

70 Thirteenth Annual Report of the Commissioners for Administering the Laws for the Relief of the Poor in Ireland, HC, 1860 2654, xxxvii, 327 at 199. The six large cities made up 24 per cent of the total – broadly in line with their population share.

The debate about union rating

As outlined above, unions were divided for rating (and electoral) purposes into several electoral divisions. The rate payable by property owners varied according to the electoral division in which the property was situated and was largely influenced by the number of paupers chargeable to that electoral division. This system had not formed part of the original proposals set out by Sir George Nicholls but had been introduced in the House of Lords by the Duke of Wellington.[71] This system led to considerable variations in the level of rates paid within the union. In general, towns were much more heavily rated than were rural divisions.

This issue had been raised before the 1861 Committee but had been dismissed without great debate. A small number of motions had been submitted to the Committee by the boards of guardians on this issue. The balance opposed any change in the existing system (eight for and three against) but the report indicates that the voting in a number of cases was close. The Committee did recommend a change in the period of residence required for chargeability. This proposal was implemented in the 1862 Act and led a considerable increase in the amount of the maintenance charged to the union rather than to the individual electoral divisions.[72] However, the adoption in England and Wales of union rating in 1865 appears to have given greater impetus to calls for a similar approach in Ireland.[73] Reporting on the English legislation, the *Freeman's Journal* supported union rating and predicted that would be extended to Ireland.[74] From the mid-1860s on there was an extensive debate about whether union rating should be

71 Sir G. Nicholls, *A History of the Irish Poor Law*, John Murray, London, 1856, 219–21.

72 See the evidence of Sir Alfred Power to the 1871 Select Committee: Law of Rating (Ireland): Report from the Select Committee…, HC 1871 (423), x, 1.

73 On the English legislation see M. Caplan, 'The New Poor Law and the Struggle for Union Chargeability,' *International Review of Social History*, 23 (2), 1978, 267–300.

74 *Freeman's Journal*, 31 March 1865. The *Dublin Evening Post* also called for the extension of union rating to Ireland, 6 April 1865.

extended to Ireland and a number of publications were in print on the issue.[75] A number of public meetings were held and deputations met the Lord Lieutenant in 1866 both for and against union rating. However, he refused to express any particular position on the issue stating that the chief secretary Chichester Fortescue would state the government's view to Parliament. It appears that Fortescue, who served as chief secretary under the short lived Russell administration in 1865–6 and again under Gladstone from 1868 to 1871, strongly considered introducing union rating at the time but, for reasons which are unclear, this proposal did not proceed.[76] Private members' bills were introduced by Irish MPs in 1866, 1867–8 and 1868–9.

Given the pressure for reform, a Select Committee of the House of Commons was established in 1871 and received extensive evidence on the existing position, on the implementation of union rating in England and Wales,[77] and on its likely impact in Ireland. The Committee was unable to complete its inquiry in the 1871 session and was re-established in 1872.[78] Official witnesses, including Sir Alfred Power, were strongly in favour of union rating. Power attributed the reluctance of some unions to provide adequate food and to meet proper establishment charges to the opposition of wealthy electoral divisions which opposed additional spending. Resolutions were submitted to the Select Committee by 139 unions: the vast majority of them were opposed to any change in the law on rating. In total, 108 unions opposed union rating, eighteen supported it, five supported a national rate, while eight expressed split views.[79] This opposition

75 See NLI Larcom Ms. 7781.

76 See Sir Alfred Power's evidence to the 1871 Select Committee: Law of Rating (Ireland): Report from the Select Committee…, HC 1871 (423), x, 1.

77 It generally found that the impact of union rating on the implementation and administration of poor relief had been positive.

78 Law of Rating (Ireland): Report from the Select Committee…, HC 1871 (423), x, 1; Law of Rating (Ireland): Report from the Select Committee…, HC 1872 (361), xi, 1.

79 In a number of cases, it is somewhat difficult to interpret the views expressed. The Poor Law Commission presented a somewhat different tally with the 114 unions against, twenty-two for and three unions supporting both positions. In a number of

is unsurprising in that each electoral division was represented on the board of guardians. Insofar as a small number of electoral divisions in the union stood to gain (sometimes considerably) from the introduction of union rating, a much larger group of divisions stood to lose.[80]

The Select Committee finally set out its recommendations in May 1872. The Committee was sceptical about arguments as to the wider effects of a change in the system of rating and took the view that it was probable that the employment of labour and the destruction or erection of dwellings for labourers were 'matters governed by personal interests and local circumstances rather than by the pressure of poor rates'. Rather it felt that the more material issues were the inequality in rating, and the impact of rating on the administration of unions. The Committee reported that there was broad agreement on setting an upper limit on the rate payable by any electoral division and on charging the cost of relief to blind persons and the deaf and dumb to the union. However, there were practical difficulties in setting such a limit. Accordingly, based on the evidence of the impact of union rating in England and Wales, the Committee decided to recommend that union rating be extended to Ireland. However, the Committee was much divided on the issue with Conservative (including Irish) members voting against this recommendation. Despite the recommendations of the Committee, the chief secretary Lord Hartington (1871–4) did not introduce legislation, presumably on the basis that he did not think it would successfully pass both houses.

Pressure for reform continued primarily from Liberal and Home Rule members. Bills on union rating were introduced by Home Rule MPs in 1871, 1873, 1874 and 1876.[81] In February 1875, R. O'Shaughnessy, Home Rule MP for Limerick, asked Michael Hicks Beach, the Conservative chief secretary

---

unions, resolutions were passed and subsequently rescinded by boards of guardians. In any case, it is clear that the vast majority opposed union rating.

80 The Select Committee reported that union rating would lead to an increase in rates in 2,405 electoral divisions and to a fall in only 919.

81 The 1871 Bill, for example, was introduced by Patrick McMahon (Liberal, New Ross), McCarthy Downing (Liberal and later Home Rule, Cork) and William Stacpoole (Liberal and later Home Rule, Ennis).

(1874–8), if the government would introduce union rating.[82] Hicks-Beach stated that he did not intend to propose union rating but instead proposed to adopt a new area for local government taxation which would be small enough to guard against extravagance but large enough to relieve poor law electoral divisions which required it. However, the following year Hicks-Beach adopted a simpler measure which set a maximum limit on the amount chargeable to any electoral division in relation to indoor relief. Anything over that amount was to be charged equally to all the divisions. Outdoor relief was to remain chargeable to the individual divisions with a view to discouraging a further increase in the level of outdoor relief. While this measure did not mean that each division now paid a standard rate, it did considerably reduce the disparity in rating between divisions. For example the maximum rate payable in New Ross fell from 4*s.* 1¼*d.* to only 1*s.* 4½*d.*[83] The rise in rates in other electoral divisions was quite modest.

Archival research reveals some of the background to this policy change and the extent to which the views of Irish Conservatives peers and MPs were taken into account. The impetus for the change arose from the long-standing pressure from Irish MPs and, in particular, the Bill on union rating then before the house.[84] Hicks-Beach was keen to find a resolution to this problem and, initially, suggested applying union rating in respect of indoor relief while leaving out door relief to the electoral divisions.[85] However, the Lord Lieutenant, the Duke of Abercorn, an Ulster landlord, was resistant to any change and suggested instead the establishment of a further Com-

82 Hansard, 222, 214 et seq., 11 February 1875.

83 See the Fifth Annual Report of the Local Government Board for Ireland, HC 1878 [c.1761] xxxviii, 1 at 20.

84 See the correspondence between Hicks-Beach and his secretary Le Poer Trench and Abercorn in February–May 1876: PRONI, Abercorn papers D/623/A/317/1, 5, 7, 9, 10, and 14 and D/623/A/321/26–27, 29–31 and T.H. Burke to Abercorn and D/623/A/321/28. See also the correspondence from J.T. Ball to Abercorn: PRONI, Abercorn papers D/623/A/321/16, 17, 19, 20 and 22. Ball, the Lord Chancellor and former Conservative MP for Dublin University, generally opposed union rating and supported Abercorn's position.

85 Hicks-Beach to Abercorn 21 February 1876: PRONI, Abercorn papers D/623/A/317/1.

mission to enquire and report as to the area of chargeability. Hicks-Beach objected to this approach suggesting that it might reopen the whole question of union rating. A number of different proposals were discussed by the two in March 1876 and, in April a large group of Conservative peers and MPs met to discuss the issue. The meeting appointed a committee of a number of Irish Conservative Lords and members of Parliament (including Abercorn's brother) to go into the details of the different proposals with the chief secretary and to settle a scheme. By May 1876, the committee, having examined the implications of different approaches, agreed on the scheme outlined above. This affected very few unions in Ulster (which were generally quite evenly rated) having a much more significant impact in the three remaining provinces. It also limited the extent to which the larger towns gained at the expense of rural ratepayers.[86] The report stated that 'it would obviously not be desirable to shift any portion of the cost of outdoor relief from an electoral division to the union at large' and, therefore, confined its recommendations to the rating of indoor relief. It described outdoor relief as the class of expenditure 'most requiring the check of local responsibility to prevent extravagant growth'.[87] Following the report a Bill reflecting its recommendations was quickly finalised.[88]

The relationship between those unions expressing views on the rating issue, by way of motions to the Select Committee, and the published data on the level of rates paid and the degree of internal equality in rating can

86 In Ulster seven out of forty-four unions would be affected and only ten electoral divisions; in Munster thirty-eight out of fifty unions and seventy-two divisions; in Leinster twenty-four of forty unions and thirty-nine divisions; and in Connaught twenty-two of twenty-nine unions and forty divisions: Hicks-Beach to Abercorn, 12 May 1876, PRONI, Abecorn papers D/623/A/317/14.

87 For the committee's report see Le Poer Trench to Abercorn, 10 May 1876, PRONI, Abecorn papers D/623/A/321/29.

88 Le Poer Trench to Abercorn, 6 May 1876 and 15 May 1876: PRONI, Abecron papers D/623/A/321/27 and 30. Abercorn appears to have agreed somewhat reluctantly on the basis that if the proposal was acceptable to Conservative supporters he had no objection to its being tried: T.H. Burke to Abercorn, 9 May 1876, PRONI, Abecron papers D/623/A/321/28.

be examined.[89] Unions supporting union or national rating were generally highly rated and had above-average internal inequality. The two highest rated unions in the country, Millstreet (albeit with low internal inequality) and Oughterard (one of the most internally unequal) supported national and union rating respectively. Only one union with rates below one shilling supported union rating (Celbridge) and only three with low internal equality (Cork, North Dublin and Millstreet – all highly or very highly rated) did so. Most unions supporting union or national rating paid rates of 1*s.* 6*d.* or more and had an electoral division paying at least 150 per cent of the average rate. However, while a largely *necessary* factor, high or unequal rating is not *sufficient* to explain who did and did not support union rating. Local politics clearly played a key role. This is unsurprising given that internal inequality, if it meant some electoral divisions would gain significantly from union rating, also meant others (and usually more) would lose. Highly rated and highly unequal Dungarvan, for example, expressed split views on the issue while other highly unequal unions such as Carrick-on-Shannon and Cashel supported the existing position. Very unequal Granard supported the status quo but only by two votes. Support for union rating was concentrated in southern Ireland with the lowly rated northern unions (which were generally also quite equal internally) having little incentive to seek change. The Home Rule party won seats in the 1874 general election in all the areas which supported union or national rating but this would appear to reflect the broader north-south split which applied both to electoral support and rating issues rather than a direct link between the party's policies on poor law and electoral results.[90]

Data are also available as to the unions which benefited significantly from the implementation of the 1876 Act. However, it does not appear that

89 Internal equality in rating is measured by expressing the highest rated electoral division as a percentage of the average. While the precise pattern varies from union to union, the general tendency is for most divisions to be rated at about the average level, with one division (often but not always the main town in the union) or a small number of divisions paying significantly higher rates.

90 For example, highly rated and highly unequal New Ross supported the existing system but returned a Home Rule MP in 1874.

all those unions which supported union rating in fact benefited considerably from the measure. Of the twenty-two/twenty-three unions which supported union or national rating, only eleven benefited through a considerable reduction in internal inequality. Although the measure introduced appeared to have addressed the most serious inequalities, data for the late 1880s indicate that widespread inequality of rating remained with unions in all four provinces where the highest rated electoral division paid over 200 per cent of the average rate.[91] However, perhaps surprisingly, the issue does not seem to have generated political controversy after the 1870s.

Conclusion

Overall the story of this period is one of consolidation of the poor law rather than dramatic change. The most important development was its expansion into the area of medical and public health services. In the area of relief, the poor law played a relatively limited role, providing support in workhouses, at any one time, to less than 1 per cent of the population with the further 0.6 per cent receiving outdoor relief.[92]

Politically the poor law became more of an issue at national level from the mid-1860s on. Politicians associated with the Home Rule party, or who would in future be associated with that party, raised a number of poor law related issues including union rating, the ballot and removal. This is significant from a number of aspects. Firstly, the social and economic aspects of Home Rule, outside the area of land reform, tend to receive relatively little attention. Secondly, the conversion of many former Liberals to Home Rule is often portrayed as opportunistic. However this examination of poor law policy shows that a number of future Home Rule MPs had established distinctive policies on poor law issues long before the establishment of the

91 Calculated from the data on NAI CSORP 1891/25518.

92 Although the total numbers relieved in any one year are significantly larger.

Home Rule party itself. Thirdly, the advocacy of these issues attracted very limited success. It is noteworthy that the United Kingdom government which was, in the near future, to attempt to introduce Home Rule for Ireland was not prepared in the 1870s even to allow ballot voting in poor law elections. In terms of the governance of Ireland, the poor law did play an important role, in conjunction with private efforts, in responding to issues such as the agricultural depression of 1859–64. The role which the poor law was to play in the serious depression after 1879 will be studied in future chapters.

In terms of broader politicisation, the local boards were involved in major debates about who should pay for the poor law (the union rating issue), about the structure of the poor law (whether it should provide hospital services and outdoor relief) and about the relationship between the poor law and religion. These issues will also be pursued in subsequent chapters.

CHAPTER 5

The Land War and Local Politics, 1879–1891

This chapter looks at the key developments in the Irish poor law in the period from 1879 to 1891. Having set out the political context, the chapter examines poor law trends, outlining the establishment of the boards of guardians and the electoral processes involved, and looking at the extent of politicisation of the boards. As Feingold has shown, the 1870s and, in particular, the 1880s marked the 'nationalisation' of the boards of guardians with, mainly Catholic and Nationalist, tenant guardians taking over control of the boards from the, mainly Protestant, landlords. This chapter develops on and refines Feingold's work in this area.

Context

Political change

In contrast to the earlier decades, the 1879–91 period saw dramatic political changes.[1] A combination of factors – including bad weather from 1878 and the fall in world markets – led to an agricultural depression in

1 See generally P. Bew, *Land and the National Question in Ireland 1858–82*, Gill & Macmillan, Dublin, 1979; S. Clark, *Social Origins of the Irish Land War*; Princeton University Press, New Jersey, 1979; M. O'Callaghan *British High Politics and Nationalist Ireland: Criminality, Land and the Law under Forster and Balfour*, Cork University Press, Cork, 1994, amongst others.

1879–82.[2] However, in marked contrast to the 1859–64 period, the response to this was one of tenant mobilisation, leading to what became known as the Land War. Politically the period saw a more determined and coherent Irish Parliamentary Party led by Charles Parnell.[3] The Land War led to important concessions by the Gladstone government in the 1881 Land Act. This and an improvement in agricultural returns led to the end of the first phase of the Land War around 1882.[4] However the world economic downturn meant that prices did not return to a pre-1879 height and political unrest continued. The third Reform Act (1884) contributed to a significant increase in Irish Parliamentary Party members in the house of Parliament to 85 in 1885 and the end of Liberal representation. These developments led to the first failed Home Rule Bill in 1886.[5] The return to office of the Conservative government in 1886, ruling for the remainder of the period, marked a dramatic decline in political opportunities for the Irish Parliamentary Party and the shift by some of its leaders to further land agitation in the plan of campaign (1886–91). The appointment as chief secretary of Arthur Balfour (1887–91) saw a consistent policy combining coercion with limited conciliation, cynically referred to as 'kicks and halfpence'.[6]

Poor law trends

This political unrest was mirrored in the operation of the poor law during the period. Indoor relief rose significantly up to 1881 reflecting the economic crisis but fell back over the remainder of the 1880s. In contrast, outdoor

2 On the resultant distress see NAI CSORP/1879/ 18213 and 20510; 1880/7070, 4115, 4267, 9293, 17648, 4922, 15619, 7865; 1881/1350.

3 See C.C. O'Brien, *Parnell and his Party, 1880–90,* Oxford University Press, Oxford, 1957.

4 Although some localised distress continued: NAI CSORP/1883/9455, 9710, 17625.

5 See A. O'Day, *Irish Home Rule, 1867–1921*, Manchester University Press, Manchester, 1998.

6 See L.P. Curtis, *Coercion and Conciliation in Ireland, 1880–92: A Study in Conservative Unionism*, Princeton University Press, New Jersey, 1963.

relief rose very sharply in 1881 and again, in response to a localised crisis in the west, in 1886. While the number on outdoor relief fell back after 1887, overall payment of outdoor relief rose over the period from only 0.4 per 100 population in 1871 to 1.3 by 1891 (although the level of outdoor relief remained lower than in England and Wales) (see table 1.2). The rise in outdoor relief was neither linear nor uniform across Ireland (see chapter 6).

In contrast to the very limited response of the Liberal government to the 1859–64 depression, there was a much more comprehensive response to the 1879 downturn – initially by the Conservative government.[7] Initially distress was supported through competing Marlborough and Mansion House Relief Funds. The Conservative government introduced the Relief of Distress Act 1880 which allowed payment of outdoor relief to the able-bodied in authorised unions. The Act allowed outdoor relief in food or fuel only, subject, insofar as possible, to a labour test (breaking stones was recommended).[8] Irish Parliamentary Party MP Joseph Biggar moved an amendment to ensure that outdoor relief under the bill was charged on the union at large rather than to the individual electoral divisions. A modification of this was accepted whereby anything over a set amount was charged to the union but a proposal to make payments in cash was opposed by James Lowther (chief secretary 1878–80).[9] The Act led to a sharp rise in outdoor relief particularly in western unions.[10] The Commissioners of Public Works were authorized to advance money to landowners for works in 90 scheduled unions in 1880. Funds were also made available for the supply of potato seed in the Seed Supply Act 1880. The Relief of Distress Act expired generally in March 1881. However, it was continued in force in relation to the families of persons arrested under the Protection

7 Although it seems likely that this difference owed more to a change in approach over the period than to a change in governing party. A subsequent report put the total Exchequer cost (in addition to poor law expenditure) at £2.5M: NAI CSORP/1891/17944.

8 See Hansard, 250, 533 et seq. 12 February 1880; 688 et seq. 16 February 1880.

9 Hansard, 250, 937 19 February 1880 and 688, 16 February 1880 respectively.

10 In fact the Local Government Board allowed fifty-six unions to 'anticipate the sanction of Parliament' and pay outdoor relief before the bill was even passed.

of Persons and Property Act, 1881 (better known as the Coercion Act).[11] However, distress continued into 1882 and the Arrears of Rent Act, 1882 included a clause allowing additional emigration which was widely used in the 1880s.[12] In December 1882, Dublin Castle, reflecting the views of Lord Spencer (Lord Lieutenant, 1882–5) and his opposition to outdoor relief,[13] announced that it was not prepared to adopt further emergency measures and that it intended to rely solely on the poor law to relieve distress, although loans would be made to distressed unions.[14] However, the numbers on outdoor relief remained high.

A similar approach to expanding outdoor relief was adopted by the Liberal government in 1886 in the context of the rising, but largely local, distress in the west and the pending Home Rule Bill.[15] The Relief Bill, published in the run-up to the Government of Ireland Bill, was warmly welcomed by Irish Parliamentary Party members who also ensured that those relieved under the bill would not be disenfranchised.[16] This Act, in the belief of local guardians that the cost would be met by the Imperial exchequer, led to dramatic rises in outdoor relief. In some unions over 50 per cent of the population was in receipt of outdoor relief and in Ough-

11 The amendment of the 'Coercion' Act to include this provision concerning relief arose from the intervention of Parnellite MP, R.H. Metge.

12 George Otto Trevelyan (chief secretary 1882–4) acknowledged in the Commons that the emigration clause had been brought forward in response to pressure from (unidentified) private members. They do not appear to have been members of the Irish Parliamentary Party who generally opposed the clause: Hansard, 272 1139 et seq (Trevelyan comment, 1255).

13 See, for example, Spencer to Hartington, 10 November 1882, Gladstone to Spencer 1 December 1882, in P. Gordon ed., *The Red Earl: The Papers of the Fifth Earl Spencer, 1835–1910. Volume 1, 1835–1885*, Northamptonshire Record Society, Northhampton, 1982, at 225, 227–8; NA CAB 37/9/106, 29 November 1882.

14 Annual Report of the Local Government Board for Ireland…, HC 1883 [C. 3581] xxix, 1.

15 Hansard, 304, 566 et seq., 29 March 1886. A provision allowing pubic works through, for example, the building of piers, was added to the bill during its passage. On its implementation, which again 'anticipated' the passage of the Act, see CSORP/1886/8230.

16 Hansard, 304, 574, 29 March 1886.

terard this reached 80 per cent. Warnings from the Local Government Board that unions would have to meet the cost led to boards of guardians temporarily terminating all outdoor relief under the 1886 Act. The maladministration of outdoor relief in these unions was investigated by a poor law inquiry Commission.[17] In August 1887 the Local Government Board issued a circular requesting boards to reduce reliance on outdoor relief – albeit to little effect as the fall which occurred relates primarily to the expiry of the temporary 1886 Act.[18] In subsequent years the numbers on outdoor relief declined very marginally.

The introduction of the outdoor relief legislation in 1881 and 1886 did not originate with the Local Government Board. In the case of the 1881 legislation the CSORP files suggest that the then Lord Lieutenant the Duke of Marlborough proposed the legislation.[19] As we have seen, the initiative to extend out door relief in 1881 came from a Parnellite MP and was accepted by the Liberal majority in Parliament. In 1886, the decision to opt for extended use of outdoor relief in the distressed west appears to have been made either by Liberal chief secretary John Morley or by the Imperial government – unsurprisingly, given the pending Home Rule legislation.

The behaviour of the western boards in 1886 was a key factor in the subsequent decision by Arthur Balfour not to rely on local unions in cases of future relief and development work. Balfour instead adopted a two-pronged approach in disadvantaged western unions. Firstly, a Congested Districts Board was established under the 1891 Land Act to support the long-term development of these areas.[20] Secondly, when local distress returned in 1890–1, the boards of guardians were bypassed and relief was provided through relief works and supervised directly by Dublin Castle

17 Poor Relief (Ireland) Inquiry Commission. Report and Evidence,... HC 1887 [C.5043] xxxviii, 1.

18 Annual Report of the Local Government Board for Ireland, being the Sixteenth Report under the Local Government Board (Ireland) Act, HC 1888 [C.5455] l, 1 at 62–4.

19 NAI CSORP/1880/24230.

20 C. Breathnach, *The Congested Districts Board, 1891–1923*, Four Courts, Dublin, 2005.

and through a charitable relief fund controlled by key administrators.[21] Access to local relief was controlled by the Royal Irish Constabulary and poor law inspectors rather than by the local poor law machinery. This led to a stabilisation of the level of outdoor relief, albeit at a much higher level than pre-1879.

1883 saw the introduction of the Labourers Act (proposed by the Irish Parliamentary Party and based on existing United Kingdom legislation) which allowed unions to build cottages for agricultural labourers.[22] The Act was little used at first and amending legislation was introduced in 1885 and 1886.

The Conservative government led a relative clampdown on 'wayward' boards with a sharp rise in boards warned about dissolution or actually dissolved. From 1880 to 1891, thirteen boards were dissolved and thirty-one warned, of which nine dissolutions and nineteen warnings occurred from 1886 onwards. This generally represented a clampdown on boards which were refusing to obey the instructions of the Local Government Board either through failing to apply normal workhouse rules to evicted persons admitted to the workhouse (New Ross),[23] paying 'excessive' relief to evicted tenants (Athy, Portumna) or by attempting to adopt political resolutions (Cork).[24] As can be seen, the dissolutions were fundamentally for political reasons in many cases.[25]

21 See Curtis, *Coercion and Conciliation in Ireland*; NAI CSORP/1891/17944 and 26481; NAI Relief of Distress papers 1891.

22 See M. Fraser, *John Bull's Other Homes*, 28–9; Crossman, *Politics*, chapter 6.

23 See V. Crossman, 'The New Ross Workhouse Riot of 1887: Nationalism, Class and the Irish Poor Laws', *Past and Present*, 179 (2003), 135–58.

24 The Athy and Portumna cases are discussed in chapter 7. For Cork see NAI CSORP/1889/19304; CSORP/1889/16849; CSORP/1890/2412. The Cork dissolution is discussed briefly in C. O'Mahony, *Cork's Poor Law Palace: Workhouse Life 1838–1890*, Rosmathún Press, Cork, 2005, 290–1.

25 Due to the fact that many files recorded in the records of the CSORP cannot currently be located, it is not always possible to establish the precise reason for dissolution.

While the Irish Parliamentary Party was much more active in Parliament, there was a, perhaps surprising, lack of focus on poor law issues.[26] In the previous period, a Home Rule party lacking in internal coherence had regularly introduced poor law legislation on union rating, removal and the election of guardians – albeit to little if any effect. The much more coherent party of the 1880s did introduce the labourers' cottages legislation. Apart from that, however, its main poor law-related proposals concerned the election of guardians.[27] The legislation proposed to introduce ballot voting, and to abolish ex-officio guardians and proxy voting. After winning support from the Liberal government in the mid-1880s the legislation finally passed the Commons (twice in 1884). However, the Lords deferred the first Bill and referred the second to a Select Committee which gutted the proposal to such an extent that it was dropped on its return to the Commons.[28] The landed proprietors of Ireland clearly wished to retain their control of the poor law boards.[29]

26 This is more surprising as a significant number of Irish Parliamentary Party MPs were involved as guardians. In 1890 five MPs were chairs of boards and a further ten were or had been guardians (18 per cent of all Irish Parliamentary Party MPs): Hansard, 341, 1298, 26 February 1890.

27 Legislation was proposed in 1879, 1883, 1884 (twice), 1885, 1886, 1887, 1888, 1890 and 1891. Home Rule MPs did introduce a bill on removal in 1880 but it was dropped. Legislation providing for union rating, ballot elections and a three year term of office was prepared by the Liberal government but never introduced: BL Althorp (Spencer) MS 77315.

28 See Hansard, 290, 1064, 1271, 1282, 1293 (deferral), 1707, 14 November 1884; 294, 26, 20 November 1884 (referral to Select Committee); 299, 391, 13 July 1885; and 300, 1454, 7 August 1885. The report of the Select Committee (1885) is interesting as – in the absence of any more general examination of the poor law in the period – it reports evidence from a wide range of witnesses on issues ranging well beyond purely electoral matters: Report from the Select Committee of the House of Lords on the Poor Law Guardians (Ireland) Bill HL 1884–5 (297), x, 364.

29 Although not to the extent of actually attending meetings: Return of… attendances… at board meetings, HC 1884 (335) lxviii, 55; NAI CSORP/1889/3812.

The nationalisation of the poor law boards

One of the key issues in this period is the takeover of the poor law boards of guardians by Nationalist guardians (which Feingold, following contemporary usage, refers to as 'nationalisation'). This has been well discussed by Feingold and this research complements and refines his findings.

The boards of guardians and the poor law electoral system

Prior to the establishment of the boards in 1838 the main form of county government was the unelected grand jury.[30] Members of the jury were selected from amongst the leading property owners. As a result the grand juries tended to be both predominantly Protestant and drawn from a very limited sector of society. The grand jury system was heavily criticised for both its inefficiency and for its exercise of local patronage. In urban areas, local government consisted of municipal corporations (borough councils) which existed in a small number of larger towns and cities, with town commissioners established in sixty-six towns.[31] Obviously this meant that the poor law boards had a much wider geographical coverage. In addition many of the town commissioners had very limited powers so that the boards of guardians were often the more important local body. As Hoppen shows, mass involvement in national politics (at least in the formal sense of voting) was quite limited and he estimates a parliamentary electorate post-1850 of about 164,000 rising to 226,000 prior to the 1884 reform law (out of total population of 6.5 million in 1851 declining to 5.2 by 1881).[32]

30 See Crossman's very helpful overview: V. Crossman, *Local Government in Nineteenth Century Ireland*, IIS, Belfast, 1994, 25–41.

31 See again Crossman, *Local Government*, 65–85.

32 K.T. Hoppen, *Elections, Politics and Society in Ireland, 1832–1885*, Clarendon, Oxford, 1984, 18 and 87–8. In 1878, Benjamin Banks, secretary to the Local Government Board, made the point to a Select Committee that the constituency for poor law elections went 'much lower down' (i.e. was much broader) than the parliamentary franchise. Report of the Select Committee on poor law guardians… HC 1878 (297), xvii, 263, Q. 4796.

The boards of guardians were established under the 1838 legislation and largely followed the English model. George Nicholls, in his 1837 report to the government, assumed that, as in England, local governance of the poor law would be the responsibility of largely elected boards of guardians subject to the control of a central authority. In England the local magistrates were ex-officio members of the board of guardians. However, Nicholls noted that the number of the magistracy (or justices of the peace) in Ireland required some modification in this rule. In England the number of magistrates was such that the elected members always far exceeded that of the ex-officio guardians. However, in Ireland, the number of magistrates who would be entitled to act as ex-officio guardians was such that it might outnumber the elected guardians. Nicholls was of the view that if this was to happen 'the elective character of the board would of course be destroyed' and even if this was not to occur 'any undue preponderance of the permanent ex-officio guardians would detract from the popular character of the goal of the body, and lower it in the confidence of the people'.[33] Accordingly Nicholls recommended that the number of ex-officio guardians should not exceed one-third of the number of elected guardians (i.e. one-quarter of the total board). Nicholls also recommended a further change in that no clergyman or Minister of any religious denomination should be eligible to act as an elected or ex-officio guardian in Ireland.

The first Poor Law Bill, which followed closely on these recommendations, was introduced by the Home Secretary, Lord John Russell on 13 February 1837.[34] The Bill provided that the boards of guardians should consist of both elected and ex-officio members with the latter limited to one-third, rather than one-quarter, as Nicholls had recommended, of the board. The composition of the boards of guardians generated debate in the House of Commons. Daniel O'Connell MP opposed ex-officio members at all, unsurprisingly as few ex-officios would be Repeal supporters. Lord Morpeth, the chief secretary, offered to reduce the proportion to one-quarter of the members but his offer was not accepted and the opposition to the provision was defeated.[35] A proposal to have magistrates elected by

33 Nicholls, *Irish Poor Law*, 173–4.

34 Hansard, 36, 453 et seq., 13 February 1837.

35 Ibid. at 1095, 26 May 1837.

the ratepayers was also defeated. The composition of the boards was raised again on the discussion of the Bill in 1838 (the original Bill having lapsed on the death of the King) but without any important change. Overall supervision of the operation of the poor law was the responsibility of the Poor Law Commissioners (from 1872 the Local Government Board).

This was the system under which the Irish poor law initially operated. Elections were held annually in March of the year.[36] Ratepayers, subject to a minimum valuation requirement,[37] were entitled to vote and the number of votes to which each person was entitled increased in accordance with the valuation of their property. Voting was not by ballot and, instead, voting papers were delivered to the address of the voter by the constabulary and subsequently collected when they had been completed. Proxy voting for landowners (but not tenants) was also allowed, something which led to considerable controversy and claims of abuse as it allowed landowners (or, in many cases, political agents) to concentrate votes in support of the 'landlord' candidate. In the 1870s about 540,000 people were entitled to vote in the poor law elections out of a total population in 1871 of 5.4 million.[38] Unions were divided, for rating purposes, into electoral divisions and one or more guardians were elected for each division.[39] This meant that the total number of guardians in each union varied depending on the number of electoral divisions. Initially 130 unions with over 2,000 electoral divisions were established but this was subsequently increased, in the late 1840s and early 1850s, to 163 unions and about 3,400 electoral divisions.

Elections were organised in 1839 and annually thereafter. It is clear that, in many areas, elections were strongly contested often with considerable

36 See Feingold, *Tenantry*, 15–26 and the Report of the Select Committee on poor law guardians... HC 1878 (297), xvii, 263.

37 All ratepayers had a vote but, from 1843, there was a minimum valuation requirement to be a ratepayer.

38 Return from each poor law union in Ireland, of the number of persons entitled to vote in each such union for poor law guardians..., HC 1874, (253), lvi, 1. This ranged from 8.8 per cent of the total population in Munster to 11.6 per cent in Ulster.

39 In 350 small divisions, arrangements were made to combine with another division to elect a guardian.

party feeling.[40] Fraud and partiality were also alleged although Nicholls claims that there were no more irregularities than might be expected in the circumstances.[41] Allegations of partiality on the part of returning officers were common.[42] In many places, however, elections were unopposed. By March 1841, ninety-nine boards had been elected of which twenty-five were without a contest. But of the 1,234 electoral districts in the contested boards, elections had taken place in only 254 (21 per cent).[43] Nonetheless this is not to say that the there was no electoral competition in the 'uncontested' divisions.[44] As Gash argues in relation to uncontested parliamentary elections, the person nominated was:

> not infrequently the result of an agreement by the influential leaders of the constituency, of personal bargains between rival candidates, or of compromises between the organized parties themselves.[45]

Given the small size of poor law electorates, similar practices seem likely in an Irish poor law context.

40 See G. O'Brien, 'The Establishment of Poor-Law Unions in Ireland, 1838–43', *Irish Historical Studies*, xxiii, 90 (1982), 97–120; P. Gray, *The Making of the Irish Poor Law, 1815–1843*, Manchester University Press, 2009, 293–7. See also the complaints of the Marquess of Westmeath: Hansard, 53, 1004 et seq., 13 April 1840 and the evidence to the 1846 Select Committee on the Poor Law: Report of the Select Committee of the House of Lords on the Laws relating to the Relief of the Destitute Poor... in Ireland, HL 1846 (694), xxiv, 1. One enterprising candidate dressed his supporters as constables and collected the voting papers from the houses of his opponents' supporters before disposing of them. Unfortunately his enterprise did not pay off as the Poor Law Commission ordered new elections.

41 Nicholls, *Irish Poor Law*, 267.

42 In one case, a returning officer cast some doubt on his impartiality by saying 'As returning officer, I am precluded from interfering with the election of Poor-law Guardians, but vote for the men that the priests desired you'. The Poor Law Commission reprimanded but did not dismiss him from his post: Hansard, 53, 1007 et seq. See O'Brien, 'The Establishment of Poor-Law Unions', 109–10.

43 Nicholls, *Irish Poor* Law, 267.

44 N. Gash, *Politics in the Age of Peel*, Longmans, London, 1953, 239–69.

45 Ibid., 240.

The 1846 Lords Select Committee provides an interesting overview of the operation of the poor law just before it was caught up in the devastation of the Famine.[46] Although the Famine had begun by this stage, the Committee heard evidence in the first part of 1846 and it was clear that nobody expected the Famine to continue in the manner in which it did. The report provides a picture of how the poor law was operating (almost fully nationwide) in a relatively 'normal' period. Evidence was taken from many of the administrators of the poor law and many chairmen of boards of guardians. Their evidence makes it clear that there was still a high level of politicisation amongst the boards of guardians. Both administrators and guardians gave evidence that elections were frequently influenced by political and religious feeling.[47] There was also evidence that both Roman Catholic clergy and landlords sought to influence the outcome of elections.[48]

Significant changes were made to the poor law legislation as a result of the impact of the Great Famine – in particular the legislation was altered in 1847 to allow the payment of outdoor relief in certain circumstances.[49] This legislation was strongly resisted by the Irish landed proprietors and in the House of Lords and as an apparent quid pro quo the number of ex-officio guardians was increased at this time to 50 per cent of the total,

46 Report of the Select Committee of the House of Lords on the Laws relating to the Relief of the Destitute Poor… in Ireland, HL 1846 (694), xxiv, 1. The Lords, many of whom were fundamentally opposed to such legislation, had expressed concerns about the implementation of the poor law on many occasions. The Committee was appointed by the Conservative government to allow these concerns to be expressed in a controlled environment.

47 Ibid. at 10–11, 83, 278, 599, 620. Assistant Poor Law Commissioner Edward Gulson stated, in addition, that board officers were often replaced on political grounds, that contractors sought to ensure the election of guardians favourably disposed to them, and that many petitions for Repeal emanated from 'political' boards: at 10–11. Feingold reports that at least three boards passed repeal resolutions: *Nation*, 26 May, 24 June and 7 October 1843.

48 At 11, 172, 420–1, 686.

49 P. Gray, *Famine, Land and Politics: British Government and Irish Society, 1843–50*, Irish Academic Press, Dublin, 1999, 276–83.

that is equivalent to the number of elected guardians.[50] The system continued in operation without major legal change until the 1898 Local Government Act (see chapter 8). As discussed in chapter 4, it appears that the involvement of boards in party and national politics may have declined compared to the pre-Famine period.[51] In contrast to the 1846 report, there is, for example, little reference to such issues in the report of the 1861 Select Committee on the poor law.[52]

The growth of nationalisation

Although the local boards of guardians consisted of 50 per cent elected guardians and 50 per cent ex-officio guardians (who were generally landowners), as Feingold has shown, in the 1870s the vast majority of officers came from the ranks of the landowners. In 1877, 88 per cent of all officers were landowners rather than tenants. This rose to no less than 99 per cent of board chairmen and 93 per cent of vice-chairman. Only amongst the deputy vice chairmen did tenants appear in any considerable numbers and even here the landowners remained a significant majority (72 per cent).[53] As Feingold also shows the officers were often very extensive landowners with the median rateable valuation of the land owned by the chairmen being £2,034. The status of the board officers in the 1870s is discussed in more detail in chapter 9.

However, clearly related to the broader politicisation of the 1880s, the more democratic element of the poor law boards gradually began to challenge the landowners for formal power. On the basis of a sample of

50 In a small number of cases there were insufficient local justices of the peace in the county to reach the 50 per cent.

51 For example, Feingold reports that only two boards of guardians passed a resolution in support of G.H. Moore's land bill in 1856 (citing the *Nation*, 3 May and 7 June 1856).

52 Report from the Select Committee on Poor Relief, HC 1861 (408), x, 1. Although there clearly was electoral competition in Dublin: see the evidence to the Committee of H.J. Mac Farlane, D.F. Brady and John Byrne.

53 Feingold, *Tenantry*, 31.

unions, Feingold estimates that the number of electoral districts which were contested rose from less than 10 per cent in the 1870s to over 20 per cent by the early 1880s.[54] This estimate is confirmed by contemporary evidence that by 1885, 17 per cent of electoral divisions were contested – up from 7 per cent in 1878.[55] Reflecting the increased level of electoral challenge, the number of tenant officers rose sharply during the 1880s rising from 12 per cent in 1877 to 35 per cent by 1882 and half of all officers by 1886.[56] But this trend was geographically varied. It was strongest in Munster, where by 1886 tenant officers had risen to 68 per cent of all officers, while in the Ulster unions this was only 24 per cent.

	1877	1886
Munster	21	68
Leinster	11	53
Connaught	9	53
Ulster	10	24
Ireland	12	50

Table 5.1 Tenant officerships by province (per cent), 1877–86
Source: Feingold, *Revolt of the Tenatry*, 174, 177.

The change is nicely captured in the case of the Navan board. In March 1880 the *Drogheda Argus* reported that the landlord chair of the board, S. Garnet JP, had been re-elected to the chair 'which he has so ably filled for over a quarter of a century'.[57] The following year the same paper reported that Garnet had been defeated by (soon to be Parnellite MP) Robert H.

54 Feingold, *Tenantry*, 105, 121 and 152.
55 Evidence of Henry Robinson to the 1884 Select Committee on the Poor Law Guardians (Ireland) Bill.
56 Feingold, *Revolt of the Tenantry*, 174.
57 *Drogheda Argus*, 3 April 1880.

Metge by thirteen votes to four. The *Argus* commented on Garnet's support for coercion as the reason for his overthrow.[58]

A sample of newspaper reports of poor law elections generally confirms Feingold's political categorisation of the boards. For example, Feingold classifies Kells, Limerick and Killmallock as tenant controlled in 1882. This is broadly confirmed in newspaper reports as the Marquis of Headford (Kells) and Lord Emly (Limerick) were defeated in the March 1882 elections with all 'Nationalist' boards (or as the unsympathetic *Limerick Chronicle* put it 'the unruly radical element') being elected in their place while in Kilmallock 'land leaguers' and 'suspects' were elected unopposed.[59] Conversely, Feingold shows Oldcastle and Rathkeale as entirely landlord dominated and indeed the papers show that the existing chairs (clearly landlord in one case) were re-elected. However, by 1886 Rathkeale is shown (by Feingold) as tenant controlled and the newspapers confirm that Nationalists were elected to all three officerships.[60] However a confidential return prepared for the Lord Lieutenant shows the complexity of changes in the political composition of boards.[61] In total there were changes in the political composition of forty-two officers as a result of the 1884 elections. The bulk of these, as one would expect, represented a change from either a Conservative (11) or Liberal (14) officer to a Nationalist one. However, there were also a number of changes from Nationalists to Conservative (6) or Liberal (3) control.

58 *Drogheda Argus*, 2 April 1881. On 10 April 1880 Metge and Parnell were elected MPs for Meath with Metge almost equalling Parnell's vote (2,252 to 2,283).

59 *Meath Herald*, 8 and 15 April 1882; *Limerick Chronicle*, 30 March 1882; 1 April 1882; *Munster Express*, 29 March, 1 April 1882. However, the newspaper reports appear to indicate that all the Kells officers were Nationalist while Feingold reports that one was a landlord while, conversely, one of the Limerick officers denied having any partisan views although all were apparently tenants. It is obviously possible that some landlords had Nationalist views (or that tenants were conservative) and this suggests that while the broad thrust of Feingold's work is correct, it would be unwise to place too much reliance on the precise difference between boards in his categorisation.

60 *Limerick Chronicle*, 1 April 1886. In Limerick the Nationalist officers were re-elected unanimously in 1886.

61 NAI CSORP 1884/10989. Unfortunately the source of information about the political affiliations of the local officers is not specified.

Nationalisation – local or national politics?

An important issue is the relationship between the take over of the poor law boards and the direction of Parnell and the national leadership of the Home Rule (later Irish) Party and the Land League (and later Irish National League). To what extent was the takeover a spontaneous local act and to what extent was it directed centrally? On the one hand, Feingold outlines the (somewhat limited) efforts made by the leadership in 1881 to encourage challenges to landlord guardians and suggests that these efforts 'had the desired effect'.[62] On the other hand, he also emphasises the extent to which local guardians acted independently of central direction and in fact highlights the lack of direction by the national movement.[63] The latter assessment seems more correct. While there can be no doubt that the movement to take over control of the poor law boards was heavily influenced by the broader political struggle of the period and that activity may, on occasion (as perhaps in 1881), have been influenced by the national leaders, in general it appears to have primarily a movement driven by individuals at a local level with, as Feingold correctly points out, very limited direction from the national level.

An analysis of the Irish Parliamentary Party's voting record in the 1880s throws some light on the party's broader views on social issues.[64] The division lists of the House of Commons on a sample of about twenty votes on 'social issues' were analysed to establish the extent to which the Irish Parliamentary Party resembled other parties/factions.[65] In the period

62 Feingold, *Tenantry*, 113–17, quote at 115.

63 Ibid., 168, 173 and 240.

64 M. Cousins, 'The voting behaviour of the Irish parliamentary party on social issues, 1881–90', paper to the Irish Historical Society, November, 2007. The analysis used the Rice Cohesion index which measures the extent to which a group of voters votes in the same way (on a scale of 0–100) and the Rice Likeness index which measures the extent to which the structure of party votes resembles another (again on a scale of 0–100).

65 About twenty votes in the period were analysed on broadly 'social' issues such as women's enfranchisement, marriage, taxation, liquor licensing, contagious diseases, employers' liability, and wages. All were larger votes (with at least 20 per cent of MPs voting) and contested.

1880–5 when the party remained a very loose alliance with a Parnellite and non-Parnellite section, one finds that turnout is lower than for the Liberal and Conservative parties (only 40 per cent of overall turnout), and cohesion is also low compared to other parties (37 on a scale of 0–100 compared to 80 for the Liberals). Perhaps surprisingly there does not appear to be a strong division between the Parnellite and non-Parnellite wings. Voting is generally closer to that of the Liberals and closer to the body of Liberals than to Radicals.[66] This is hardly a surprise given the background of many Irish Parliamentary Party MPs. In the short 1886 Parliament (which was, of course, exceptional), turnout was up considerably (to 78 per cent of overall). Cohesion also shows a marked improvement (to 74). Party cohesion was consistent (with the exception of some liquor issues) and voting is consistently closer to the Liberals and now closer to the Radical MPs. Conversely any likeness to Conservatives disappears. But voting on social issues is still relatively weak compared both to other parties and to Irish Parliamentary Party votes on other issues (and the leadership rarely votes). Finally, in the Conservative-controlled Parliament from 1886 to 1890 (before the Parnell split), turnout falls again. Cohesion remains high on most issues (79) but is overstated due to high non-voting and disappears on a number of issues. The voting likeness to the Liberals remains but is overstated due to non-voting and split votes but there is no likeness to the Conservatives.

Looking at the period as a whole, there is a clear and expected change between the pre- and post-1886 party. The Parnellite controlled party (post-1885) becomes much more cohesive and the party votes more closely with the Liberals. Overall, however, the record of consistently low turnout does not provide any clear indications that the Irish Parliamentary Party was strongly committed on social issues. As will be seen in future chapters, it is argued that there is also little indication that the local 'Nationalist' or tenant representatives adopted any very distinctive policies on a left-right political spectrum.

66 Radical members are identified on the basis of T.W. Heyck's work, *The Dimensions of British Radicalism: The Case of Ireland, 1874–1895*, University of Illinois Press, Urbana, 1974.

Despite the volume of publications on the Land War period, there has been surprisingly little study of the Irish National League, established in October 1882, at either a national or local level.[67] However, the role of the League can be examined both through the archives of some key figures (such as Timothy Harrington secretary of the Irish National League), the pages of *United Ireland*, and the surviving minute books of a number of branches. Research indicates that the head office of the Irish National League did attempt to encourage local branches to take action on specific aspects of the poor law such as, for example, the implementation of the labourers' cottages legislation and attempted to discourage boards from becoming involved in jobbery.[68] An examination of two surviving minute books indicates that some local branches were very actively involved in putting forward candidates for poor law elections, sanctioning members who did not vote for the 'popular' candidate (despite the objections of Harrington) and in attempting to influence guardians on issues such as the wages of poor law staff, appointment of officials, union rating, implementation of the labourers acts, election of chairman, and a range of other issues.[69] Again, however, the main initiative for action appears to have come locally.

How the new guardians exercised control

A second key issue is the question of what the Nationalist guardians did with the power once they had taken over. A number of activities emerge from this research. The first is that boards of guardians increasingly passed

67 See D. Jordan, 'The Irish National League and the "Unwritten Law": Rural Protest and Nation-Building in Ireland 1882–1890', *Past & Present*, 158 (1998), 146–71; D.S. Lucey, *The Irish National League in the Dingle Poor Law Union, 1885–91*, Four Courts, 2003.

68 NLI Ms. 9454.

69 NLI Ms. 33561 and 34909.

resolutions supporting political objectives.[70] One clear sign of the change of control was the passing of such resolutions by the 'Nationalist' boards.[71]

The second activity involved the use of poor law funds to support political activity, specifically the payment of outdoor relief to suspects and evicted tenants and the provision of cottages to such persons.[72] The Evicted Tenants Act 1847 allowed payment of outdoor relief to evicted tenants – who would otherwise only have qualified for indoor relief – for up to one month. This does not appear to have been widely used in the period to 1879 but in the 1880s tenant controlled boards increasingly used these powers to support evicted tenants and to penalise evicting landlords who had to contribute considerably to the cost of outdoor relief paid by way of increased rates.[73] In addition, the government had allowed boards

70 E.g. NAI CSORP/1881/494, 1884/23450, 1889/19371, 10197. And see H. Robinson to AJ Balfour, 10 February 1888, NAI CSORP/1890/20219.

71 For example, the Limerick board passed a motion of support for Mr Gray MP on his imprisonment in August 1882. In contrast, Lord Inchiquin in the (landlord controlled) Ennis board refused to accept a similar motion: *Limerick Chronicle*, 24 August 1882. Other examples include motions concerning the operation of the Land Acts passed by Newcastle (*Munster News*, 18 March 1882), and one supporting Home Rule passed by the Limerick board (*Limerick Chronicle*, 1 April 1886).

72 See NAI CSORP/1881/26500, 1882/19779, 1886/11762, 1888/13520; 1891/15787. Payment of outdoor relief was described by Robinson as the 'most striking instance' of abuse of power: H. Robinson to AJ Balfour 10 February 1888, NAI CSORP/1890/20219.

73 See, for example, NAI CSORP/1886/11762; CSORP/1886/22627; CSORP/1888/13250; CSORP/1889/10197. The Local Government Board generally did not intervene directly in these cases leaving it to the auditor to decide if a surcharge should be imposed on the guardians. In his evidence to a 1884–5 Select Committee, Local Government Board inspector Richard Bourke described a case in Tulla union where a landlord who evicted a large number of tenants in one division (of which he owned 'the greater part') was saddled with rates of about 6 *s.* (as opposed to the normal 10*d.* to 1*s.* 2*d.*) as a result of the guardians paying high outdoor relief (£1 to 25*s.*) to evicted tenants: Report from the Select Committee of the House of Lords on the Poor Law Guardians (Ireland) Bill, 1884–5 (297) x, 364, Qs. 337–53. However, in this case, it appears from the evidence that a surcharge was imposed and eventually paid by the guardians. See also a similar case In Roscommon union in 1881–2: evidence of Henry Smyth, ex-officio guardian: Q. 1260 et seq. and the resulting legal proceedings in *R. (Jephson) v Justices of Roscommon*, 12 Lr. Ir. 331.

of guardians to support the families of arrested suspects through the Protection of Person and Property Act 1881 which had extended the powers in relation to payment of outdoor relief contained in the Relief of Distress Act of 1880 to such persons. It is difficult to establish the extent to which boards used these powers but the Local Government Board annual reports for the period indicate that the auditor surcharged up to forty boards of guardians annually for excessive or unauthorised payments of outdoor relief.[74] However, given the degree of discretion which local boards had in establishing an appropriate level of payment and the difficulty the auditor faced in detecting excessive expenditure, it seems likely that the cases in which surcharges were actually recorded represented only a small proportion of total expenditure on relief to evicted tenants. The New Ross case, studied by Crossman, is a further, albeit atypical, example of a board of guardians acting to support evicted tenants.[75] This is discussed in more detail in chapter 6.

Another area of board activity was the building of labourers' cottages under the 1883 Act. A considerable number of houses were built in the first few years of the operation of the Acts although this fell off considerably after 1888–9. The building of cottages was a complex matter. Firstly an application had to be made to the board of guardians which had then to agree a scheme. This was considered at an inquiry by a Local Government Board inspector and the Local Government Board then made a provisional order which often varied the scheme originally proposed by the board of guardians. Finally, this order had to be confirmed by Parliament or, after 1885, the Judicial Committee of the Irish Privy Council and the landowners involved could petition the Council not to confirm the scheme. The Privy Council was, based on the reports of its decisions, clearly unfavourable to any attempt by Nationalist guardians to make what it saw as improper use of the Acts. There are a number of cases where the Council refused to

74 The largest surcharge appears to have been £139 in Athy, see NAI CSORP/1888/12739, 19910; 1890/7728. This case is examined further in chapter 7, as it is linked to the plan of campaign struggle between the Marquis of Lansdowne and his tenants.

75 V. Crossman, 'The New Ross Workhouse Riot of 1887: Nationalism, Class and the Irish Poor Laws', *Past and Present*, 179, (2003), 135–58.

authorise schemes (which had already been passed by the Local Government Board) such as cases involving an attempt to return an evicted tenant to the land from which he had been evicted.[76] Both these issues are considered in more detail in chapter 6.

A further area in which the boards exercised their powers was in favouring businesses who supported 'national' as opposed to Conservative interests (although the definition of this might be very loose). An example is the decision by the Athy board of guardians to award a printing contract to a local Nationalist newspaper as opposed to the Conservative newspaper which had the contract during the period in which vice guardians controlled the union. Again it is difficult to assess how widely these type of powers were exercised although at least one board of guardians was dissolved for accepting a higher tender (Dungarvan).[77] Conversely, however, the Local Government Board (at least under the active leadership of Arthur Balfour) attempted to prevent boards giving contracts to newspapers which, in Balfour's words, 'habitually break the law'.[78] Balfour blithely argued that, in doing so, the Board had no regard to politics although as J.J. Clancy MP (Dublin North) pointed out this was a bit like saying that no question of religion entered into jury-packing.[79]

76 Although these made up a very small number of the total applications. See the reports of hearings of the Privy Council in the *Daily* Express, 23 and 25 February, 5 and 10 April, 20 and 23 May and 15 September1887.

77 Annual Report of the Local Government Board for Ireland, HC 1889 [C. 5769] xxxvi, 695 at 79.

78 Hansard, 346, 1625 et seq., 14 July 1890 (Balfour comment at 1629). It appears that the *Carlow Nationalist*, the *Cork Herald* and *Cork Examiner* amongst others had been so 'boycotted'.

79 Ibid., 1636.

Conclusion

The 1880s saw very significant changes in the operation of poor relief. In particular, the proportion of the population on outdoor relief exceeded that on indoor relief for the first time. In addition, this period saw the dramatic take-over of the boards of guardians throughout much of southern Ireland by Nationalist, tenant guardians. Interestingly this take-over followed rather than preceded the take-over which had already happened at a national level.[80] So, in one sense, the struggle for control of the boards can be seen as an example of landlord resistance to the growing power of Nationalism.[81] However, by the end of the 1880s, Nationalist guardians had taken control of the majority of boards in southern Ireland. Nonetheless, it is important also to emphasise the degree of continuity in poor relief policies in that the regional divisions identified in chapter 2 survived largely intact despite the changes which occurred in board composition.

1891 marked the end of the period of struggle. Balfour's 'kicks and halfpence' approach was now well established, and the rise in outdoor relief which had occurred in the 1880s was not continued in the 1890s. The Parnell split seriously weakened the Nationalist movement both nationally and locally. For example, the powerful Mothel (Co. Waterford) branch of the Irish National League – which was effectively nominating five guardians to its local board by 1890 – disbanded to avoid taking sides in the split.[82] In Meath the Parnell split led to heated disputes between pro- and anti-Parnell factions which were, in part, fought out in the boards of guardians.[83]

80 K.T. Hoppen, *Elections, Politics and Society in Ireland, 1832–1885*, Clarendon, Oxford, 1984, 329, points out that landlords had already lost electoral power at the parliamentary level by about 1880.

81 See, in a similar vein, L.P. Curtis, 'Landlord Responses to the Irish Land War, 1879–1887,' *Éire-Ireland*, 38:3–4 (2003), 134–88.

82 NLI MS 34909 (Minute book of Mothel branch, INL).

83 D. Lawlor, *Divine Right? The Parnell Split in Meath*, Cork University Press, Cork, 2007.

CHAPTER 6

Outdoor Relief and Labourers' Cottages: Nationalism and/or Economics?

This chapter looks at issues concerning the growth in outdoor relief over the period of its expansion from the 1860s to the 1880s, and at the building of cottages for agricultural labourers, on the basis of legislation adopted in 1883, in the period up to 1911. It examines, in particular, some of the possible causes of the growth in outdoor relief and the subsequent expansion of labourers' cottages. In doing so, it looks at whether or not a link can be seen between these developments and the nationalisation of the boards of guardians which took place in the 1880s.

Outdoor relief

The rise in outdoor relief, 1860–1870s

One of the most interesting questions to arise in the study of the post-Famine poor law is the reason for the rise in outdoor relief in the period after 1860. As has been seen, the original 1838 legislation required that all relief be provided in workhouses but outdoor relief was introduced during the Famine in 1847. This Act allowed payment of outdoor relief to limited categories of persons[1] but excluded able-bodied persons from any entitle-

1 S. 1 of the 1847 Act allowed relief outdoors of all destitute poor persons disabled by old age, infirmity, sickness and serious accident, and of destitute poor widows having two or more dependent legitimate children.

ment unless the local workhouse was full or unfit to admit poor persons due to fever or infectious disease.[2] During the Famine, outdoor relief was paid extensively but this declined rapidly in the 1850s to a situation where by 1859 outdoor relief had been reduced to very low levels (only about 1,500 received outdoor relief daily) (see figure 1.1). These were almost all non-able-bodied and outdoor relief was rarely allowed for able-bodied persons in the period.

The agricultural depression of 1859–64 saw a significant rise in the average daily level of outdoor relief but – unlike the post-Famine period – this continued after the end of the depression, rising to about 20,000 by 1870 and over 30,000 by 1878. However, this was not a uniform picture and there was a great deal of variation in how boards of guardians responded (see map 2.5). Geographically, Leinster unions were most likely to pay outdoor relief, followed by Munster and Connaught with few Ulster unions paying extensive outdoor relief. Boards of guardians in cities, while paying high amounts of outdoor relief in absolute terms, all paid a relatively low proportion of relief outdoors. The rise in outdoor relief in the period was, of course, precisely the opposite tendency to that occurring in England and Wales where a 'crusade against outdoor relief' led to a fall in the numbers on outdoor relief, although this remained significantly higher than in Ireland.[3]

The matter received some consideration by the 1861 Select Committee (discussed in chapter 4). The issue of outdoor relief was the subject of the largest number of motions by the local boards of guardians to the Committee with no less than 24 (mainly from Ulster and Munster) submitting motions opposed to any extension of outdoor relief.[4] The bulk of witnesses giving evidence to the Committee were also opposed to outdoor relief although former assistant Poor Law Commissioner Dr Phelan sup-

2 S. 2 of the 1847 Act. Even where these conditions were satisfied an order of the Poor Law Commission was necessary to allow admission of the able-bodied.

3 See A. Brundage, *The English Poor Laws, 1700–1930*, Palgrave, Basingstoke, 2002, 112–17, and E. Hurren, *Protesting about Pauperism: Poverty, Politics and Poor Relief in Late-Victorian England, 1870–1900*, Royal Historical Society, Woodbridge, 2007.

4 Report from the Select Committee on poor relief, HC 1861 (408), x, 1. A number of motions were however submitted in favour of the boarding out of children.

ported greater outdoor relief.[5] The Committee supported the retention of the status quo and a proposal by Laurence Waldron (Liberal, Tipperary County) that boards of guardians should give outdoor relief more freely was defeated.[6]

In 1864, J.P. Hennessy MP introduced a Bill allowing for the extension of outdoor relief. Hennessy was a Conservative MP (Kings) but his views on outdoor relief did not reflect those of most Irish Conservatives. He argued that an extension of outdoor relief would, in fact, reduce the cost. More broadly he argued for such an extension on grounds of public policy for 'if Irish persons were more harshly treated than those who live nearer the centre of government, the loyal attachment to the government that should exist in Ireland was necessarily disturbed'.[7] However, the chief secretary Lord Naas (Conservative, 1852, 1858–9, 1866–8) opposed the measure as did a number of Irish Conservative and Liberal MPs. Despite support from a number of Liberal MPs, including some who would in future be associated with Home Rule, the Bill was deferred.

The Poor Law Commission/Local Government Board remained opposed to outdoor relief but its opposition appears to have been quite muted and it was largely unable to stop local boards of guardians acting as they wished. It is clear that individual inspectors did attempt to persuade boards of the 'error' of using outdoor relief. Lord Spencer, one of the very few Lords Lieutenant to display an interest in the poor law, also attempted to limit poor law expenditure encouraging the publication by Sir Alfred Power of *A Paper on Out-door Relief in Ireland* in 1875, and (as noted in chapter 5) deciding in 1882 not to renew the broader powers of the boards to pay out relief under the Relief of Distress Act.[8] However, these efforts and occasional efforts by the Commission/Board – such as the circular on outdoor relief in 1887 – clearly did not have the desired effect in the

5 See, for example, Henry Robinson (Q. 6679 et seq.) and Edward Senior (Q. 7305).

6 The proposal was supported by three Liberal members and one Conservative but opposed by eight members (both Conservative and Liberal).

7 Hansard, 176, 449 et seq. at 452–3, 29 June 1864.

8 On Spencer's role in the English 'crusade against outdoor relief' see Hurren, *Protesting about Pauperism*, passim.

longer term.[9] The 1887 circular was notable mainly for its aspirational character with the Board 'hoping' that local boards would give the question of outdoor relief 'their earnest consideration and endeavour to lessen the charges on the ratepayers…'.

The question arises as to why boards of guardians increasingly, but to varying degrees, relied on outdoor relief. There is some correlation between levels of indoor relief and outdoor relief (0.42 in 1877). Thus unions which pay indoor relief to more people are more likely to pay outdoor relief as well. However, one cannot simply explain the level of outdoor relief payable by a particular the union by reference to its policies on indoor relief.

Why would boards of guardians pay outdoor relief?

The thirteen unions with the highest level of outdoor relief in 1863 (as ratio of indoor relief: outdoor relief) were all, with one exception, high outdoor relief unions in 1877. The initial rise in outdoor relief occurred during the agricultural depression and it might be argued that this was related to humanitarian and/or social control reasons, i.e. maintenance of public order. However, when one compares the unions (all in Leinster) in which the highest levels of outdoor relief were paid in the period to 1863, there is, in fact, no correspondence between these unions and the unions identified by Richard Griffiths, head of the Irish Board of Works, as unions worst affected by distress in 1863 – all of which were on the western seaboard.[10] This would suggest that while the agricultural depression may have indeed triggered outdoor relief payments in some unions, the reason was not specifically distress-related. Indeed, the period saw a number of large-scale protests in western unions seeking, in part, outdoor relief (in Limerick in 1861, Westport in 1863 and Galway in 1865).[11] These were

9 Annual Report of the Local Government Board for Ireland, being the Sixteenth Report under the Local Government Board (Ireland) Act, HC 1888 [C.5455] l, 1 at 62–4.

10 Griffiths to Larcom, 21 February 1865, NLI Larcom Ms. 7785.

11 For Galway see NAI CSORP/1865/1141; NLI Larcom Ms. 7609. For Westport see *Mayo Constitution*, 23 and 30 June, 7 and 14 July 1863. For Limerick, NLI Larcom Ms. 7783; *Limerick Reporter*, January 1861.

resisted by the local bourgeoisie by a variety of means including an offer of relief in the workhouse.[12]

There is a relationship between the level of outdoor relief paid and the wealth (in terms of valuation per head of population) of the union (0.52).[13] Thus one might suggest that the regional variation was to some extent related to the ability to pay additional support.

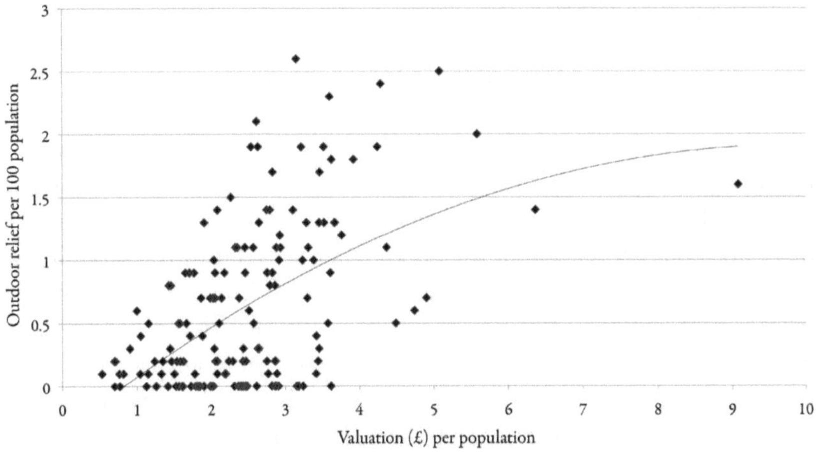

Figure 6.1 Outdoor relief and valuation by union, 1877
Source: Database of poor law statistics

As can be seen, there is a general trend for the level of outdoor relief to rise with a rise in the valuation. However, the wealthiest unions are *not* those with the highest levels of outdoor relief. The relationship between outdoor relief levels and valuation is not dissimilar to that which has already been

12 Although it is noteworthy that such protests generally led to alternative measures to improve the position of the protestors. See M. Cousins, 'Collective Action and the Poor Law: The Political Mobilisation of the Irish Poor, 1851–1878', in W. Sheehan and M. Cronin (eds), *Riotous Assemblies: Riots, Rebels, & Revolts,* Mercier Press, Cork, 2011, 110–26.

13 That is the number of persons supported by way of outdoor relief per 100 population.

seen in relation to indoor relief and valuation (in chapter 1) and it is not clear it can explain the separate patterns as to payment of outdoor relief.[14]

Looking at the continued rise after 1864, studies would suggest that boards of guardians might pay outdoor, as opposed to indoor, relief (i) if changing standards of living led boards of guardians to provide greater support to older and disabled persons outside the workhouse; (ii) if it was cheaper than indoor relief; and/or (iii) if boards of guardians wished to support a pool of labour.[15]

If one looks at the composition of those receiving outdoor relief, it is found that persons permanently disabled from labour by old age, infirmity or bodily or mental defect make up from half to two-thirds of those receiving out relief and that this proportion, albeit with some year-on-year variation, rises from half in the early 1860s to two-thirds by the late 1870s.[16] In contrast, those disabled from labour by reason of severe sickness or serious accident make up about 40 per cent of total poor relief cases during the agricultural depression but fall to less than one-quarter by 1878.[17] This might suggest that the rise in numbers *was* driven by rising generosity towards older and permanently disabled persons. However, this explanation cannot explain why such rising levels of generosity are regionally varied. In addition one must bear in mind that (i) this classification (especially at an aggregate level) was not very exact and may well have varied greatly from one union to another; and (ii) unions were not supposed to support able-bodied persons by way of out relief so it would be surprising if their records showed that they did so.[18]

14 Controlling for the level of indoor relief weakens the relationship between outdoor relief and valuation (0.42).

15 G.R. Boyer, 'The Old Poor Law and the Agricultural Labour Market in Southern England: an Empirical Analysis', *Journal of Economic History*, xlvi, (1986) 1, 113–36. In the Irish case all unions had a recently built workhouse which was, in most cases, much larger than required in normal circumstances so the lack of institutional provision seen in some British unions should not have been a factor in Ireland.

16 Data relates to the number of *cases* rather than *persons*, i.e. it does not include the family members of the main claimant.

17 About 10 per cent of cases involved widows with large families.

18 See below for a more detailed analysis of one of the few outstanding outdoor relief registers of the period.

It is clear that it did cost much less per head to support an individual through outdoor relief than through indoor relief. As has been seen in chapter 1, the average total outdoor relief payment in 1877 was only 40 per cent of the maintenance cost of a person in a workhouse. However, the argument – with which boards of guardians would be familiar – was that payment of outdoor relief would increase the total claim-load and therefore that overall costs would be higher under an outdoor relief system. In addition, Irish boards of guardians were saddled with large underused workhouses, and their standing costs, so that the marginal cost of adding small numbers to the indoor relief lists might not have been considerably higher than paying outdoor relief. Finally, it is difficult to see why a regional pattern would emerge if the decisive factor was relative cost.

The Poor Law Inquiry (1879) used a somewhat selective comparison of unions not using out relief with those using such relief to argue that the use of out relief added considerably to poor relief costs.[19] An analysis of poor relief data for the period 1859–77 does broadly support this argument. Firstly, poor law spending per 100 persons is positively correlated with the numbers on outdoor relief in 1877 – even controlling for variations in valuation per head. This indicates that the more persons on outdoor relief the greater the cost, suggesting that unions with high outdoor relief costs were doing so in addition to, rather than in substitution of, indoor relief costs.

Similarly, a comparison of overall spending by unions in 1859 and 1877 does show that while spending per head more than doubled overall, it increased most rapidly in those unions which paid extensive out relief and least in those which paid no or very limited relief outside the workhouse.[20]

19 Poor Law Union and Lunacy Inquiry (Ireland) Report, HC 1878–9 [c.2239] xxxi, 1.

20 Although it should also be noted that the higher-spending unions also spent much more in 1859, when outdoor relief made little difference to costs.

	1859	1877	Change per cent	N
No OR	5.46	10.13	86	42
Low OR (0.1–0.3)	5.61	10.64	90	40
Average OR (0.4–0.7)	6.42	13.98	118	25
High OR (>0.5)	9.12	21.06	131	56
Average	6.90	14.90	116	163

Table 6.1 Poor law spending per union by variation in outdoor relief, 1859–77
Source: Database of poor law statistics.

There are at least two basic reasons why local employers might wish to use the poor law for labour supply purposes: (i) to 'pension off' old or sick workers; and (ii) to maintain a pool of labour to meet seasonal demand. The two purposes, although different, are not inconsistent and an older worker might be both 'retired' and kept available for light or short-term seasonal work. In both cases, this would suggest that outdoor relief payments should be higher in areas of 'waged' employment. In an Irish context, this would suggest that outdoor relief should be highest where there are large numbers of farm workers employed as opposed to small scale tenant farmers. That such an effect might exist is consistent with Fitzpatrick's argument that in most regions in post-Famine Ireland the supply of agricultural labour was excessive in winter and inadequate at harvest time and that few labourers were employed throughout the year.[21]

Outdoor relief payments *were* broadly cyclical, i.e. high at times of slack labour demand and conversely low when demand for labour was high. However, all poor relief payments, including indoor relief for sick persons, followed roughly the same cyclical pattern so the best that can be said is that the data are not inconsistent with the labour supply thesis.[22] Outdoor

21 D. Fitzpatrick, 'Disappearance of the Irish Agricultural Labourer', 66–92.

22 Strangely, movements in outdoor relief figures lag behind trends in indoor relief while, intuitively, one would have expected movements in outdoor relief to precede changes in indoor relief.

relief payments appear to be related to large farm size, as per Clark's factor analysis,[23] and to the ratio of farm labourers to farmers, as measured by Fitzpatrick.[24] However, such a comparison involves matching union level data as to relief levels with county data as to employment and given the considerable variations within counties, this is not very satisfactory. In order to explore this issue further, the union level data in the 1881 Census have been examined to identify variations in the significance of agricultural labourers in the population.[25] It is found that there is a clear and positive correlation between the level of outdoor relief provided in 1881 and the proportion of agricultural labourers in the union population (0.47). In other words, the larger the proportion of agricultural labourers in the working population, the higher the level of outdoor relief paid in the union. This correlation is clearly consistent with the argument that outdoor relief was used by guardians for labour supply purposes.

23 S. Clark, *Social Origins of the Irish Land War*, Princeton University Press, New Jersey, 1979.

24 Unfortunately neither indicator is published at a union level and there may be significant intra-county variation in some cases. Both large farm size and the labourer ratio are themselves closely correlated (+0.82).

25 This data is only available from 1871 but in that year it does not distinguish between labourers and assisting relatives. As the data is provided on a county basis, we focus here on the more than 100 unions which did not cross county boundaries. There is no reason to believe that this distorts the results. As Fitzpatrick has pointed out there are a number of difficulties with the data. In particular Census respondents often did not distinguish between the categories of agricultural and general labourer. Following Fitzpatrick it is assumed that most labourers (including general labourers) were agricultural labourers but that all labourers living in cities and 'principal towns' were not. Clearly this is a somewhat approximate adjustment but would appear to be the only way to address the issue given the absence of Census manuscripts for the period.

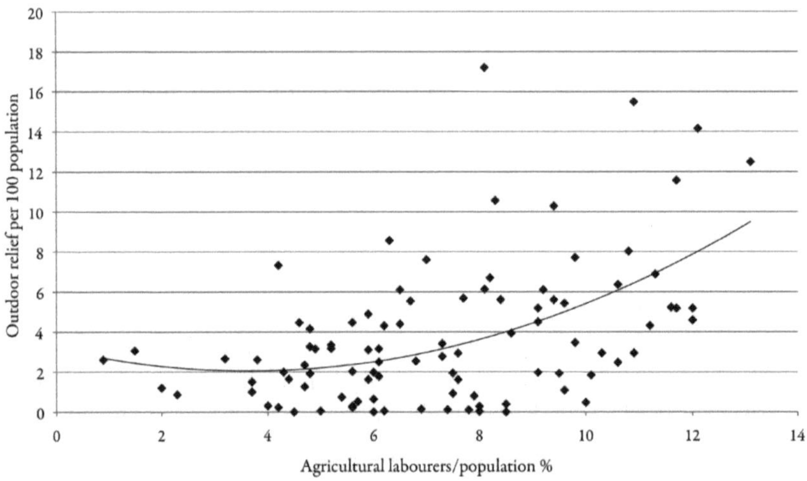

Figure 6.2 Outdoor relief and agricultural labourers/population, 1881
Source: Database of poor law statistics; Census 1881.

Obviously the importance of agricultural labourers cannot explain all the variation in outdoor relief but when one recalls that they made up (at most) 12–13 per cent of the union population and 20–3 per cent of the overall workforce, it would appear that out relief patterns were related to the importance of agricultural labour in the union.[26] Agricultural labourers are consistently the largest group of persons amongst recipients of indoor relief.[27]

Of the 103 unions included in the study, thirty-three unions with above-average outdoor relief also had an above-average proportion of agricultural labourers in the population while only four unions with high out relief had a below-average share of labourers.[28] Conversely, there were twenty-eight unions which had an above-average share of labourers, though

26 On average in the 103 unions, agricultural labourers made up 6.1 per cent of the total population and 11.5 per cent of those in occupation (aged twenty or over).

27 In 1906, 52 per cent of men in workhouses were agricultural or general labourers: Royal Commission on the Poor Law, Statistical Memoranda and Tables relating to Ireland. HC 1910 [Cd. 5244] liv, 763.

28 Longford, Ennis, Kenmare and Clifden (all unions with either two or three landlord officers in 1882).

most were just above the average at about 7–8 per cent, but below-average outdoor relief. Of these, twelve were in Ulster, all – except Newtownards – with two to three landlord officers in 1882.[29] Of the sixteen southern unions which did not have high outdoor relief despite an above-average share of labourers, three (Bantry, Dingle, and Newport) were poor western unions which were arguably constrained in expenditure by their low taxation base.[30] Of the remaining thirteen unions which do not fit the expected pattern, no clear political explanation emerges. In terms of control of the boards, four were entirely landlord controlled and a further four had two landlord officers, but three were tenant controlled and a further four had two tenant officers.[31] Thus while one cannot explain the level of outdoor relief solely by the level of agricultural employment in a union, there is a clear and positive link between the share of agricultural labourers and the level of outdoor relief paid in the southern unions.[32]

A case study of one union

Unfortunately there is very little debate at union level as to the policy concerning payment of outdoor relief. Insofar as this is discussed at all it appears to have related to individual cases and broader policy appears to have evolved over time without explicit debate in most cases.[33] Thus it is very difficult to identify sources as to the policies of local unions. A further evidential problem is that very few outdoor relief registers have survived for

29 Feingold, *Tenantry*, 199.

30 Although Clifden and Kenmare – also poor peripheral unions – have above-average out relief.

31 Ibid. The political data again relates to 1881 and it is possible that some change of control occurred in the period 1881–2 (although four of the unions had at least one tenant officer as early as 1877). However, we look at the impact of the takeover of the boards below.

32 No northern union had a very high level of agricultural labour (the maximum was 8.5 per cent in Limavady) but within the Ulster unions the relationship between outdoor relief and agricultural labourers is weakly negative (-0.15).

33 One exception to this rule is in the Dundalk union where a series of resolutions were passed on outdoor relief policy.

the period – especially for those southern unions which paid higher levels of relief. One of the few which has is for the midlands Tullamore union for the period October 1862 to July 1863.[34] Tullamore was one of the higher outdoor relief unions of the period, although the amount of outdoor relief remained modest by later standards. A shift in policy can be seen in the period, and there is a sudden increase in outdoor relief in January 1863.[35] In the period from October to December 1862 there were only seventeen grants of outdoor relief.[36] Of these most were old (aged sixty-five or over), passing though the union,[37] 'sick and dying', or deserted children; and there were only three cases where the person was of working age.[38] In contrast, in the period January to July 1863 there were seventy-five cases of outdoor relief and of these no less than thirty were of working age. In many cases these are shown as 'sick', but in several it is a child or spouse who is sick and the reason in one is specifically recorded as 'want of work'.

	1862	1863
In transit	4	10
Deserted child	4	0
Old	5	26
Sick and dying	1	6
Working age	3	30
Not known	0	3
Total	17	75

Table 6.2 Persons granted outdoor relief in Tullamore union 1862–3
Source: Tullamore union application and report book, 1862–3.

34 Application and report book, Tullamore union 1862–3, Offaly County Archives.
35 Unfortunately the minute book for this period is not extant and there is no relevant coverage in the local newspapers.
36 Each case can involve a number of people as dependents are normally (but not always) recorded as part of the main claim.
37 Recorded as being 'on the way' from or to a certain place.
38 The 'sick and dying' category can include persons of any age, although most are elderly.

Thus one can see that in 1862, the Tullamore union adopted a restrictive approach to outdoor relief and it could not be argued that out relief was being used as a wage subsidy in any number of cases. However, there is a large increase in the level of outdoor relief granted in 1863 and this is not due to an increase in the number of those types of case supported in 1862. Rather there is a change of policy so that far more working age people are supported on out relief in 1863. While the reasons for this are not known, it is consistent with the wage subsidy argument.

The rise of outdoor relief, 1877–1881

Outdoor relief increased at a much more dramatic rate in the period from 1879 – corresponding with the onset of the Land War. The average numbers on outdoor relief increased from 36,300 in 1879 to 60,000 in 1881. However, outdoor relief reached extremely high levels in 1881 following the introduction of legislation allowing the payment of outdoor relief to able-bodied persons on a temporary basis. The average number on outdoor relief remained at about the 1881 level throughout the 1880s, with the exception of a further sharp increase in 1886 relating to further legislation allowing relief to be paid to the able-bodied in a small number of distressed western unions.[39]

The rise in outdoor relief over this period corresponds with a number of factors which might be thought to be possible causes for the rise in outdoor relief. Firstly the onset of the Land War around 1879 gave rise to very considerable agitation including large-scale meetings and agrarian crimes. It might be suggested that the rise in outdoor relief may have been related to this agitation and that it would be seen as a means of seeking to calm down the situation.

The rise in outdoor relief also corresponds with the beginning of the takeover of poor law boards by the tenantry (discussed in chapter 5), a factor also related to the Land War. Feingold suggests that this takeover

39 Annual Reports of the Local Government Board, 1879–91. See chapter 5 and V. Crossman, *Politics, Pauperism and Power*, 2006.

of the boards may have been related to the rise in outdoor relief.[40] In a similar vein Crossman suggests that the increasing influence of elected poor law guardians 'encouraged a more populist approach to poor law administration, most evident in the provision of labourers' cottages and outdoor relief'.[41] Thus one might expect to find that the rise in outdoor relief took place primarily in those unions dominated by tenants. Feingold provides evidence as to the number of officerships controlled by landlords and tenants in 1881 and this can be related to the level of outdoor relief paid in that union.[42]

Thirdly, the Land War related to a broader economic downturn in the United Kingdom and led to significant hardship in parts of Ireland.[43] So it might be suggested that the rise in outdoor relief was a straightforward response to increased need at a local level. It is normally difficult to obtain any independent indicator of need. However, in this case, presumably as part of the preparation of relief measures, the Royal Irish Constabulary carried out a nationwide survey of persons in want of employment which can be used to give an indicator of need which can be measured against the rise in outdoor relief.[44]

Agitation

Clark developed a measure of agitation consisting of three variables: (1) the number of land meetings per capita in the period 1879–80; (2) number of agrarian crimes per capita in the same period; and (3) the number of arrests per capita under the Protection of Person and Property Act (more

40 Feingold, *Tenantry*, 180.
41 Crossman, *Politics*, 217.
42 While the indicator of the number of officerships controlled was perfectly valid for Feingold's purpose of showing the takeover of the boards by tenants, it is a somewhat crude indicator of the extent to which different groups actually influenced policies in different unions. However, in the absence of detailed local studies in all areas it is the only indicator available to us.
43 See S. Clark, *Social Origins of the Irish Land War*, passim.
44 NAI CSORP/1880/3112.

commonly known as the Coercion Act) of 1881.[45] This provides a measure of agitation ranging from very low to very high. It is, unfortunately, only available on a county basis. The increase in outdoor relief (annual expenditure per 100 population) between the years 1877 and 1882 for each union was compared with the level of agitation for the county in which the union was located. In short, there is only a weak correlation (0.28) between the two measures. If one compares unions in counties (8) with very high agitation with those in counties (6) with very low agitation (all in Ulster), there does appear to be some relationship in that outdoor relief expenditure is higher in the agitated counties (£3.33 compared to £1.18) and increased much more rapidly over the period. However, looking at the broader picture it is clear that outdoor relief increased most rapidly in a wide range of counties in which agitation was not very high (further details are provided below).

Nationalisation

The rise in outdoor relief in the period for each union was also compared with the governance of that union. Feingold provides information as to the extent to which, in 1882, landlords or tenants controlled the three officerships on each board. Thus one has a scale from 0 to 4 of possible tenant influence ranging from a situation where tenants hold no officerships whatsoever to that where they control the entire board. Again, however, there is almost no correlation between the level of increase in outdoor relief and the governance of the board (0.17). As suggested above, it may be that the index is a somewhat inappropriate or imprecise one. Accordingly, the research also looked at those boards in which tenants or landlords controlled all three officerships on the assumption that these might more clearly reflect tenant and/or a landlord policy. Again, the findings do indicate that tenant controlled boards spent more on outdoor relief (£5.28 compared to £3.08) and that expenditure in these unions rose more rapidly over the period. However, once again, turning to the broader picture it can be seen

45 Clark, *Social Origins of the Irish Land War*, 252–6.

that those boards in which the largest increase (all unions saw an *increase* of over £6 p.a.) took place do not show any clear pattern of tenant control or agitation although none of the boards include 'low' agitation areas (almost all in Ulster).

Board	Control (number of tenant officers)	Agitation*
Tralee	1	Very high
Croom	1	High
Kilmallock	3	High
Limerick	0	High
Rathkeale	3	High
Tipperary	3	High
Kilkenny	0	Medium
Navan	1	Medium
Trim	0	Medium

Table 6.3 Boards with highest increases in outdoor relief, 1877–81
Source: Annual Reports of the Local Government Board; Control of boards from Feingold, *Revolt of the Tenatry*, map 3; Agitation scale from Clark, *Social Origins of the Irish Land War*, figure 5.
* It should be noted that on Clark's index almost all counties outside Ulster are categorised as from medium to high in terms of agitation (only Waterford and Wicklow are classified as low).

In making any such comparisons, we are faced with one might call the Ulster problem. This relates to the fact that Ulster unions were overwhelmingly landlord controlled and (as discussed in chapter 2) had different policies as to the provision of indoor and outdoor relief, and building labourers' cottages.[46] Thus, any general comparison of Irish unions will tend to show that

46 Brandes points to the need for caution in using 'Ulster' as a generic label (including all kinds of unspoken socio-political preconceptions), and the need to be sensitive to variations in practice within Ulster. (Personal communication.)

landlord controlled unions paid less outdoor relief and built fewer labourers' cottages. However, the Ulster unions had adopted quite distinctive policies decades before the Land War. Ulster unions always tended to pay less outdoor relief, and have lower rates, than the average for Irish unions. The extent to which this can be explained by Ulster politics, sectarianism, the regional economy and labour market, or a combination of these and other factors has been discussed in chapter 2. However, it does mean that one needs to be sensitive to the fact that one cannot simply compare southern and Ulster unions and assume that any differences between them are accounted for by the different political makeup of the boards.

Need

If politics do not appear to help greatly in explaining the rise in outdoor relief, does a response to need do any better? As explained above, the RIC carried out a survey of the number of agricultural labourers and their families 'in want of employment' and the number of occupiers of land 'in distress and requiring employment'. No doubt these somewhat subjective definitions were not interpreted in the same manner in all areas. However, the RIC were experienced collectors of information and the data do look plausible.[47] The level 'need' is broadly correlated with that for agitation although some Ulster counties appear to be less agitated than might be expected given their level of 'need', while some southern counties (Kings, Westmeath, and – to a lesser extent – Kerry) are more agitated than might be expected. Again, however, there is no correlation at all (-0.095) between this indicator of need and the rise in outdoor relief which increases most rapidly in counties with low-moderate levels of need.

47 For example, need is highest in the western counties, need is highest amongst labourers (as opposed to farmers) in those counties where labourers dominate, etc.

Outdoor relief 1881–1886

Turning to the period to 1886, agrarian crime decreased significantly and there is no reason to expect that agitation might explain relief patterns in this period. Similarly, the main period of distress ended about 1882–3 and the rise in distress in 1886 was mainly confined to a relatively small number of western unions. However, as discussed in chapter 5, the nationalisation of the boards did continue in this period so that by 1886, tenants controlled 50 per cent of all officerships. The data for the increase in outdoor relief from 1877 to 1886 were compared to the composition of the boards in 1886. Here one can see a reasonable correlation between the composition of boards and both the level of expenditure in 1886 (0.40) and the increase over the period from 1877 (0.41).[48] However, there is an equally strong correlation between the pattern of relief in 1877 and that in 1886 (0.44) which suggests that in increasing the level of out relief boards may have been influenced as much by policy legacies as by a specific 'Nationalist' preference for this form of relief.

Farm labourers again

If the above factors only go some way to explaining the rise in relief, what other factors might explain this? As set out in figure 6.3, there remains a strong, if by no means perfect, correlation between the prevalence of farm labourers in a unions (in 1881) and the level of outdoor relief paid by that union in 1886 (0.49).

48 Data for five western unions with extremely high outdoor relief due to the 1886 Act are excluded from this exercise.

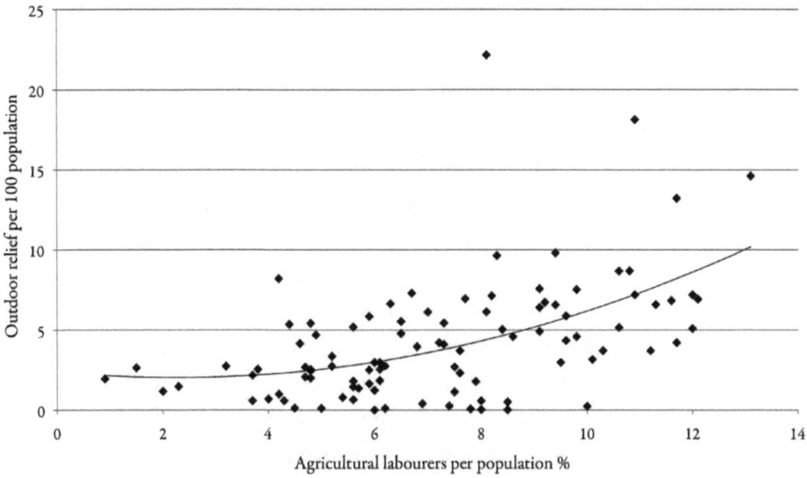

Figure 6.3 Outdoor relief and agricultural labourers/population, 1886
Source: Database of poor law statistics; Census 1881.

But why would that explain the dramatic increase in outdoor relief which took place over the period from 1877 to 1882? An argument concerning labour supply and demand might help to explain this increase. Emigration – mainly to the USA – increased significantly in that period from 7.7 emigrants per 1,000 population in 1878 to 21.6 by 1883.[49] And these were mainly labourers as the proportion of labourers amongst the total male emigrants was between two-thirds and three-quarters in the period.[50] Although the short-run evidence is somewhat limited, there is no sign that the Land War led to a fall in agricultural wages.[51] And looking at the longer-term picture, it has been convincingly argued that the level of emigration was related to the increase in agricultural wages over the period.[52] Thus if certain parts

49 Data in *Irish Historical Statistics – Population 1821–1971*.

50 Emigration Statistics for Ireland for the year 1878, HC 1878–9 [C. 2221] lxxv, 703; Emigration Statistics for Ireland for the year 1883, HC 1884 [C. 3899] lxxxv, 493.

51 Turner, *After the Famine: Irish Agriculture 1850–1940*, 192.

52 T.J. Hatton and J.G. Williamson, 'After the Famine: Emigration from Ireland, 1850–1913', *Journal of Economic History*, 53 (3) (1993) 575–600.

of the country had a demand for agricultural labour and if the increased emigration of labourers, attracted by higher wages in America, led to a shortage of labour supply, it would be rational for the medium-sized and larger farmers who employed the labour both to increase wages and to improve other benefits such as outdoor relief and to provide benefits such as labourers' cottages, a topic discussed in more detail below.

Unfortunately, one can not relate in any clear way the level of emigration by county to patterns in outdoor relief. It is clear that those unions in which outdoor relief increased most where those were farm labourers were prevalent and that there was either a high level of emigration from those counties or a considerable increase in the rate of emigration in the period in question. However, there was also a high rate of emigration from a number of western counties where a much more limited increase in outdoor relief occurred. The key factor distinguishing these two outcomes is arguably the different regional demand for labour. However, there does not appear to be any readily available indicator of such demand in the period.

Labourers' cottages

Legislation allowing poor law unions to build cottages for agricultural labourers was introduced by the Irish Parliamentary Party in 1883.[53] Crossman provides a detailed outline of the background to and implementation of this legislation. She does not, however, provide data as to the unions in which houses were built nor examine, in a statistical manner, the relationship between house building and various factors which might be thought to influence it. The data on the number of houses built in each county in 1892 were compared both with the prevalence of agricultural labourers in

53 See Crossman, *Politics*, chapter 5 for a discussion of the background to and implementation of the legislation.

the county (in 1881)[54] and the composition of the boards of guardians in the county in 1886.[55] As can be seen in figure 6.7, there is a strong correlation (0.77) between the number of labourers' cottages built (as a proportion of the county population) and the prevalence of farm labourers in that county. This, in itself, is unsurprising – it would be much more surprising if one did not find such a correlation – but does warn against looking at the distribution of labourers' cottages without having regard to the fundamental issue of the distribution of the labourers themselves.

Figure 6.4 Labourers' cottages and prevalence of agricultural labourers by county, 1892
Source: Annual Report of the Local Government Board, Fitzpatrick 'Disappearance of the Irish Agricultural Labourer'.

54 On the assumption that there was a considerable lag between 'demand' for and supply of houses due to the slow and bureaucratic process involved.

55 It would be preferable to be able to draw on a longer-term indicator of the level of control of tenants over poor law boards but this is only available for 1886. The categorisation of counties in terms of board governance is based on that in Feingold (*Tenantry*, 202) where he categorises counties as being tenant controlled if tenants hold more than 60 per cent of board officerships in the county. Landlord controlled boards are categorised in a similar manner and there are a small number of counties (6) which satisfy neither criterion and which are treated here as being neither tenant nor landlord controlled. Again, at county level, this is obviously a somewhat imprecise measure.

The comparison of the building of cottages with board control also gives a reasonably strong correlation (0.58). As stated above, this measure of board control is somewhat imprecise and should be taken here only as a general indicator. The correlation is driven primarily by (1) a high level of building in three largely tenant-controlled counties: Limerick, Meath and Westmeath; and (2) by very low levels of house-building in the largely landlord controlled Ulster counties. As discussed above, this does raise again the difficulty that the (post-1880s) landlord-controlled Ulster unions tend to make the tenant-controlled southern unions look more generous whereas, in fact, the landlord-controlled Ulster unions also made the landlord-controlled southern unions look more generous in the earlier period.

The annual number of houses built under the Labourers Acts declined (after an initial peak in the mid-1880s) to under 500 by 1895. However, the number of applications rose dramatically from 1899 leading to a significant rise in houses built from 1903 on.[56] The Local Government Board, which was well placed to judge, attributed this rise to the impact of the democratisation of local government through the Local Government Act in 1898.[57] By this time, spending had become less concentrated in Munster and Leinster although these two provinces continued to dominate house building. By 1906–7, 47 per cent of cumulative spending had been in Munster and 38 per cent in Leinster (compared to 99 per cent in both provinces in 1892–3). The number of houses built in 1910 (reflecting the considerable increase in the early 1900s) was compared with the prevalence of farm labourers by county. As in 1892, there remains a very strong correlation between the two (0.79). Unfortunately, there do not appear to be any published data as to control of the rural district councils in this period although it does appear that 'Nationalist' representatives controlled most southern councils.[58] Thus one cannot replicate the examination of the extent to which the building of houses is related to the different political composition of councils.

56 Annual Reports of the Local Government Board, 1892–1908.

57 Annual Report of the Local Government Board for Ireland… 1901, HC 1902 [Cd. 1259] xxxvii, 1 at. xxxi et seq. See also Crossman, *Politics*, chapter 5 and Fraser, *John Bull's Other Homes*, 35.

58 Crossman reports an estimate by the then undersecretary, Sir David Harrell, who suggested that Labour representatives formed one-sixth of the elected councillors in urban areas (*Politics*, 165).

However, it is noteworthy that there is a very strong correlation between the distribution of labourers' cottages in 1892 and that found in 1910 (0.94) despite the very significant increase in the number of houses over that period (rising from 2.4 per thousand population in 1892 to 7.8 per thousand in 1910). This would indicate that the distribution of cottages geographically did not change dramatically over that period. It should be noted that, to a certain extent, the Local Government Board compelled the building of houses in some northern unions but it is unclear whether this would have any significant effect of the overall patterns.[59]

Discussion

This chapter reports the findings of research into the rise in outdoor relief in the 1880s and the later rise in the building of agricultural labourers' cottages. In the case of outdoor relief, it suggests that there is no clear pattern to be seen between the considerable rise in relief in the early 1880s and either the Land War agitation nor the estimates of distress and lack of employment arising from the overall depression of the period. It also suggests that there is little indication of any clear link between the rise in outdoor relief in the initial phase in the nationalisation of boards of guardians to 1882. While there is slightly more appearance of a link between patterns of outdoor relief and the political composition of boards by 1886, it would appear the policy legacy of existing high levels of out relief payments may also play an important role.

In relation to agricultural labourers' cottages, the research indicates that, unsurprisingly, the main factor driving the building of cottages was the prevalence of agricultural labourers in a particular area. However, the statistical data do suggest that Nationalist, or tenant controlled, boards were somewhat more likely to build labourers' cottages than landlord controlled boards. Nonetheless the data upon which these indications are based are somewhat imprecise.

59 See Crossman, *Politics*, 165.

Unfortunately there is an almost total absence of any explicit discussion at board level as to policy on outdoor relief payments. Boards rarely debated in general terms the approach to outdoor relief and discussion as to individual applications is almost never reported in minutes and only rarely in local newspapers. The only real discussion is on quite exceptional 'political' cases, such as support for evicted tenants. Even where an opportunity to discuss the issues arises, one finds no record that the board did so.[60] In contrast, in the case of labourers' cottages, there is a significant body of evidence which would require a separate study to investigate fully.[61] However, it was very clear from a detailed examination of Kells union that it was the change in the franchise and the advent of various 'labour' representatives which led to the decision to build more houses and, in fact, pressure from labourers can be seen in the area going back to the 1880–1890s.[62]

This chapter suggests that there is limited evidence that the political composition of the boards played an important role in the policy adopted on outdoor relief. Clearly there may well have been tenant controlled boards which adopted an outdoor relief policy and landlord controlled boards which resisted such an approach.[63] On aggregate, however, there seems

60 For example, the Local Government Board inspector's 1882 report on Limerick commented on the doubling of outdoor relief in the period from 1880 but no discussion on this is recorded in the local papers: *Limerick Chronicle*, 7 September 1882.

61 This includes initial discussion at board level in relation to building/not building cottages (newspapers/minutes); newspaper reports of local enquiries by Local Government Board inspectors; newspaper reports of subsequent appeals to the Irish Privy Council; and various parliamentary returns.

62 *Meath Herald*, 27 May, 3, 17 June, 15 July, 28 September, 14 October, 4, 25 November 1899. For the earlier period see, for example, *Meath Reporter*, 4 October 1890 demonstration in Kells re 'The labourer's question' including housing.

63 In his evidence to an 1884–5 Select Committee, Colonel Spaight, Local Government Board inspector, gave the example of Kerry where, he argued, three unions 'under the control' of ex-officios (Dingle, Cahirciveen and Kenmare) provided low outdoor relief while three unions controlled by tenant guardians (Listowel, Tralee and Killarney) provided high outdoor relief. However, Spaight's evidence is somewhat weakened by the fact that he defines 'under the control' as meaning that the chair is an ex-officio while, as he himself admits, one of the unions allegedly under the control of elected guardians (Killarney) was chaired by an ex-officio (at Q. 683): Report from the Select

to be only a limited link between changes in political composition and changes in poor relief patterns. It has been argued that the importance of agricultural labourers in the local labour force and changes in the demand for agricultural labour had a more important influence on outdoor relief patters. Obviously the northern boards did generally adopt a most restrictive policy to both outdoor relief and building of labourers' cottages. However, it is argued that this was not simply because they were landlord controlled but rather that policy on outdoor relief and cottages was shaped by the broader range of factors discussed in chapter 2.

Committee of the House of Lords on the Poor Law Guardians (Ireland) Bill. 1884–5 (297) x, 364, Qs. 672–707; 738–45. Our research for 1886 indicates that (per capita) out relief in Listowel was lower than that in Cahirciveen and Kenmare.

CHAPTER 7

The Poor Law and the 'Plan of Campaign', 1886–1891

In the previous chapter the rise in outdoor relief was examined and it was argued that this was, at best, only loosely related to the 'nationalisation' of the boards of guardians and the take-over of power by (mainly) Catholic, Nationalist guardians. However, that study relied mainly on aggregate data and in this chapter one specific episode – the plan of campaign – is examined more closely. During the 'plan', it might be thought that Nationalist boards would be particularly likely to try to pay outdoor relief in order to compensate evicted tenants and to 'punish' rate-paying landlords. In the initial Land War period (1879–82) agitation was widely dispersed throughout Ireland and, as has been seen in the previous chapter, there is no clear link between Land War activities, nationalisation and payment of outdoor relief. However, it may be that this is due to data issues, and the much more tightly focused plan of campaign (1886–91) allows a case study which can look in detail at the activities of the local boards.

The plan of campaign

The plan of campaign was initiated by senior members of the Irish Parliamentary Party in late 1886 and promulgated through *United Ireland*, local meetings and through the local branches of the Irish National League.[1] In contrast to the earlier period, where land agitation was widely dispersed, the plan of campaign was confined to specific estates. The plan involved

1 See L.M. Geary, *The Plan of Campaign*, Cork University Press, Cork, 1986.

the tenants in agreeing on a demand for a reduction in rent levels which they presented to the landlord. If agreement was not reached between the parties, the tenants paid the proposed rent to a fund which was to be used to support the struggle with the landlord. In many cases where landlords did not agree to the terms demanded and rent was not paid, this led to evictions. Unfortunately, the different sources provide different estimates of the total number of estates involved in the Plan ranging up to over 200.[2] However, in many cases activity was short lived and resulted in either a quick settlement by the landlord or a cessation of activities by the tenants. In these cases, therefore, there would, in any case, have been no additional poor law expenditure. Fortunately, the CSORP archives contain a list of seventeen estates on which the plan of campaign was still in force in 1891 and information is also available in the report of the Evicted Tenants Commission (which adds a further two small Donegal estates).[3] It is possible to identify the unions in which these estates were based and to compare expenditure in these unions over the period from 1886 to overall trends in poor law expenditure (both nationally and province wide).[4]

Aggregate data

If it was the case that Nationalist boards of guardians used the poor law, to a significant extent, to support evicted tenants and penalise evicting landlords as part of the plan of campaign, one would expect to find that Nationalist boards increased the amount which they spent on relief and/or paid more relief by way of outdoor relief during the period of the plan

2 Geary, *Plan of Campaign*.

3 NAI CSORP/1891/12731. These are listed in M. Cousins, 'Poor Relief in Ireland, 1851–1914', PhD, Glasgow Caledonian University, 2010, annex 2. The methodological issues involved in identifying the relevant estates and the unions in which they were located are discussed in more detail therein.

4 While it would be preferable to compare the trends in unions to those in the surrounding counties, this would greatly increase the amount of data required to be collected given that county level data was not published by the Local Government Board.

than did comparable boards in other unions, i.e. in the cases examined from 1886–91, although disputes were not active in all cases for the entire period.

The unions in which the nineteen estates in which the plan was still ongoing in 1891 were primarily located have been identified.[5] The nineteen estates fell into seventeen unions, although some estates were in two unions while in other cases two or more were in the same union. The amount spent in each union on indoor and outdoor relief in the period from 1886–91 was then identified. Some indication of the political complexion of the boards can be obtained from Feingold's analysis. Feingold provides data on the composition of the officerships in 1886.[6] Only two of the boards – Dunfanaghy (where the chairman of the board was also the landlord involved in the dispute) and Skibbereen – were entirely landlord controlled ('conservative' in Feingold's terminology). The majority were tenant controlled ('radical'). This is unsurprising as it is likely that Nationalist areas would both elect Nationalist guardians and support the plan of campaign.

The evidence at an aggregate level does *not* provide any indication that Nationalist boards in plan areas used the poor law to provide significant support to evicted tenants. As set out in figure 7.1, spending in the seventeen plan of campaign unions, and in the fifteen unions excluding the two entirely conservative unions, fell over the period, and this fall was broadly in line with national trends.

5 All of the nineteen estates are included in Geary's list of over 200 participating estates. However, the address which Geary gives is usually that of the landowner which does not necessarily correspond with the location of the estate (or that part of the estate) involved in the plan. Some estates – such as Clanricarde's – were very large while others were scattered across a number of different areas. I have identified the areas where disputes took place through contemporary accounts, local history projects, etc.

6 It is, of course, possible that the political complexion of boards changed during the period and, as will be seen, in two cases boards were dissolved and replaced by vice-guardians.

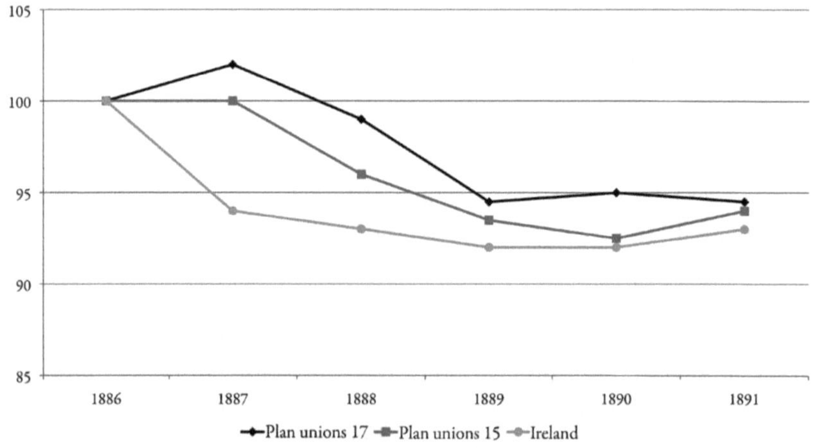

Figure 7.1 Trends in poor relief expenditure (%) in plan of campaign unions, 1886–91
Source: Annual Reports of the Local Government Board, 1886–91.

Similarly, outdoor relief as a percentage of total relief fell in the fifteen unions from 70 per cent to under 65 per cent. Although these unions, on average, were more inclined to pay outdoor relief, the trend was in line with the national picture and, in fact, there was more of a shift away from outdoor relief in the plan unions than there was nationally.

If we examine the overall trends in the amount and composition of relief spending by the political composition of the board of guardians, there is also no support for the thesis that Nationalist unions used the poor law to support tenants. When we look at overall trends in expenditure in the period, i.e. total spending in the period 1887–91 compared to total spending in 1886, we find that all – except the two 'conservative' unions – spent, on average, somewhat less in the period than they had in 1886. Finally, as shown in figure 7.2, the data indicate that the more 'radical' the composition of the board the greater the shift away from outdoor relief. It seems unlikely that this is related to the political composition of the board and is presumably related to local variations in relief demand and practices.

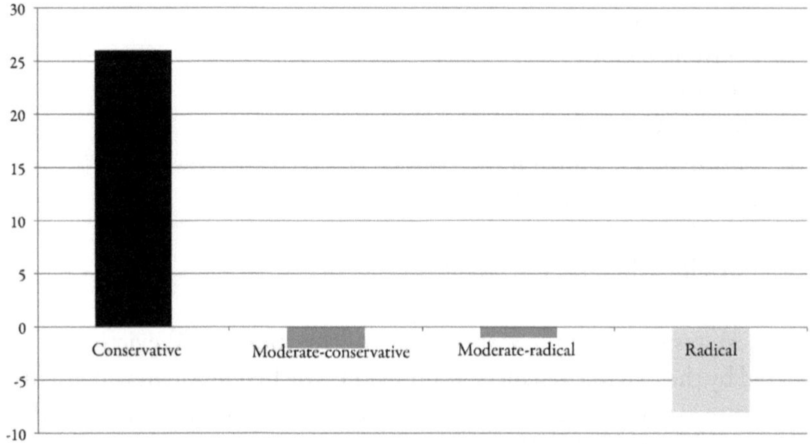

Figure 7.2 Change in the structure of spending (%) by political composition of board, 1886–91
Source: As figure 7.1.[7]

Individual unions

The evidence from the aggregate data do not fit particularly well with what might be expected in the period. Accordingly individual unions were examined to establish if there were specific unions which appeared to fit the expected pattern.[8] The principal estates affected by the plan of campaign, in order of the number of tenants evicted, were:

7 The figure shows the change in the percentage of total spending made up by outdoor relief. The figure shows that all groups – except the two 'conservative' unions – shifted away from outdoor relief.

8 It should be noted that in a number of unions, particularly in Limerick, the size of the estate involved would be too small to affect spending in any case. Conversely, of course, evictions went on in non-Plan estates over the period.

1) Wybrants Olphert, Donegal
2) Ponsonby, Cork
3) Clanricarde, Galway
4) Brooke, Coolgreany, Wexford
5) Smith-Barry, Tipperary
6) Massereene, Louth and Meath
7) Lansdowne, Luggacurran, Kildare
8) O'Kelly, Clongorey, Kildare

These estates included the vast majority of the (post-1886) evictions considered by the Evicted Tenants Commission. The first union in which a dispute arose in this period was New Ross which Crossman has considered in detail in a recent article.[9] The New Ross dispute was not, in fact, concerned with the plan of campaign having originated in March 1886 before the plan was formally established. The New Ross board of guardians decided to set aside a special ward in the workhouse for tenants evicted following a dispute with the Marquis of Ely. This ultimately led to the dissolution of the board of guardians and the appointment of paid vice guardians by the Local Government Board. While it appears that a number of boards considered establishing similar special wards for evicted tenants, in the event none did. Setting aside special wards was a somewhat cumbersome approach and one unlikely to find favour with many evicted tenants who preferred to remain on or close to their former farm and receive outdoor relief.

Lansdowne, Luggacurran (Athy)

The first major dispute as to the plan of campaign took place on the estate of the Marquis of Lansdowne in Luggacurran in the Athy union, Co Kildare. As this was, in many ways, a test case for both sides it is worth considering it in some detail.[10] The dispute took place on the large Lansdowne

9 V. Crossman 'The New Ross Workhouse Riot of 1887: Nationalism, Class and the Irish Poor Laws', *Past and Present*, 179, (2003), 135–58.

10 The focus here is on those aspects of relevance to the poor law. Space does not allow a detailed account of the background to, development and final outcome of the plan of campaign dispute on which see Geary, op. cit.

estate. The Marquis of Lansdowne was a senior Liberal (and later a Liberal Unionist) politician and was, at the time of the dispute, Governor General of Canada. The dispute arose when Lansdowne refused to agree to a reduction in rent demanded by some of his tenants and they refused his counter offer.[11] It appears that the relationship between Lansdowne and his tenants had been relatively harmonious until recent years. Certainly Lansdowne was not in the same category as the uncompromising Clanricarde and in November 1886, as part of an effort to resolve the dispute, had offered his tenants help with establishing a creamery or to buy bulls.[12] However, when negotiations broke down Lansdowne moved very quickly to evict his tenants and proceedings were issued in January and February 1887. In total over 80 tenants and sub tenants were evicted from 1887 onwards. Of course, this involved a much larger number of people having regard to family members. While there was a large variation in the size of holding involved, a number of the tenants had very considerable farms. Nine tenants had holdings of 100 acres or more including the two leaders of the dispute. J.W. Dunne JP had a holding of 970 acres and was the long-standing chairman of the local board of guardians. Dennis Kilbride held 868 acres and had previously been deputy vice-chairman of the board. Both had a significant number of sub-tenants who appear to have been agricultural labourers and family members.

Evictions commenced, amidst considerable but non-violent resistance, on 22 March 1887.[13] Kilbride was the first to be evicted and there were further evictions in April 1887 and throughout the following years into 1889. The evicted families largely continued to live in the area in huts erected on land of the Roman Catholic Church and with family members. Considerable tension continued throughout this period. The landlord attempted to make use of the land and took legal proceedings against the Church to remove the huts erected on its property and against former tenants who

11 For the details of the offer and counter offers see the evidence to the Evicted Tenants Commission.

12 Report of the Evicted Tenants Commission, HC, 1893–94 [C. 6935] xxxi, 13, Q. 3925 et seq. The tenants refused on the basis that 'before they got bulls some of them would want to have cows' (Q. 3928).

13 This section draws on reports in the *Leinster Leader* and *Leinster Express*.

allowed stock to trespass on his land. The tenants, for their part, held at number of large 'indignation' meetings about the dispute and a tenant defence fund was initiated to support the evicted families.

The Athy board of guardians appears to have been one of the earliest boards to have been taken over by tenants. As has been seen, J.W. Dunne had been chairman of the board since 1883 and Daniel Whelan, the vice-chairman, was even longer serving. Thomas Orford, the deputy vice-chairman, had also held his post since 1883. However, the reports of board meetings at the time show a board going about its normal business and, before the evictions began, paying relatively little attention to political issues.[14] In early 1887 the board, as required by law, received notice of eviction in relation to the initial Luggacurran evictions including an eviction notice concerning its chairman, J.W. Dunne.[15] Later in February, the Irish Lord Chancellor removed the Commissionership of the Peace from Dunne because of his participation in the plan of campaign. This meant that he was no longer entitled to sit as ex-officio member of the board. The board condemned the Lord Chancellor for this action and Dunne was offered and accepted a vacant seat on the board which allowed him to continue as chairman.[16] Following the evictions in March 1887, the relieving officer applied to the board for relief for all the labourers affected and the board, which also condemned the evictions, granted outdoor relief at the relatively high level of £1 per week to families of up to eight and *2s. 6d.* per head for larger families. The Nationalist *Leinster Leader* estimated that this would amount to about £20 per week and would cost the landlord about half of this. It predicted that Luggacurran would not be a 'paying concern' for his Lordship.[17] It is possible to identify the persons to whom outdoor relief was

14 While the minute books of the Athy board are no longer extant, we are fortunate that detailed accounts of the board meetings are reported in the local newspapers. I have examined the reports of the meetings in both the *Leinster Express* (Conservative) and the *Leinster Leader* (Nationalist). The meetings were also covered by the *Carlow Nationalist* and the *Kildare Observer*.

15 *Leinster Leader*, 5 February 1887.

16 Ibid., 26 February 1887. The *Leinster Express*, in contrast, supported the Lord Chancellor in calling Dunne to account: *Leinster Express*, 19 February 1887.

17 *Leinster Leader*, 2 April 1887. See also *Leinster Express*, 2 April 1887.

paid as these are listed in the auditor's subsequent report (and published in the local papers). These can be compared to the list of evicted tenants and sub-tenants compiled by the Evicted Tenants Commission This indicates that relief was mainly paid to the sub-tenants of both Dunne and Kilbride and to many of the 'smaller' tenants whose former farms ranged from 19 to 80 acres in size.

Following the annual poor law elections in late March, Dunne, Whelan and Dennis Kilbride, described as 'three campaigners', were elected as the three officers of the board. The dispute continued with various meetings and further evictions in April and unsuccessful negotiations to resolve the dispute. Kilbride, now becoming involved in more national politics, went to Canada with William O'Brien MP to highlight the dispute with Governor General Lansdowne (continuing the trip to the United States).[18] In late May the board of guardians discussed the payment of outdoor relief to the Lansdowne tenants. The acting chairman John McLaughlin argued that they should not exceed the amount allowed by law but no decision was taken at that meeting.[19] Following further discussion at the next meeting of the board, the guardians were of the opinion that the tenants should get as much as the law allowed.[20] Subsequently during a consideration of the renewal of the outdoor relief lists, the chairman Daniel Whelan asked if he should give the usual relief to the Luggacurran tenants. The clerk to the board recommended against this approach as it would give rise to a surcharge. However, Whelan asked rhetorically 'what can you do but as they did in New Ross?' and the usual relief was given. The dispute continued throughout the summer period with further meetings, prosecutions for allowing cattle trespass and for assaulting emergencymen and, in September, the election of Dennis Kilbride as member of Parliament in South Kerry.

In October application was made to the board from tenants evicted in September and amounts varying between 10*s.* and £1 per week were

18 On his return in June 1887, Kilbride went to live with his brother, the solicitor P.J. Kilbride in Athy, having fallen seriously ill.

19 *Leinster Leader*, 28 May 1887.

20 *Leinster Leader*, 4 June 1887.

granted. Later that month, an inquiry was held by the Local Government Board into irregularities concerning the administration of outdoor relief by a local relieving officer. This inquiry was held by Henry A. Robinson, Local Government Board inspector.[21] Although the inquiry was unrelated to the board's action on payment of evicted tenants, the issue of the payments came up and Robinson advised the clerk to notify the board of guardians of the limit of one month concerning the payment of outdoor relief to evicted tenants. Robinson is reported as having expressed the view that the chair would have to pay a surcharge where this limit was exceeded.

Around the same time three families, some of whose members had acted as emergency men in Luggacurran, came before the board of guardians and applied for admission to the workhouse. The board refused to allow admission although the evidence was that they were destitute. However, as a result of the courageous action of the relieving officer concerned, it appears that the men and their families were in fact admitted to the workhouse as the relieving officer took the view that his legal duties under the Poor Law Act had to be complied with regardless of the orders of the board of guardians.[22] The fact that the board's concern was primarily for evicted tenants was also illustrated by an application by destitute labourers for relief in late 1887.[23] About 100 labourers had assembled outside the board to seek relief and three men were asked in to state their case. Having heard the circumstances the board ordered the relieving officer to investigate the cases and agreed to seek Local Government Board approval for the payment of outdoor relief. At a subsequent meeting, the board received the Local Government Board's refusal as there was room in the workhouse

21 *Leinster Leader*, 22 October 1887.

22 *Leinster Leader*, 22 and 29 October, 5, 12 and 19 November 1887. The board prosecuted one of the men concerned for refusing to leave the house but, unsurprisingly, the magistrates refused to convict. The magistrates were, generally, also members of the board of guardians. Hearing the case, a Mr Keogh, one of the magistrates, asked for the circumstances as, he said, he did not understand anything about the case. The workhouse master, John Hyland, pointed out that Keogh was at the board where the incident had occurred.

23 *Leinster Express*, 3 December 1887.

and it could not legally accede to the board's request, as the board must have known all along. Following a lengthy discussion the board explained to the labourers' delegation that it could not give outdoor relief in the circumstances.

In contrast in November 1887 the board had allowed outdoor relief to William Cranny. Cranny was an evicted tenant with twelve in his family. He had previously been on outdoor relief but had been taken off. The board agreed to pay an amount of 7*s.* 6*d.* per week. Subsequently it appears that Lansdowne's agent, Townsend Trench, wrote to the Local Government Board complaining about the grant of outdoor relief to Cranny as an able-bodied person and the Board subsequently wrote to the guardians for their observations. Daniel Whelan stated that when persons were 'thrown out in the ditch, we would not allow them to starve'.[24] The Local Government Board again wrote to the guardians pointing out that it was only lawful to give outdoor relief to an evicted tenant for one month but the board effectively ignored the complaint and, when the relieving officer sought directions about the case, Whelan stated that he didn't care if he was surcharged or not and the outdoor relief was continued.[25]

The issue arose again in early 1888 when the Local Government Board auditor audited the accounts and surcharged over £130 in relation to excess outdoor relief, mainly against Daniel Whelan.[26] At the subsequent meeting of the board, the board agreed a resolution which referred to a previous outdoor relief case to which the Local Government Board had not objected, argued that it was cheaper to relieve people through outdoor relief and that there was no accommodation for so many in the workhouse. The resolution also complained that the Local Government Board had not advised the board that their actions were illegal. The clerk advised the chairman that he should strike Cranny off or he would be surcharged but Whelan again refused.[27] The Local Government Board quickly rejected the board's

24 *Leinster Express*, 3 December 1887.

25 *Leinster Express*, 17 December 1887.

26 The auditor's comments are to be found on NAI CSORP/1888/12739.

27 *Leinster Leader*, 4 February 1888.

arguments but the guardians, after further discussion, resolved that the auditor had acted in an illegal and arbitrary manner.[28] However, the Local Government Board did not intervene and enforcement proceedings went ahead against Whelan.[29] After some delays arising from procedural issues, a decree was issued against Whelan and his goods seized.[30] This was discussed by the board in May and, following some discussion, the board agreed at a special meeting to sign a cheque for Whelan.[31] When the guardians who signed it were surcharged, it was proposed that others would do the same for them. The Local Government Board immediately wrote to the board warning that the proposed action was illegal and, implicitly, threatening dissolution of the board. The Local Government Board had responded slowly, if at all, to the initial unlawful payment of outdoor relief. However, perhaps encouraged by the more proactive approach adopted by Arthur Balfour as chief secretary, the board responded much more rapidly to the issuing of a cheque to Whelan. On 14 June 1888 Henry Robinson, vice-president of the Local Government Board (1880–91),[32] sent a telegram to the Irish office in London to explain the background. On the same day the papers were sent to the chief secretary asking him for a decision on the proposal to dissolve the board. Balfour quickly agreed and the Local Government Board dissolved the board and appointed vice-guardians.[33]

The elected guardians initially attempted to offer some resistance. At the final meeting of the board, they resolved to meet again the following week and a public meeting was called in Athy. The meeting passed a resolution protesting against the dismissal of the guardians. However the

28 *Leinster Leader*, 25 February and 3 March 1888.

29 The issue was considered at the highest levels. In March Henry Robinson, vice-president of the Local Government Board, wrote to Balfour explaining the background to the surcharge and stating that he was satisfied that it was correct: Robinson to Balfour, 24 March 1888, NAI CSORP/1888/12739.

30 *Leinster Leader*, 31 March, 14 April and 26 May 1888.

31 *Leinster Leader*, 26 May, 2 and 9 June 1888.

32 Henry Robinson was the father of Henry A. Robinson, sometime local government inspector and himself a future vice-president of the Local Government Board (1898–1922).

33 *Leinster Leader*, 16 and 23 June 1888.

board was refused admission to the workhouse by the vice-guardians and the board members appear to have allowed their resistance largely to collapse. Although it was proposed that ratepayers would not pay rates to the vice-guardians, even the Nationalist *Leinster Leader* admitted that this had little effect.[34] A further meeting in Athy in October also appears to have had limited impact. The auditor recorded a further surcharge against Whelan in August 1888 and subsequently disallowed the payment to Whelan and surcharged the guardians who had signed the cheque (Dunne, M.J. Minch and James McLaughlin).[35]

The vice-guardians, initially referred to by the *Leader* as 'the office grabbers' or 'their emergencyships', quickly got down to work to reduce the amount of outdoor relief paid. In July 1888 the board met a delegation of ratepayers which protested against the amount of outdoor relief and was allowed to inspect the relief lists and object to specific cases.[36] In March 1889 Henry A. Robinson was able to express his admiration of the 'unprecedentedly large collection' of rates.[37] It had originally been intended to restore the board at the time of the annual elections in March 1889 but it appears that due to residual unrest, this decision was postponed for a number of months and it was not until May that Balfour announced that it had been decided to restore the board at the time of the supplementary elections during the summer. It was not until July 1889 that the new board met. M.J. Minch, one of the signatories of the Whelan cheque, was appointed as chair with Orford as vice chair and James McLaughlin as deputy.[38] Minch made a stirring speech regretting the absence of Dunne and Whelan, praising the Luggacurran campaign and the Irish National League. However, while outdoor relief subsequently rose, there was no resumption of the previous level of expenditure. The aggregate data show

34 *Leinster Leader*, 28 July 1888.

35 *Leinster Leader*, 18 August and 22 December 1888.

36 *Leinster Leader*, 28 July 1888.

37 *Leinster Express*, 30 March 1889.

38 Whelan was an elderly man and died in 1890. Minch went on to be MP for Kildare South from 1892 to 1903 and he and Orford were both members of the first county council for King's County in 1899.

a rise in outdoor relief in 1887 but a fall thereafter in 1888–9 reflecting the appointment of the vice-guardians. Outdoor relief rose thereafter but not to former levels.

The Local Government Board took considerable satisfaction in the imposition of the surcharge. Henry Robinson stated that the incident had attracted a great deal of attention and that the auditor's actions had taught the guardians a lesson, the salutary effect of which it was impossible to exaggerate.[39] In relation to a subsequent dispute in May 1889 (concerning a printing contract), Henry A. Robinson, the local government inspector, provided an interesting commentary on the guardians. He stated that the old guardians had been replaced by small farmers and shopkeepers but did not agree that the new guardians were not intelligent or that the old guardians had been representative of industry. He stated that if the large landlords used their proxy votes properly they could secure representation and if they did so and attended the meetings they would lessen much of the alleged abuse. He criticised the ex-officios for non attendance.[40] While, he believed, the new guardians would 'openly perpetrate a job… which the exigencies of patriotism oblige them to' he stated that it was nevertheless the fact that they were extremely sensitive about their capabilities of transacting the ordinary poor law business.[41]

39 NAI CSORP/1888/12739.

40 An 1884 return shows only 102 attendances by the twenty-nine ex-offico guardians compared to 511 by the same number of elected guardians. Return of… attendances… at board meetings, HC 1884 (335) lxviii, 55.

41 Report of Henry A. Robinson, NAI CSORP/1890/7728. The dispute concerned the fact that the restored guardians had taken the printing contract away from the Conservative *Leinster Express* and given it instead to the *Carlow Nationalist* despite the fact that the latter's quote was higher. Following several weeks of discussion and correspondence from the Local Government Board to the guardians the editor of the *Nationalist* reduced his price to that of the *Express* and the matter was allowed to rest.

O'Kelly, Clongorey (Naas)

The impact of the dissolution of the Athy board could clearly be seen when evictions occurred on the O'Kelly estate in the neighbouring Naas union. In late November 1888 evictions occurred in Clongorey and an application for outdoor relief was made for the evicted tenants. However, in contrast to the actions in Athy, the chairman of the Naas board read from the Compendium concerning the legal position.[42] The view was expressed that the board should go as far as the law allowed but the chairman said that he would not press the board to give unlawful relief so that the board would not be dissolved as in Athy. Following a long discussion on the appropriate amount of relief various amounts were agreed up to a maximum of £1 per week for a family of eleven.[43] There was further discussion at the next meeting of the board and the clerk drew the board's attention to the fact that many of the children included in the initial payment of outdoor relief were over the age of fifteen and, he said, should not be relieved. The chair again expressed concern about a surcharge and the allowances were reduced. The Local Government Board had, by this time, adopted a more proactive approach and a warning letter had been received pointing out the legal position on evicted tenants based on the minutes of the previous week.[44] There appears to have been relatively little political dispute in the Naas union and the officers were all re-elected following the annual elec-

42 Perhaps the version recently updated by Mooney: T.A. Mooney, *Compendium of the Irish Poor Laws; and general manual for the Poor Law Guardians and their officers*, Thom, Dublin, 1887.

43 *Leinster Leader*, 1 December 1888.

44 *Leinster Leader*, 8 December 1888. In fact, the Local Government Board subsequently clarified that while the children over fifteen must be dealt with separately they could be relieved as evicted tenants, and the relieving officer was asked to visit those who had been struck off the previous week.

tion in March 1889.[45] However, despite occasional political resolutions,[46] the board appears to have been careful not to breach the law in its support for evicted tenants.[47]

Clanricarde (Portumna and Loughrea) and Lewis (Loughrea)

One of the bitterest disputes took place at the large Clanricarde estate which was located in both the Portumna and Loughrea unions.[48] The Evicted Tenants Commission indicates that the bulk of outdoor relief to evicted tenants was paid by the Portumna union, possibly because the larger number of tenants fell within its remit. Unfortunately, the minute books of the union are not extant and nor is there a consistent series of reports of board meetings in the local press. However, it does appear that the guardians took steps to support evicted tenants and exceeded their legal powers in doing so. Although the board was chaired by a landlord – Captain Eyre of Eyrecourt, Galway – newspaper reports indicate that it took a generally Nationalist position on political issues.[49] In September 1886, strictly speaking before the plan of campaign, the board discussed granting outdoor relief to some of Clanricarde's evicted tenants. Eyre was fearful that he would be surcharged but was prepared, he said, to pay his

45 The *Leinster Express* reports that the ex-officios did not appear and that the Nationalists took two offices but selected a Unionist for deputy chair: 6 April 1889. The *Express* condemned this 'compromise'.

46 *Leinster Express*, 26 January 1889 (condemning threatened evictions); *Leinster Leader*, 2 March 1889 (protesting against the sentence of Mr Carew MP).

47 While the amount of relief paid (as reported by the Evicted Tenants Commission) was one of the larger amounts, this must be seen in the light of the fact that Naas spent about £3,000 per annum on outdoor relief.

48 Useful background information is provided in two collections of local history published by the Woodford Heritage Group, *A forgotten campaign* and *Clanricarde country*.

49 For example, the board passed a resolution condemning the local grand jury resolution against Home Rule: *Connaught People*, 3 April 1886. Eyre had been chair for several years and had previously been vice chair under the old Marquis of Clanricarde (as had his father, who died in a hunting accident in 1856).

share. Large amounts of outdoor relief were granted to a number of tenants and this presumably explains the fact that a surcharge of £45 15 *s.* was imposed by the Local Government Board auditor in January 1887.[50] The awards made included an extraordinarily high amount of £5 to Thomas Saunders of 'Saunders Fort', a scene of strong resistance to the evictions. In October 1889 the Portumna board was dissolved, ostensibly for failure to levy sufficient rates and replaced by vice guardians. However, the fact that the Local Government Board auditor raised a further surcharge of £50 in respect of illegal outdoor relief in January 1890 suggests that political issues may also have been involved.[51]

In Loughrea union, although the aggregate data show no major rise in outdoor relief, spending shifts towards outdoor relief over the period from 74 per cent to 88 per cent. An examination of the minute books for the Loughrea union for the period throws some interesting light on the issue.[52] Loughrea was, at least in theory, a landlord-dominated board. Feingold shows it as moderate-conservative board with two (out of three) landlord officers. In fact, over the period in question the landed interest clearly dominated the election of officers with Colonel Daly being elected as chair and Major Rogers as vice-chair despite challenges from Nationalist guardians in 1886, 1887 and 1888.[53] However, their control over the board was limited. Daly rarely sat and Rogers was more often in the chair. Both generally refused to accept 'political' resolutions and the Loughrea Nationalist guardians – unlike some other boards –

50 *Connaught People*, 25 September 1886.

51 Unfortunately, it has not been possible to locate any consistent coverage of the Portumna board in the local newspapers and the file in relation to the dissolution of the board was not found in the National Archives. Legal proceedings were subsequently brought against several Portumna guardians to recover the surcharge: Hansard, 346, 1564 et seq., 11 July 1890; 1620 et seq., 14 July 1890.

52 Galway County Archives (GCA).

53 GCA, Minutes of 10 April 1886, 2 April 1887 and 31 March 1888. The board included several active Nationalist guardians including future MP John Roche; Laurence Egan and Martin Egan both jailed during the plan of campaign, and Peter Broderick who had served two years in Galway prison as a suspect in 1880–1. His prison notebook is in the NUI Galway archives. This information was provided by Ina Scherder.

did not push the issue.[54] However, the extent to which the chairs could control the board in this regard depended on their actual presence. A good example of their limited power is shown by the fact that Colonel Daly refused to put a motion condemning the ill-treatment of W. Scawen Blunt and his wife in November 1887. The elected guardians although, no doubt, in a majority did not push the issue at that board. However, at the next meeting, at which Daly was not present, the board passed a motion condemning the ill-treatment and, for good measure, adding its congratulations on William O'Brien's 'noble stand'.[55]

When it came to financial issues the Nationalists were less deferential. The board, with Rogers in the chair, had awarded £1 per week for one month to tenants evicted from the Lewis estate in September 1886. This led to a £12 surcharge and despite the pleas of the board, the Local Government Board refused to interfere in the enforcement of this against individual guardians.[56] The board actually withheld its own rent due to Lord Clanricarde and an attempt to rescind this motion was resoundingly beaten.[57] The board did subsequently pass a number of resolutions granting outdoor relief to evicted tenants at a rate of £1 per family per week with only the chair objecting.[58] However, the dangers of further surcharges appear to have had an effect and, after August 1887[59] although frequent notices of intended evictions are recorded in the minutes there is a long gap without any such resolution and when the board next agreed such a payment the amount was reduced to only 10 *s*.[60]

54 GCA, Minutes of 23 April 1887 (resolution condemning coercion bill); 12 May 1888 (resolution condemning actions of sessional crown solicitor). The first was passed at the following meeting 30 April 1887.

55 GCA, Minutes of 5 and 12 November 1887. See also the board's condemnation of the Lewis evictions in the absence of Daly and Rogers: minutes 18 September 1886.

56 GCA, Minutes of 9 and 23 April 1887.

57 GCA, Minutes of 28 January 1888 and 16 June 1888.

58 GCA, Minutes of 16 and 30 July 1887.

59 GCA, Minutes of 6 August 1887 in which the Local Government Board warned that the awards of £1 would come under the notice of the auditor.

60 GCA, Minutes of 16 June 1888.

Ponsonby, Youghal

The Ponsonby estate was located in the Youghal poor law union. In Youghal, the board was controlled by Nationalist guardians and the ex-officios rarely attended. The board passed a motion of support for New Ross and indicated that they would also set aside a ward for evicted tenants.[61] But the Youghal guardians were committed to verbal rather than fiscal Nationalism. There is no indication that a 'ward of honour' was ever prepared and the auditor could only find one evicted tenant who had received a generous payment. Giving the board the benefit of the doubt, the auditor did not surcharge them but warned them for their future guidance.[62] The board continued to pass anti-eviction resolutions but neither the (brief) minutes nor the aggregate data indicate any significant financial support.[63] The Youghal guardians' main act of defiance was to pay 12 *s.* and 6 *d.* for a bust of William O'Brien for which they were duly surcharged.[64]

Unions which provided little or no outdoor relief

In a number of these estates, it is clear that boards gave very little assistance to evicted tenants. Wybrants Olphert was both the landlord of the main Donegal estate involved in the dispute and the chair of the Dunfanaghy board of guardians and, unsurprisingly, the data provided to the Evicted Tenants Commission indicate that no outdoor relief at all was provided to evicted tenants.[65] The Evicted Tenants Commission also indicates that no outdoor relief was paid to evicted tenants on the Smith Barry estate

61 Cork City and County Archives (CCCA), Youghal Minute book of 17 December 1886.

62 CCCA, Minutes of 4 February 1887.

63 This is confirmed by the Evicted Tenants Commission data which found that only £30 had been paid in outdoor relief to evicted tenants.

64 CCCA, Minutes of 5 July 1889.

65 The same applies to the neighbouring Sweeney and Stewart Estates. In fact Rev. James McFadden PP claimed that Olphert turned evicted tenants out of the workhouse: Report of the Evicted Tenants Commission, op cit. Q. 13688–90.

(Tipperary union). The aggregate data do indicate that outdoor relief rises to 1888 and falls thereafter. However, the main body of evictions on this estate did not occur until February–March 1890 and so this rise was unrelated to the plan of campaign.[66] The report of the Evicted Tenants Commission suggests that little if any outdoor relief was provided to evicted tenants on the Brooke estate (Gorey union) and this is confirmed by aggregate spending data which show no particular change. This approach is unsurprising when it can be seen that the Gorey board was chaired by the Earl of Courtown who had been re-elected unopposed in April 1887.[67] In May 1887, fifty notices of eviction were received by the relieving officer in relation to the Brooke tenantry. A resolution was proposed to the board condemning the landlord but the acting chair (Henry Ringwood) declined to read it as it had nothing to do with the poor law. Despite further evictions on the estate in July there is no sign that the board responded by providing outdoor relief and the figures for the number and cost of outdoor relief (already very low) show almost no variation over the period.[68]

The Evicted Tenants Commission indicated that only a very small amount of outdoor relief was provided to evicted tenants on the Massereene estates which fell in the Ardee and Drogheda unions.[69] The records of both boards – particularly Ardee – indicate that, like Youghal, they were committed to at least verbal Nationalism[70] and the aggregate data indicate that

66 The newspaper reports of Tipperary board meetings do not indicate that the board attempted to provide any support to evicted tenants.

67 *Gorey Correspondent*, 9 April 1887.

68 See the *Gorey Correspondent* for the period. For example in June 1887 there were 111 cases on outdoor relief at a cost of £12 per week. In October there were 107 at a cost of £11.

69 Unfortunately the Drogheda minutes are largely missing from March 1887 to December 1888 although the minute book which starts in December 1888 in fact includes some incorrectly bound minutes from October–December 1887 (Louth County Archives (LCA), Dundalk). However, the local papers do provide extensive coverage.

70 The Ardee board passed motions supporting Home Rule (March and June 1886) on the release of political prisoners (July 1886), condemning the Coercion Act (April 1887) and the 'inhuman' treatment of William O'Brien and other prisoners (October

outdoor relief in Drogheda did rise to 1888. However, although evictions on this estate commenced in October 1887, it appears that the rise in relief was largely unrelated to the evictions. Amongst those evicted in October 1887 was James Byrne of Dunleer, a member of the Ardee board. Although the board passed a vote of sympathy with him and the Drogheda board pledged itself to admit evicted tenants to the workhouse following the example of New Ross, there is little indication from the reports of the meetings of either board or from the statistics provided as to relief that any significant level of outdoor or indoor relief was provided to evicted tenants.[71] In fact the Drogheda guardians expressed considerable concern about the rise in outdoor relief and this was discussed at a number of meetings.[72]

Discussion

A number of points arise from this examination. Firstly and more generally, it is clear that the plan of campaign played a very important role in providing a focus for political activity in the post-Home Rule Bill period when the Irish Parliamentary Party was able to achieve little in a Conservative dominated Parliament. The importance of the plan from this point of view has perhaps been understated in much historiography to date. Secondly, it

1887). The Drogheda board was less given to expressing general political views but did condemn an ex-officio member for bringing 'Orange emergencymen' into the area in relation to a tenant dispute (September 1886), condemned the imprisonment of Fr. Fahey (October 1886), the 'brutal outrage' on the Blunts at Woodlawn (26 November 1887) and the treatment of O'Brien (12 November 1887). All references are to LCA, Ardee and Drogheda Minutes.

71 The board described Byrne as a victim of 'felonious landlordism': LCA, Ardee minute book October 1887. Another member of the board was subsequently evicted and the board again expressed sympathy and congratulated him on his support for the plan of campaign.

72 *Drogheda Argus* and *Drogheda Conservative*, 29 October 1887.

emphasises the extent to which the Land War was not, or not simply, a struggle between repressive, alien Protestant landlords and a poor, oppressed, Catholic tenantry but rather a class war between repressive, alien Protestant landlords and a developing wealthy Catholic bourgeoisie represented by people like Dunne and Kilbride. Unlike the Protestant gentry, however, the Nationalists both recognised the need for, and generally managed to build, a cross-class alliance with the poorer Catholic tenantry. This point supports Clark's thesis of a reciprocal relationship between large and small farmers in the post-Famine period rather than Bew's emphasis on animosity between these groups.[73]

Turning more specifically to the poor law, there is little indication of any strategic approach to the use of the poor law as part of the plan of campaign. New Ross is an example of a board which deliberately planned to provide a 'ward of honour' for evicted tenants but this approach was somewhat impractical and quickly led to the board's dissolution. While a number of boards (including Drogheda and Youghal) passed resolutions pledging to adopt a similar approach, there is no indication that these boards gave any serious consideration to doing so.[74] Even in Athy, there is little indication of any co-coordinated plan to use the poor law as part of the plan of campaign, although the guardians clearly knew the implications of their decisions in terms of the landlord's rates.[75] Rather a decision was made to grant 'high' allowances in the heat of the initial evictions and this remained in place largely due to the reluctance of Daniel Whelan to reduce payments to evicted tenants. Clearly the other guardians – to a

73 See S. Clark *Social Origins of the Irish Land War*, Princeton University Press, 1979; P. Bew, *Land and the National Question in Ireland 1858–82*; Gill & Macmillan, 1979. The arguments are helpfully reviewed in N.P. Canny 'Fusion and Faction in Modern Ireland. A Review Article', *Comparative Studies in Society and History*, 26(2), (1984).352–65.

74 An official report stated that Fermoy, Kanturk, Mallow and Millsteet had also adopted resolutions pledging to follow New Ross's example: NAI CSORP 1890/20219. None did.

75 Although the level of cost involved was unlikely to have any impact on the landlord's approach.

greater or lesser degree – supported this decision but there is no sign that this formed part of a wider strategy. Both Dunne and, especially, Kilbride who played key roles in the broader plan of campaign had little involvement in the poor law debates. In other unions, as has been seen, there was even less use of the poor law to support evicted tenants.

The fact that the aggregate data indicate that the boards did not use the poor law to support the plan is explained to some extent by looking at what happened in individual unions. Unions which tried to, or might have tried to, use the poor law to support evicted tenants as part of the plan were dissolved (Athy and New Ross) or surcharged (Athy, Portumna and Loughrea). This clearly had an impact on spending in these unions and may well have had a demonstration effect in other unions. Thus while it is argued that there was no strategic plan to use the poor law, such a plan might have developed had the Local Government Board not clamped down on unions such as New Ross and Athy. The government and the Local Government Board appear to have won the battle to prevent boards using the poor law to support the plan.

Finally, however, some boards (such as Loughrea) appear to have used the plan (if not very strategically) as part of a Gramscian 'war of position'.[76] Even if they lost this particular battle, the energy expended must have had an important effect in wearing down the resistance of the (much less numerous) local landlords. Evidence to the 1884–5 Select Committee on the Poor Law Guardians (Ireland) Bill indicates that this was a feature of many boards. Witnesses claimed that ex-officios were 'swamped' and given 'no voice' in the activities of some boards, that their attendance was made 'very disagreeable' and that they were liable to 'very gross insults'.[77]

76 A. Gramsci, *Prison Notebooks, Volume 3*, Columbia University Press, New York, 2007, 168.

77 See, in particular, the evidence of Colonel Spaight, Local Government Board Inspector, *passim*; Richard Bagwell, ex-officio guardian of Clonmel and Clogheen, Qs. 882–4: Garrett C. Tyrrell, ex-officio guardian of Edenderry union, Qs. 1029–30; Henry Smyth, ex-officio guardian in Roscommon union. Q. 1252: Report from the Select Committee of the House of Lords on the Poor Law Guardians (Ireland) Bill, op. cit.

These findings again raise the important questions as to whether the 'nationalisation' of the boards had any major impact on poor law practices and whether there was anything distinctive about Nationalist 'policies' on the poor law. They tend to confirm the view outlined in chapter 6 that Nationalists did not have a strongly distinctive view on poor relief practices and that, even in extreme circumstances such as the plan of campaign, the nationalisation of the boards had a limited impact on poor law practices.

CHAPTER 8

The Democratisation of Local Government and the Poor Law, 1892–1906

This chapter provides an overview of developments in the Irish poor law in the period from 1892 to 1906. As will be seen, there was a considerable degree of stability as to the actual operation of the poor law in this period. Reflecting both the gains won during the 1880s, in terms of control of the boards of guardians, and the divisions arising from the split in the Irish Parliamentary Party, there was a considerable fall-off in the party political nature of the poor law in the 1890s. A key feature in the period was the Local Government Act in 1898 which led to very important changes in the composition of the boards of guardians and the establishment of union rating. However, perhaps surprisingly, this appears to have had little impact on poor relief practice (although it did lead to a significant increase in the building of labourers' cottages). Reflecting rising political tensions after 1900, a return of politics to the poor law can be seen but again this appears to have relatively little impact on poor law administration. This relative stability led to a growth in the influence of the Local Government Board in policy formation. The end of this period sees the establishment of two important bodies to examine proposals for reform of the poor law: firstly, the Viceregal Commission which reported in 1906 and the Royal Commission on the poor law (1909).

Political and other developments

The 1890s saw a considerable fall off in political campaigns concerning the poor law, reflecting the division of the Irish Parliamentary Party following the fall of Parnell. There were four elections in the period. Nationalist candidates won the vast majority of seats in all cases but never achieved the dominance attained by the Irish Parliamentary Party in the late 1880s. Even after the reunion of the Irish Parliamentary Party in 1900, there remained (at most periods) a number of independent or quasi-independent factions led by Tim Healy and William O'Brien. In addition, the balance of power in Westminster in this period meant that the Irish Parliamentary Party rarely was able to deploy significant political influence (i.e. its votes were not required to support a British government).[1] The population continued to fall in the period, to 4.4 million in 1911.

Poor law developments

There was considerable stability in terms of the numbers in receipt of indoor and outdoor relief over the period-in marked contrast to the previous period. The numbers on indoor relief rose slightly from 40,740 in 1892 (8.9 per 100) to 42,829 in 1906–7 (10.0). However, in contrast to the previous decade the numbers on outdoor relief fell somewhat from 62,229 to 56,861 (though given the falling population, relief as a proportion of the population remained broadly stable). Nor were there are any significant variations in the intervening years. Expenditure did increase from £871,000 in 1891 to just over £1m by 1906 (a rise of 16 per cent). As seen in chapter 6, the annual number of houses built under the Labourers Acts continued to decline (after an initial peak in the mid 1880s) to under

1 See generally F.S.L. Lyons, *The Irish Parliamentary Party, 1890–1910*, Faber & Faber, London, 1951.

500 by 1895. The number of applications rose dramatically from 1899 leading to a considerable rise in houses built from 1904 onwards. As has been seen in chapter 6, the impact of the democratisation of local government through the Local Government Act in 1898 appears to have played a major role in this increase in house building.[2]

Provision of poor relief

Given the stability as to the overall numbers in receipt of relief and rising standards of living generally, poor law debates tended to reflect concerns about the standard of treatment of those in workhouses.[3] In particular, there were a number of reforms on the treatment of older people in workhouses including a relaxation of regulations on the use of tobacco and, following an investigation of practices in other parts of the United Kingdom, older couples were allowed to share an apartment.[4]

There was also significant concern about the treatment and continued high mortality rates of children in workhouses.[5] Policy tended to favour boarding out although there were also concerns as to the quality of care provided. Interestingly, the members of the 1906–9 Royal Commission visited a number of boarded out children in Ireland. Their reports of the children's treatment and relationship with the foster parents are almost universally positive.[6] These developments must, of course, be seen in the

2 Annual report of the Local Government Board for Ireland…, 1901, 1902 [Cd. 1259] xxxvii, 1 at. xxxi et seq. See also Fraser, *John Bull's Other Homes*, 35.

3 See, for example, an improved diet (Annual report of the Local Government Board for Ireland…, 1901, 1902 [Cd. 1259] xxxvii, 1, 362–3).

4 Twenty-second Annual Report of the Local Government Board for Ireland, 1894 [C. 7454], xli, 1 at. 5 and 52–3; NAI, CSORP/1896/5444 (resolution from Banbridge BG on this issue); and see the National Archive files re the correspondence with the English Local Government Board: NA MH 19/53.

5 For example NAI, CSORP/1897/5761 and CSORP/1899/11869.

6 Royal Commission on the Poor Laws and Relief of Distress. Appendix volume XXVIII. Reports of visits to Poor Law and charitable institutions and to meetings of local authorities in the United Kingdom, 1910 [Cd. 4974] liv, 99.

context of broader trends at the time, reflected in the Prevention of Cruelty and Protection of Children Act, 1889 (repealed by the Prevention of Cruelty to Children Act, 1894), the Custody of Children Act, 1891 and the Infant Life Protection Act, 1897.[7]

There was also a general tendency towards the professionalisation of medical care. From 1898 on nurses were required to be qualified and the Local Government Board issued a circular forbidding boards to use inmates as nurses. Two unions (Athlone in 1896 and Clogher in 1898) were dissolved for failing to appoint qualified nurses.

Although falling outside the scope of the poor law proper, an important issue in this period was the significant rise in the number of 'lunatics' in asylums. Finnane shows that the first admission rates to Irish district asylums rose dramatically between 1871 and 1911, rising between 110 per cent in Downpatrick and 300 per cent in Ballinasloe and Cork. Expenditure on district lunatic asylums rose from £270,000 in 1891 to almost £500,000 by 1911 (a rise of 83 per cent). The numbers in district asylums rose from about 11,700 in 1892 to over 19,000 in 1908 (close to half the workhouse population at that time).[8] This issue is discussed in more detail in chapter 10. As will be seen below, Gerald Balfour proposed legislation addressing issues (in particular financial issues) concerning asylums and their relationship with workhouses in 1896 although this was not adopted.

A further area of concern related to a perceived rise in vagrancy.[9] In 1908, statistics indicate that there had been 5,400 night lodgers accommodated representing 900 people.[10] However, public concern related to the

7 See R. Dingwall, J.M. Eekelaar, T. Murray, 'Childhood as a Social Problem: a Survey of the History of Legal Regulation', *Journal of Law and Society*, 11, 2 (1984), 207–32.

8 Forty-second Report... of the Inspectors of Lunatics (Ireland), 1893–94 [C.7125] xlvi, 369 at 1; Fifty-sixth Report... of the Inspectors of Lunatics (Ireland), for the year ending 31st December, 1906, 1908 [Cd. 3745] xxxiii, 575 at 1.

9 See, for example, the Thirty-fourth Annual Report of the Local Government Board for Ireland, for the year ended 31st March, 1906, 1906 [Cd. 3102] xxxvi, 495 at xv–xvi.

10 However, these figures do not show the whole picture as, particularly in Dublin, the provision of night accommodation was mainly outside the remit of the poor law itself, being provided by voluntary organisations.

perceived excessive number of vagrants and insufficiently punitive treatment rather than the quality of care provided.[11] In many unions, overnight admissions formed the majority of admissions on any one day. However, an overemphasis on the importance of such vagrants in the 'flow' of admissions would greatly overstate their importance amongst the 'stock' of inmates where (as has been seen in chapter 1) they made up a small proportion of the total.

Finally, in relation to the provision of relief, there were ongoing issues about the need for exceptional relief in the congested districts of the west of Ireland.[12] As has been seen in previous chapters, Arthur Balfour rejected the extension of outdoor relief and, instead, established a system of public works controlled by Dublin Castle. The 1892 report of the Local Government Board favoured this approach[13] but, in 1895, policy (under the Liberal chief secretary John Morley (1886 and 1892–5)) returned to a more controlled version of extending outdoor relief and this was continued in 1897 by Balfour's brother Gerald (1895–1900).[14] Finally, Gerald Balfour took the opportunity of the Local Government Act to establish, in section 13 of that Act, a permanent mechanism for the provision of exceptional relief. However, disputes continued about whether and under what circumstances this provision would be put into place and, basically, about who would pay for it. While the need for exceptional relief continued in the west of Ireland, the extent of this need declined over time. Relief works were established in twenty-three unions in 1891 but this fell successively to fourteen in 1895, eleven in 1897–8 and only seven in 1905.[15]

11 See the evidence to the Viceregal Commission: Minutes of evidence taken before the Vice-Regal Commission on Poor Law Reform in Ireland. Volume III. Minutes of evidence and index, 1906 [Cd. 3204] lii, 1.

12 NAI CSORP/1895/230 and 634; 1897/3227 and 26957; 1909/7750.

13 Annual Report of the Local Government Board for Ireland…, 1892 [C. 6801] xxxix, 1 at 96–103.

14 See NA PRO 30/60/23, Memorandum as to relief of distress operations, 1897–8.

15 The Local Government Board also used funds provided under the Unemployed Workmen Act, 1905 in the western rural areas (although that this does not appear to have been the intention of the Act).

Governance of the poor law

Throughout the 1890s, the Irish MPs continued to introduce legislation proposing the reform of the composition and election of boards of guardians, albeit without any success. However, the Local Government Act in 1898 introduced by Gerald Balfour as part of the policy of 'constructive Unionism' made major reforms of the poor law in this area.[16] Obviously, the Act is part of the broader history of local government in Ireland and most of its provisions do not directly relate to the poor law.[17] However, the Act introduced three main changes as to the operation of the poor law.

Firstly, it replaced the existing system of elected and appointed boards with wholly elected boards and provided for an expansion in the franchise. Secondly, it made changes in payment of rates including the introduction of union rating.[18] Finally, it introduced (as discussed above) a permanent system of exceptional relief under section 13 of the Act.

The Act established county, and urban or rural district councils.[19] Councillors were elected for a three-year period. At cabinet, Gerald Balfour had rejected the argument that the qualification for the local government franchise should be set at a high level on the basis that the existing restrictive franchise had been 'perfectly useless' over the greater part of Ireland as a means of giving loyalists any real power on boards of guardians and that such a wide departure from previous United Kingdom precedent 'could scarcely be defended in Parliament'. He also rejected the idea of an ex-officio

16 On constructive unionism see A. Gailey, *Ireland and the Death of Kindness: The Experience of Constructive Unionism, 1890–1905*, Cork University Press, Cork, 1987.

17 See V. Crossman, *Local Government in Nineteenth Century Ireland*, IIS, Belfast, 1994, 91–7. On the cabinet debate on Irish local government reform see NA CAB 37/30/38.

18 It appears that this was a result of broader changes in relation to rating under the Act rather than a specific desire to introduce union rating.

19 See Crossman, *Local Government in Nineteenth Century Ireland*, 92 et seq. On the politics of the act see C. Shannon, 'The Ulster Liberal Unionists and Local Government Reform, 1885–1898', in *Reactions to Irish Nationalism, 1865–1914*, Gill and Macmillan, Dublin, 1987.

element as having 'certainly failed' in the poor law boards.[20] The franchise was based on the Parliamentary franchise but with the important addition of women who had been allowed to vote as ratepayers under the old poor law electoral system. This saw a considerable increase in the number of voters to almost 900,000 by 1901.[21] Reflecting the long-standing demands of the Irish Parliamentary Party, plural voting and ex-officio poor law guardians were abolished. In rural areas, the rural district council acted as the board of guardians so that separate elections for the boards of guardians no longer took place. However, in urban areas separate boards of guardians were retained, elected on the same franchise as urban councillors.

The Act amalgamated the poor law rate and the county cess. Whereas rates had previously been payable partially by the occupier and partially by the owner, the Act provided that the rates were to fall entirely on the occupier. In compensation for this change, the British government provided a fund equal to half the cess and rate paid in the previous year which, as Crossman points out, meant that the government was taking over that proportion of the rates previously paid by landlords. Effectively, the government bought out the objections of the landlords to a democratic reform of local government. As part of these changes, the existing system of rating according to electoral divisions was abolished and replaced by union rating.

The Local Government Act led to sweeping changes in the composition of the board officers (see chapter 9). However, the interesting thing is that these sweeping changes led to almost no discernible change in poor law practices, except in the building of cottages.[22] However, it may well be that the changes which Nationalist guardians wished to make had already taken place during the 1880s and 1890s and/or that the Nationalist guardians did not have a particularly distinctive policy on poor relief. Nonetheless, as has been seen, the Act does seem to have led to considerable increases

20 NA CAB 37/30/38.

21 Return respecting Local Government Electoral Areas, showing… the Number of… Local Government Board Electors…, 1901 [2] lxiv, 413. The precise figure is 890, 524 which represents exactly one-third of the population over twenty in 1901.

22 From 1899, labourers' cottages were formally the responsibility of the rural district councils rather than the boards of guardians.

in the building of labourers' cottages, attributed to the extension of the franchise to labourers and to the fact that labourers could now sit on the councils. The priorities of the newly enfranchised labourers clearly lay in the area of housing rather than changes in the poor law itself.

A further issue as to the governance of the poor law was the ultimately successful introduction of legislation allowing women to sit as poor law guardians in 1896. Legislation had been introduced from the early 1890s by a number of northern MPs (Liberal Unionist, Liberal and Unionist). The Irish Parliamentary Party was not united on this issue with Tim Harrington speaking against it although Tim Healy and other members supported the legislation. Subsequently there were at least two female chairs of the boards in Wexford and Clonmel. Women were also appointed as poor law inspectors for the first time (although primarily in relation to the boarding out of children). Urquhart has examined in some detail the role of women as poor law guardians in Ulster.[23] However, even here, it is clear that women only made up a very small minority of guardians. In 1911, there were only thirty-one female guardians in Ulster (3 per cent of the total) and only ten of the twenty-seven boards had any women guardians.[24] While studies have tended to emphasise the importance of allowing women to become guardians and the (no doubt considerable) contribution of women guardians,[25] it may be well not to overstate the difference which such a small minority of guardians could make. In addition, while the boards formed an important training ground in local governance for the rising Catholic bourgeoisie, there is no indication that women were able to take advantage of their poor law apprenticeship in the same manner.[26]

23 D. Urquhart, *Women in Ulster Politics, 1890–1940*, Irish Academic Press, Dublin, 2000. On the English experience see. S.A. King, *Women, Welfare and Local Politics, 1880–1920*, Sussex Academic Press, Brighton, 2006.

24 Op cit., 122.

25 Urquhart, *Women in Ulster Politics*; Crossman, *Local Government in Nineteenth Century Ireland*, 55–6.

26 Urquhart reports that less than 2 per cent of local government representatives in the period 1899–1940 were women while only 3 (2 per cent) members of the Northern Ireland Parliament were women in the period to 1940: op. cit., 155 and 175.

Amalgamation and reform

Amalgamation of the poor law unions had been on the agenda since the 1880s (and indeed earlier). However, no comprehensive proposals had been put forward in the previous period and only three small unions were amalgamated in the period to 1903 (Newport in 1885, Donaghmore in 1886 and Glin in 1896).[27] In 1896, the Conservative chief secretary Gerald Balfour published legislation proposing a general approach to amalgamation of unions and this legislation was reintroduced in 1897.[28] The legislation proposed the establishment of a commission of inquiry to draw up a draft scheme for amalgamation. It allowed the combination of unions into joint districts for the maintenance of lunatics and the care of children and provided for the transfer of lunatics from local workhouses to a central workhouse for lunatics. It also gave power to the inspectors of lunacy to inspect workhouses with regard to lunatics, reporting to the Local Government Board. The Act also proposed reforms on pauper children including allowing boards to provide for the teaching of workhouse children in national schools and restricting the hiring of pauper children under twelve. However, it appears to have been less than universally welcomed. In any case, the proposals were overtaken by the Local Government Act in 1898.

The issue was raised again by the Local Government Board with the new chief secretary George Wyndham (1900–5). In March 1901 Wyndham said that he was not aware of any intention to propose a general scheme of amalgamation but by June of that year he said that the issue was now engaging the attention of the Local Government Board.[29] In December 1902 Henry A. Robinson, now vice president of the Local Government Board, wrote to Wyndham proposing the establishment of a commission of inquiry.[30] Clearly knowing his man, Robinson described his proposal as 'a really big thing' hastening to add that by this he did not mean that it would be troublesome but rather 'a great reform of the system' which

27 As will be recalled, Gortin was an early casualty, being amalgamated with Omagh in 1870.

28 NAI CSORP/1897/11410.

29 Hansard, 91, 865–6, 22 March 1901; 95, 913, 20 June 1901.

30 NAI CSORP/1915/9746.

would be both beneficial and politic and which would give a lead to the other parts of the United Kingdom. He attached a detailed memorandum on the issue. Robinson argued that the case for amalgamation was not as clear as appeared at first sight and that it would only be beneficial if it achieved other objectives, i.e. allowing classification of workhouse inmates and the use of existing workhouses for different purposes. He suggested the establishment of a commission to investigate this issue and the Viceregal Commission on Poor Law Reform in Ireland was ultimately established in 1903. It consisted of W.L. Micks,[31] a member of the Local Government Board, George Murnaghan, Irish Parliamentary Party MP for Tyrone,[32] and Dr E. Coey Bigger, one of the medical inspectors of the Board. The Commission reported in 1906 and its recommendations were very widely welcomed by a range of organisations.

The recommendations of the Commission were generally of an evolutionary rather than revolutionary nature.[33] The Commission began with a stirring retelling of the history of the Whately Commission in the 1830s and how its proposals had been 'put aside' by the government of the day in favour of those of Sir George Nicholls based on his 'hurried inspection'. In the spirit of Whately the Commission took the view that the poverty of Ireland could not 'be adequately dealt with by any Poor Relief Law such as that of 1838, but by the development of the country's resources' which it, therefore 'most strongly urged'. Having expressed these politically

31 Micks had previously been a local government inspector and then secretary of the Congested Districts Board.

32 Murnaghan was an Irish Parliamentary Party MP from 1895 but in April 1908, he voted (in a minority of fifteen) with William O'Brien on a Party motion favouring conciliation. In the first 1910 election he was replaced as Party candidate, stood as an independent Nationalist but lost (the split vote allowing the Unionist candidate to take the seat): see P. Bew, *Conflict and Conciliation in Ireland, 1890–1910*, Clarendon Press, Oxford, 1987, 171 and 196. Murnaghan was also a sometime chair of Omagh board of guardians.

33 The recommendations as to hospital care and other issues not directly relevant to poor relief are not addressed here. The most radical recommendation of the Commission was that an exchequer-funded State Medical service should be established, on which see R. Barrington, *Health, Medicine and Politics in Ireland 1900–1970*, IPA, Dublin, 1987.

appropriate views, the Commission dropped the topic and got down to the nuts and bolts of reforming the poor relief law. Key principles underlying the Commission's recommendations were a move away from the union as the area of responsibility[34] and towards a larger unit such as the county and a greater degree of segregation of different classes of inmates. It recommended that workhouses should be abolished and that the various classes of inmates should be segregated into different institutions.[35] However, by this it appears simply to have meant that within a county the existing workhouses should be set aside for use by particular categories of inmate. The 'aged and infirm', for example, were to be placed in a 'disused workhouse to be known as the County or District "Almshouse"'.[36] Unmarried mothers were, 'on the occasion of their first lapse', to be sent to institutions run by religious or philanthropic bodies or, where no such institution existed, to a specialist 'disused workhouse'.[37] 'More depraved cases' were to be sent to separate institutions and could be detained in a 'labour house'.[38] The Commission, reflecting the views of many in Irish (and indeed British) society, took a dim view of casuals and vagrants who were to be detained 'for long periods' in 'labour houses' under the control of the General Prisons Board.[39]

The Commission remained largely wedded to a system of indoor relief and, despite evidence in favour of outdoor relief, on the grounds that it

34 It recommended (Murnaghan dissenting) that expenditure on the sick, aged and infirm, epileptics, lunatics, infants and unmarried mothers should be a county charge while vagrants and others compulsorily detained were to be supported by the Exchequer.

35 Report of the Vice-Regal Commission on Poor Law Reform in Ireland. Volume I, 1906 [Cd. 3202] li, 349: paras 63, 81, 133 and 137.

36 Paras 138–40.

37 Paras 169–70.

38 Para 226.

39 Paras. 215, 229. The Commission was anxious that surroundings in these houses should be of the 'plainest roughest kind' and that the inmates 'be individually made to feel the necessity for personal exertion' (at para 216). Only 'old and infirm people well known in a locality who exist on the charity of friends and neighbours' and 'genuine ballad-singers' ought not to be detainable in the labour house. In an unusual display of humanity, the Commission opined that 'few in Ireland' would wish to interfere with genuine ballad-singers (at 228). In this case at least musick obviously did have Charms to sooth an otherwise 'savage Breast, To soften Rocks, or bend a knotted Oak' (Congreve).

would be better for the poor and more economical for the ratepayers,[40] the Commission did not recommend any change in policy and, in fact, proposed that the area of charge revert to the electoral district.[41] It did, however, recommend some modification to the outdoor relief rules, including the abolition of the quarter-acre clause.[42] As can be seen, despite its platitudes about the development of the country's resources, its recommendations were generally driven by economy and involved compulsory detention for several groups[43] and treatment of vagrants of which the 1830 English Poor Law Commission might well have approved. In this context, and again in support of the view that Nationalists did not take a particularly different (or positive) policy as regard poor relief, the recommendations of the Commission were widely supported.

However, by the time the report was published, Wyndham had resigned in disgrace,[44] the Liberals were in office and the Royal Commission on reform of the poor law had been established. The reports of the Viceregal Commission were effectively shelved pending the considerations of the Royal Commission which, itself reported in 1908.[45] However, by this time, public policy had taken an entirely different direction with the introduction of the Old Age Pensions Act, 1908.

40 Para 224.
41 Paras 245 and 254.
42 Para. 250.
43 For an (uninspired) attempt to defend the philosophical basis of these recommendations (which it acknowledged involved 'very great interference with the liberty of such classes') see para. 236.
44 See Gailey, *Ireland and the Death of Kindness*.
45 Robinson had proposed that one of the other members of the Local Government Board (Micks) should be on the Viceregal Commission and this was agreed. However, he himself was a member of the Royal Commission and, whether reflecting political realities or for other reasons, appears to have become less supportive of the implementation of the Viceregal Commission's recommendations over time. See, in particular, his detailed memo to Birrell of 10 May 1907, NAI CSORP/1915/9746. The new chief secretary, Augustine Birrell (1907–16), meeting a large delegation, damned the report with faint praise and vague promises of unspecified activity while warning of the need to have regard to the Royal Commission and the old age pensions issue: *Daily Express*, 13 December 1907.

The return of politics

There appears to have been a falloff in political contests for seats at the boards of guardians after 1891.[46] However, the rateable qualification to sit as a guardian was reduced in 1894 (under the secretaryship of John Morley). With the return of land agitation in the late 1890s, the establishment of the United Irish League and the reunification of the Irish Parliamentary Party in 1900, politics returned to the poor law. However, as discussed above, there is relatively little indication that this affected the day-to-day practice. Rather politics took the form of resolutions, the giving over of the use of workhouse boardrooms for political meetings,[47] and attempts to confine union contracts to Nationalist suppliers.[48] Firstly, and showing the symbolic importance attached to the boards, a number of boards allowed the use of the boardroom to bodies such as the United Irish League of which, in many cases, the guardians were also leading members. Middleton union, in particular allowed the local executive of the UIL to use the boardroom on several occasions in 1902. Secondly, and while one can find earlier instances of Nationalist unions contracting with Nationalist providers (as in Athy in chapter 7), there appears to have been a loose campaign in 1902 amongst a range of local government bodies, including the boards of guardians, to favour Nationalists. However, achieving this in practice – without leaving the guardians open to surcharge – proved more difficult.[49] In addition, guardians were also mindful of the potential impact of such patriotism on the rates.

46 In 1892 disputes appear to have been primarily intra-Nationalist: NAI CSORP/1892/8144, 8991 and 9611. See also D. Lawlor, *Divine Right? The Parnell Split in Meath*, Cork University Press, Cork, 2007, who outlines the struggles between the Parnellite and Ant-Parnellite factions in the Meath boards, a battle resoundingly won by the latter with the support of Bishop Nulty.

47 See NA PRO 30/60 15, 23 October 1899. The fact that the boardrooms were seen as having political significance locally is interesting, and throws light on the role of the poor law in the politicisation of rural Ireland (see chapter 9).

48 NAI CSORP/1902/26100; 1903/11365 and 11366; 1905/24658; 1906/3867; 1907/22826.

49 See the newspaper coverage in the *Clareman*, 25 October 1902 (Gort union), *Clonmel Chronicle*, 18 October 1902 (Tipperary Union); *Nenagh Guardian*, 11 October 1902 (Nenagh union) in addition to the more extensive coverage of Mullingar (below).

A leading example was the decision by the Mullingar guardians in autumn 1902 to award contracts to Nationalist suppliers.[50] Like Athy during the plan of campaign, the guardians' actions do not appear to have been strategically planned and the issue arose, at least in part, due to the proclamation under the 'Coercion Act' of the Mullingar rural district. Nor were there actions supported by external resources. The Mullingar board also favoured Nationalist suppliers in 1901 but the lack of publicity on that occasion appears to have led to no action by the authorities.[51] However, in April 1902, there was a dispute between guardians who sought to accept the lowest tender for the milk contract and those who suggested that the board would not be 'doing good to the country and to the ratepayers generally by supporting a man of that class'. On this occasion the lowest tenderer was included in the contracts.[52] As in the case of the response to the plan of campaign (discussed in chapter 7), the approach of Nationalist boards to the award of contacts is by no means straightforward and varies over time reflecting the conflicting issues involved. The question of the tendering practices of boards requires further detailed local study.

In October 1902, Attorney General John Atkinson[53] wrote to the Crown Solicitor explaining that it had been discovered that the Nationalists wished to force the government to proclaim the United Irish League believing that they could carry on agitation through the county councils and boards of guardians.[54] The law officers in Dublin Castle (and in par-

50 NAI CSORP/1903/11366 and see the minute books of the Mullingar board in the Westmeath Co. Archives. The actions of the Mullingar guardians are discussed extensively in the local and national press. See, for example, *Westmeath Examiner*, 20, 27 September, 4, 11 October 1902; *Westmeath Guardian*, 3 October 1902; *Midland Reporter*, 2, 9, 16, 30 October 1902, 13 November 1902; *Irish Times*, 11 October 1902.

51 *Westmeath Examiner*, 28 September 1901.

52 *Westmeath Nationalist*, 5 April 1902.

53 Atkinson is an under-studied figure in the historiography. He was solicitor-general (1889–92); Attorney General 1892–3; 1895–1905, Conservative MP for Londonderry (1895–1906) and was appointed as a judicial member of the House of Lords in December 1905.

54 NAI CSORP/1903/11365. The attorney wished to establish that he had ex-officio the right to restrain all public bodies from abusing their powers. Failing this he envisaged

ticular Atkinson) developed a sophisticated legal strategy to counter these attempts and took and won legal proceedings against boards which had both given permission to the United Irish League to use their boardrooms for political meetings and which had given contracts to Nationalist providers where a cheaper alternative was available.[55] This is an interesting strategy for a number of reasons. In previous decades, such activities would simply have led to threatened or actual dissolution of the boards. However, after the local government reforms, Dublin Castle was equally worried about the activities of the county and rural district councils which could not simply be dissolved. The litigation focused on the poor law unions largely because the Local Government Board had greater powers of control over these and could more easily establish the facts as to the specific circumstances involved. It would appear that the strategy of the law officers was largely successful although reports of union workhouses being used for occasional political meetings continue throughout the period.

Ultimately, like the limited attempts to use the poor law to support evicted tenants during the plan of campaign (discussed in chapter 7), these specific efforts to use the poor law for 'Nationalist' purposes were largely unsuccessful. However, they underline the extent to which Nationalists were now the hegemonic class in southern Ireland. In addition, these efforts created the ground for the takeover of the local government system by the revolutionary Dáil Éireann in the 1919–21 period. Sinn Féin won the local elections in many local authorities in the 1920 elections and, ultimately, many local authorities broke their connection with the Local Government Board thereby creating a local, de facto state which played an important role in the success of the War of Independence.[56]

---

that it would be necessary to pass legislation giving the Local Government Board the power to dissolve Councils: Atkinson to Coll, 20 October 1902.

55 *Attorney General v. Middleton Guardians* (NAI CSORP/1903/11365); *Attorney General v. Mullingar Guardians* (NAI CSORP/1903/11366).

56 A. Mitchell, *Revolutionary Government in Ireland: Dáil Éireann 1919–1922*, Gill & Macmillan, Dublin, 1995. On the impact on poor law reform, see M. Cousins, *The Birth of Social Welfare in Ireland, 1922–1952*, Four Courts, Dublin, 2003, 24–7.

Other issues

Religious issues were much less dominant in this period than they had been in, for example, the 1860s. Occasional allegations of proselytism and/or misuse of religious services continued to arise.[57] Reflecting the dominance of Nationalist guardians, the number of nuns employed in unions had risen considerably, and by 1903 there were 415 nuns employed in eighty-five unions, mainly as nurses, at a cost of £13,500 per annum. As might be expected, these were heavily concentrated outside Ulster.[58] Finally, issues concerning removal of paupers continued to arise from time to time, although the numbers involved appear to have been relatively small. A return in 1894 indicates that 1,718 paupers had been removed to Ireland in the previous five years, 756 from England and 962 from Scotland. The addition of 340 paupers per year (even assuming all qualified for relief in Ireland) can hardly have had a very significant impact on costs but clearly a number of unions continued to resent this one-sided traffic.[59]

Conclusion

Overall, while a number of important events occurred during this period, one can already see the extent to which poor relief was no longer the key factor it had been in the earlier part of the nineteenth century. The local government reforms, which delivered many of the key reforms which had been demanded by Nationalist politicians (such as electoral reform and

57 E.g. NAI CSORP/1894/811; 1896/7461 and 20790; *Newtownards Spectator*, 24 February, 3 March, 10 March, 17 March, 31 March, 21 April, 5 May, 12 May 1901.

58 Return showing the Number of Workhouse Infirmaries in Ireland in which Nuns are employed in any capacity, showing for each Infirmary the Number of Nuns so employed and the amount paid to them by way of salaries within the last financial year, 1903 [115] lix, 497.

59 NAI CSORP/1903/2963 is an extensive file covering the issue back to 1871.

union rating), were enacted for reasons largely unconnected with the poor law itself. The establishment of a system of democratically elected local government meant that the boards were no longer a central forum for Nationalist opinion (particularly in rural areas). And, ironically, the major reforms introduced by the local government legislation led to little change in poor relief policy (with the exception, as discussed above, of the building of labourers' cottages).[60] The establishment of two important Commissions on poor law reform perhaps held out the possibility for a new and more central role for the poor law machinery. However, as will be seen in chapter 10, this hope was to be short-lived and in this area also the poor law was overtaken by broader developments.

60 A responsibility which was, in any case, no longer that of the boards of guardians after 1899.

CHAPTER 9

The Broader Role of the Boards of Guardians in Local Politics and Community

This chapter examines the broader role of the boards of guardians in the *politicisation* of Irish society. The fact that two rather different approaches to the provision of relief have been identified indicates that the role of the boards was important in the development of policy. Boards had considerable discretion in how they applied the law and could and did decide on the precise approach to the provision of relief. At the same time, the degree of continuity in poor relief patterns over the nineteenth century indicates that the major reconstruction of the boards in the 1880s did not lead to dramatic changes in poor relief policy. So if Nationalists took over 'control' of the southern boards, what use did they make of their new powers? And why did they bother to take over control of the boards at all? These questions point to the broader importance of the boards in Irish society and, in particular, in the politicisation of the Irish population. The term 'politicisation' is used in the sense that the politicisation of a group or a society is the socio-historic action by which political issues penetrate the daily lives of the members of that group or society: in the words of Catherine Ford 'the formation of a political consciousness'.[1] While some authors have presented the issue of politicisation as a contrast between 'archaic' and 'modern' forms of politics,[2] it is perhaps better seen as 'a metamorphosis

1 C. Ford, 'Tradition in the Politicisation of Rural France during the Nineteenth Century'. in *La Politisation des Campagnes au XIX e Siècle, France, Italie, Espagne, Portugal.*, École Française de Rome, Rome, 2000.

2 E. Weber, *Peasants into Frenchmen: The Modernization of Rural France 1870–1914*, Stanford University Press, Stanford, 1976; and Id., 'Comment la Politique vint aux Paysans: A Second Look at Peasant Politicization', *American Historical Review*, 87(1982), 357–89.

of attitudes and behaviours in the evolving political field'.[3] In certain ways, for example, in the mass campaigns for Catholic emancipation and repeal led by Daniel O'Connell (surely a key exponent of politicisation), Irish society was quite politically 'modern'.[4] However, one can see a clear distinction between pre-Famine Ireland and the post-local government reform Ireland 100 years later.

Who were the guardians?

The establishment of the boards and their electoral processes, and the take-over of many boards by Nationalist guardians in the 1880s have been discussed in chapter 5. In this part an analysis of the composition of the boards of guardians and, in particular the board officers, is developed over the period from the 1860s to 1911. While full listings of boards are not readily available, the names of the three officers are published annually (in Thom's directory) for the full period. Unfortunately no manuscript Census returns survive for 1861, 1871, 1881 and 1891. However, it is possible to use national and local directories to identify who the officers were in this period. Unfortunately, these are often described only as gentry, justice of the peace, etc. but one can cross-reference to the listing of all landowners in Ireland for 1876 which shows that the vast majority were large land-

3 L. Le Gall 'Des Processus de Politisation dans les Campagnes Françaises (1830–1914): Esquisse pour un État des Lieux', in J.-C. Caron, F. Chauvaud (eds), *Les Campagnes dans les Sociétés Européennes (1830–1930)*, PUR, Reims, 2005. See also the criticisms of this dichotomous approach in Ford 'Tradition' op. cit. and P.M. McPhee 'Contours Nationaux et Regionaux de l'Associationnisme Politique en France (1830–80) in *La Politisation des Campagnes*, op cit.

4 See C. Tilly, 'Social Movements and (all sorts of) other Political Interactions – Local, National and International – including Identities', *Theory and Society*, 27, (1998) 453–80; and T. Margadant, 'Comment on Charles Tilly's "Social Movements"', *Theory and Society*, 27, (1998) 481–8.

owners.[5] Feingold shows that in 1877, 99 per cent of all board chairs and 88 per cent of all board officers were landlords.[6] Table 9.2 sets out the full breakdown of the occupation of all board officers in 1877. Feingold also shows that the 1877 chairmen in particular were very extensive landlords with a median rateable valuation of about £2,000.[7]

In the period to the late 1870s, there is very strong continuity in the control of the boards. The focus here is on an analysis of the chairs of unions over the period from 1849 to 1876. Table 9.1 set out details as to the extent to which the same person remained in the position of chair over that period.

	1849	1859	1871	1876
1849	133	67	38	30
1859	–	162	85	69
1871	–	–	161	114
1876	–	–	–	163

Table 9.1 Survival of chairs of boards of guardians, 1849–76
Source: Database of board of guardians officers.[8]

The table shows that of the 133 chairs in office in 1849, 50 per cent remained in that position ten years later in 1859.[9] In fact, almost a quarter of chairs

5 The officers were obviously not necessarily representative of the guardians as a whole. It is possible to obtain published listings of guardians for some areas (e.g. Cork County in 1873). However, it seems likely that these were figures of lesser social importance and the directories available usually don't allow any identification. (The directories tend not to include farmers, who were not classified as gentry, etc.)

6 Feingold, *Tenantry*, 31.

7 Feingold, *Tenantry*, 219.

8 As part of this research, a database of officerships of the boards of guardians was compiled from the anuual Thom's directory.

9 The degree of continuity may be slightly overstated, as the data includes a number of titled figures where it is not readily apparent when a new person has succeeded to the same position of the death of the holder.

remained in that role over the full period of over twenty-five years.[10] Similarly, of the 162 chairs in office in 1859, just over half remained in office over a decade later in 1871. If one compares this to the longevity of members of Parliament, it is found that only seven of the 105 persons elected in the 1852 election were also elected in the same constituency in 1874. Thus the 'life expectancy' of a chair of the board of guardians was considerably longer than that of a member of Parliament. Over the five years from 1871 to 1876, of the 161 chairs in 1871, no less than 71 per cent were still in office in 1876. In contrast, of the 105 MPs elected in 1868 only forty-six (44 per cent) were re-elected for the same constituency in 1874. Thus even in the relatively politically volatile period of the rise of Home Rule, the position of the boards of guardians appears to have remained relatively stable.

This analysis does, however, indicate a significant change in the sort of persons who were elected as chairs over this period. In 1849, no less than eighteen chairs (14 per cent) were members of Parliament. However, this declined rapidly so that by 1876 only one chair was also a member of Parliament. In 1849, twenty-one (16 per cent) chairs were titled (most being members of the House of Lords). In contrast to the fall in the participation of MPs, this proportion rose somewhat so that by 1876 no less than thirty-three (20 per cent) of chairs were titled. Feingold shows that in 1877 only two chairmen were not landowners and there is nothing to suggest that the situation was any different in the previous decades.

Feingold has outlined in some detail the changes which took place in the boards of guardians during the Land War period (see chapter 5). Here only the impact on the composition of board officers is examined. By 1886, there has been a major shift in the composition of the officerships. The proportion of board officers who were landlords had fallen from nine out of ten in 1877 to less than half by 1886. Conversely the number of tenant officers had risen considerably. And the impact of this change was made greater by the fact that it was regionally varied with most of the change occurring outside Ulster. In 1886, half the Ulster boards had no tenant officer and a further 36 per cent had only one tenant officer holder.[11] Only two boards

10 This would be higher if account was taken of the fact that a number of unions were not yet established in 1849.

11 Feingold, *Tenantry*, table 15.

(Newtownards and Glenties) were tenant controlled. In contrast in Munster, almost half the boards were now tenant controlled (i.e. having all three tenant officers) and only 10 per cent now had three Conservative officers. Leinster and Connaught boards fell between these two extremes with about one-quarter of boards now having three tenant officers, a further quarter two tenant officers and 14 per cent (Connaught) to 23 per cent (Leinster) still having three landlord officeholders. Table 9.2 sets out the occupation of guardians in 1886, contrasting this with the position in 1877.

Occupation	1877	1886
Landowners	87.9	49.8
Farmers	6.7	26.2
Shopkeepers	1.0	8.8
Publicans and innkeepers	0.4	1.4
Professionals	0.6	1.2
Merchants and manufacturers	1.0	1.2
Members of parliament	0.2	0.2
Land agents	0.6	0.4
Business agents	0.4	0.2
Civil servants	0.2	0.2
Unidentified	1.9	9.9
Total	100.9 (n=489)	99.5 (n=486)

Table 9.2 Occupation of all board of guardians' officers, 1877 (per cent)
Source: Feingold, *Tenantry*, table 20.

As can be seen, farmers and shopkeepers were the main occupations of the new tenant officers. Not only did landlords decline overall as a proportion of the officers but the type of landlord who held office changed between 1877 and 1886. In Ulster the median valuation of the land held by chairmen rose significantly from £2,026 in 1877 to £3,474 in 1886 while, conversely, the rateable valuation of land held by southern chairs fell from £1,953 to

£1,262.[12] As Feingold puts it '[t]he removals in the southern chairmanships had occurred at the top of the scale: those in the north had occurred at the bottom'.[13] Feingold notes that the number of titled chairs actually rose in Ulster in this period (from eleven to thirteen) while in the south it fell sharply from thirty-four to thirteen, and speculates that this represented a particular attack on 'absentee' landlords. Unsurprisingly, there was a sharp fall in the 'longevity' of chairs in the period. Of those in office in 1876, only twenty-three remained in 1890 (about 15 per cent, allowing for vacancies and dissolved unions).[14] However, if one compares this to members of Parliament, again poor law chairs do not fare badly. Of the 103 MPs elected in 1874, only three were elected for a related constituency in 1892. In addition, the high level of change did not always signal a change in political allegiance. Indeed, as Feingold has noted, in a number of cases titled figures took up the chairmanship of boards in the period[15] and no fewer than twenty-two titled figures (including baronets) were chairmen in 1890.

As has been seen in chapter 8, the introduction of major local government reform in Ireland in 1898 – with the first elections in 1899 – saw a dramatic change in board composition. No less than eighty-six board chairmen (more than 50 per cent) were newly elected. In some cases, the new chairman had previously been deputy or vice chairman of the board and, it may well be that in other cases they had previously been board members. The high level of turnover may, in part, be due to the fact that about one-quarter of board officers became members of county councils.

The 1898 reforms saw the end of the widespread representation of titled figures as board chairman (only the Earl of Kilmorey in Kilkeel and Lord Ventry in Dingle survived the democratic electoral process) and other long-standing landlords (such as Colonel Daly in Loughrea)[16] also

12 In the case of the other officerships who were generally small and middling landowners, the median valuation fell generally (see Feingold, *Tenantry*, table 21).

13 Feingold, *Tenantry*, 220.

14 It does appear that in perhaps six cases the 1890 chair was a son or relative of the 1876 chair.

15 Including the Earl of Leitrim in Milford, the Earl of Kilmorey in Kilkeel, Viscount Powerscourt in Rathdown, and the Earl of Kingston in Boyle.

16 Although Daly became a member of Galway county council as a representative of the grand jury.

lost their positions. The democratisation of local government appears to have had an equally sweeping effect on the political composition of the guardians generally. It was reported that prior to the Local Government Act, Unionists constituted slightly over half the Irish guardians (3,773 to the Nationalists 3,639). After the 1899 elections, Unionists were reduced to only 1,523 guardians compared to 6,689 Nationalists.[17] This study looked at the identity of guardians for four counties in 1911: Antrim (including Belfast city), Down, Dublin (including the city) and Kerry; and for five counties in 1901: Clare and four western counties (Leitrim, Mayo, Sligo and Roscommon). This allows an analysis of occupation, religion, age, etc. of the officers in a considerable proportion of all boards (30 per cent). The counties available provided a good cross-section of the unions including a number of northern and peripheral western unions.

Area	Date	No.	None Identified	Roman Catholic	Church of Ireland	Presbyterian	Methodist	Baptist	Age
Western	1901	50	43	40	0	1	0	0	48
Clare	1901	24	21	21	0	0	0	0	51
Dublin	1911	12	12	8	3	0	0	0	55
North	1911	33	31	8	2	17	3	1	59
Kerry	1911	17	11	10	1	0	0	0	47

Table 9.3 Age and religion of board officers, 1901–11
Source: Thom's directory 1902, 1912; Census manuscripts 1901, 1911.

17 NA CO 904/184/1 quoted in P. Travers, *Settlements and Divisions: Ireland, 1870–1922*, Helicon, 1988, Dublin, 66. One might attend more to the general tendency shown than to the dubious accuracy of the precise numbers.

As set out in table 9.3, there are 136 board officers, of which it is possible to identify 118 (87 per cent).[18] In some cases, there are two (or more) individuals of the same name where it is not possible to identify which is the officer.[19] In other cases, the guardian may have died or moved away (or simply been absent on Census day).[20] The officers are overwhelmingly male. There is not one female officer in all the southern unions in 1901 and only two (Mrs. Bibiana Foran, vice-chairwoman of Listowel and Lady Rosa Gilbert, deputy vice-chairwoman of Rathdown) in 1911. The northern unions do have a somewhat higher female representation (five in Antrim) although even here there is no chairwoman and, as Urquhart has shown, women's representation never rose above about 3 per cent of total board membership.

In terms of age, officers tended to be middle-aged, with the average age varying from the late forties for the western boards in 1901 to the late fifties for the northern boards in 1911. There were only two officers in their twenties of the over 100 identified. The rural southern boards officers are overwhelmingly Roman Catholic. As might be expected the Dublin boards are somewhat more mixed with three Church of Ireland members out of eleven. The northern boards are also quite religiously mixed. In fact the surprising fact here is the underrepresentation of the Church of Ireland, which made up 22.3 per cent of the population of Down and Antrim in 1911, but only held two officer posts. Presbyterians and Methodists are correspondingly overrepresented, while Roman Catholics take up eight posts with just over a quarter, and broadly in line with their representation in the overall population.

In terms of occupation, the Census returns provide somewhat limited evidence. Many officers are returned only as 'farmer' and the Census

18 There were a number of board vacancies, so not all boards had a full complement of three officers.

19 In a number of cases, there are co-resident fathers and sons of the same name and it has been assumed that the father is the guardian, except where the father was very old (late seventies).

20 For example, the chairman of Castlerea (and future MP) John Fitzgibbon is not in the Census but his drapery, with a staff of thirty-four, can be identified.

does not include data on the size of holding. It is equally difficult to get a sense from the returns as to the size of enterprise represented by the term 'draper' or 'manufacturer'.[21] Given these limitations, table 9.4 sets out the occupations reported for the officers.

Area	Date	Farmer (incl. sons)	Trader	Manufacture	Teacher	Employee	Land-owner	Other	Not known
Western	1901	24	14	0	0	0	3	2	1
Clare	1901	15	4	0	0	0	1	1	0
Dublin	1911	1	4	0	2	1	0	3	0
North	1911	17	7	1	0	1	0	3	2
Kerry	1911	6	4	0	0	1	0	0	0
		63	33	1	2	3	4	9	3

Table 9.4 Occupations of board officers, 1901–11
Source: As table 9.3.

As can be seen, farmers were the dominant class (except in Dublin). However, traders (the term includes shopkeepers, grocers, drapers, publicans, hotel keepers, etc.) also played a very important part. Only one individual recorded himself as a 'farmer & grocer' (recorded here in the trader group) but it would seem likely that there was probably a much greater cross-over between the two categories. In the south, one still seems some (albeit limited) remnants of the old landowners. It is striking that only one manufacturer (Thomas Lavery in Newtownards) features. There are almost no professionals (e.g. lawyers or doctors). Equally striking is the lack of employees with only three employees in the more than 100 officers identified.

21 Except where the owner lives on the premises or other external information can be drawn on.

The patterns for rural southern Ireland are very clear. The officers are middle aged, Catholic men who are important locally as businessmen, shopkeepers, and farmers and were often important local political figures.[22] Jasper Tully, chairman of the Boyle board, was a long-standing MP (from 1892 to 1906 originally as a member of the Irish Parliamentary Party and subsequently independent Nationalist) and owner of the *Roscommon Herald*.[23] John Fitzgibbon, chair of the Castlerea board (and rival of Tully), was the owner of a large drapery in Castlerea while also acting as local inspector of industry for the Congested Districts Board.[24] Fitzgibbon was active in the Gaelic League, the temperance movement and as a land agitator. He was an Irish Parliamentary Party organiser and future Irish Parliamentary Party MP (from 1910). Peter Cawley, chair of Tobercurry was a UIL organiser.[25] P.N. White, chair of Sligo, was a chemist, mineral water bottler and mill owner.[26]

The Dublin officers are a heterogeneous group and in addition to the usual merchants include the secretary of the Builders and Stonelayers Trade Union (the only 'labour' representative identified), a collector of income tax, managing director of a shipping company and an author.

22 Silverman and Gulliver's study of one rural southern board (Thomastown) shows that by 1911, the overall members of the board was dominated by farmers (fifty out of fifty-four guardians) who tended to hold larger farmers: M. Silverman and P.H. Gulliver, '"Common sense" and "governmentality": local government in southeastern Ireland, 1850–1922', *Journal of the Royal Anthropological Institute*, 12 (2006), 109–27.

23 See M. Wheatley, *Nationalism and the Irish Party: Provincial Ireland 1910–16*, Oxford University Press, Oxford, 2005, 15 and 99. Wheatley describes Tully as 'the most vocal Nationalist in Boyle' and a man whose 'political influence spread across much of North Roscommon and South Leitrim'.

24 Wheatley, *Nationalism*, 35 describes Fitzgibbon as 'far and away the most influential Nationalist politician' in Co. Roscommon. See also Bew, *Conflict and Conciliation in Ireland*, passim.

25 Wheatley, *Nationalism*, 141.

26 Wheatley, *Nationalism*, 140. White is described as 'firmly part of Sligo's Nationalist, business leadership'.

It is interesting to compare these figures with the occupations of Irish Parliamentary Party MPs. Lyons shows that farmers and local merchants made up a much smaller proportion of the parliamentary party in the period 1900–10 (a third at most) while professionals (lawyers and doctors) and 'journalists', which, in fact, includes owners, managers and editors of newspapers, made up close to half the party's MPs.[27]

Urban guardians

Thus far the focus has been on board officers and it has been seen that the pattern for the Dublin unions is significantly different to that for rural unions. It is possible to explore this issue in more detail for both Dublin[28] and Belfast unions. Thom's directory contains a full annual listing of guardians for Dublin and as it also contains a full street directory, it is possible to identify a quite high percentage of guardians. Similar commercial directories exist for Belfast and it has been possible to analyse the composition of the Dublin and Belfast unions in the 1860s at least so far as occupation is identified in these directories.[29] The officers of the Belfast union in 1866 were the owner of a large wholesale and retail wollendrapers, silk merchants and general warehouse business, a solicitor with offices in both Belfast and Dublin, and a landowner.[30] The Dublin boards were chaired by two ex-officio landowners and the other officers included two barristers (both elected).[31]

27 Lyons, *Irish Parliamentary Party*, 169–76.

28 Previously, we looked at the North and South Dublin unions and the more 'rural' Balrothery and Rathdown unions which covered part of the Dublin suburbs. Here, the focus is only on the North and South Dublin city unions.

29 The 'Return of Owners of Land of one acre and upwards… ', HC, 1876, [C. 1492] lxxx, 61, was also used to check property holdings.

30 David Taylor JP, who owned property in Belfast, rated at over £1,000; John Suffern, solicitor and owner of property in Belfast, rated at over £1,000; and James Thompson, JP, owner of 693 acres.

31 The chairs were Sir Robert Shaw JP (owner of almost 1,000 acres in Dublin) and H.J. McFarlane (owner of 466 acres in Dublin, and 300 in Kilkenny). McFarlane

	Belfast			North Dublin			South Dublin		
	Ex-officio	Elected		Ex-officio	Elected		Ex-officio	Elected	
		City	Outside city		City	Outside city		City	Outside city
Landowner	8	0	0	19	0	0	14	0	2
Merchant	4	6	4	0	7	4	10	7	2
Professional	3	1	0	1	4	2	3	4	1
Manufacturer	0	2	0	0	0	0	0	2	2
MP	0	0	0	2	0	0	0	0	0
Newspaper/journal proprietor	0	0	0	(1)	1	0	0	0	0
Other	1	0	0	1	2	0	3	0	2
Not known	5	1	8	5	4	9	2	5	5
Total	21	10	12	28	18	15	32	18	14

Table 9.5 Occupations of Dublin and Belfast guardians, 1865–76
Source: Thom's *Directory* 1866 (Dublin); Wynne's *Business Directory of Belfast and principal towns in the province of Ulster for 1865–66* (Belfast).

As the results are quite different for ex-officio and elected guardians and for those guardians living within the city as opposed to the more outlying divisions, results are shown separately for each category.[32] Some caution should be applied in reading these results. They are drawn from two separate

also served as ex-officio guardian in Thomastown (Kilkenny) and Clogher (Tyrone), indicating that he was also a property-owner in Tyrone (although this cannot be identified from the 1876 Return).

32 Both directories are much more likely to allow identification of those living in a numbered street address than persons in the suburbs.

commercial directories and identification is, to a certain extent, dependent on the degree of precision used by the compliers of the directories. It is also possible that persons recorded here as 'landowners' may have also exercised another occupation. In Britain, aristocratic involvement in finance, industry, and urban development was one of that class's defining characteristics. It may well be the case that this was also true in Ireland. However, having regard to these concerns and to the fact that a significant number of guardians (up to one-third in Belfast)[33] cannot be identified, one can see both some similarities and some differences between the two cities.

In Dublin, then still the undisputed capital, the ex-officio members of the North Dublin board include two MPs (one of whom is Sir John Gray shown here also in his capacity as owner of the *Freeman's Journal*) and the Earls of Charlemont and of Howth.[34] Although the South Dublin board contains no titled figures or MPs it also includes a considerable landed section. The Dublin boards include more landowners (one-quarter to one-third, compared to one in seven in Belfast). The Belfast and South Dublin boards include more merchants (almost one-third compared to less than one-fifth in North Dublin). Manufacturers make up a surprisingly small proportion of all boards (although the extent to which merchants or landowners may have had an interest in manufacturing businesses is not known). Professionals (mainly lawyers and doctors) make up about 10 per cent of all three boards. The religious composition of the boards is not generally known, although in Belfast in 1857 only two of twelve elected members were Catholic.[35]

33 Four of the unidentified Belfast guardians can be identified from the 1876 'Return of owners of land of one acre and upwards' as owners of relatively small portions of highly rated property, so they are probably in business of some sort and are not landowners.

34 Charlemont owned property of over 200 acres in Clontarf rated at £700, while Howth was the owner of 7,377 acres in Co. Dublin and a further 2,061 acres in Co. Meath (with a total rateable value of over £13,000).

35 *Belfast Newsletter*, 27 October 1857. In contrast, H.J. McFarlane in his evidence to the 1861 Select Committee stated that Roman Catholic guardians were often in a majority on the North Dublin board (Report, Q. 5557).

For 1911, it is possible to draw on the Census data. There has been a very significant change over the fifty years in that large landowners, titled figures and MPs have almost entirely disappeared from the boards.[36] Farmers make up a relatively small proportion (although their numbers are probably somewhat undercounted here as it is again more difficult to identify persons in rural areas).[37] Persons involved (usually as the owner) in service businesses, in particular grocers (often grocers and wine/spirit merchants) but also traders of various kinds (chemists, hairdressers, etc), form the largest block in all three unions, from about one-third in Belfast to about one-half in Dublin. As in the 1860s manufacturers are hardly represented on the boards. Professionals make up a relatively small group while there has been an increase, especially in Dublin, in white collar workers (teachers, an insurance inspector). Only in South Dublin is there any sign of a 'labour' representation (including two labourers, a chimney sweep and bricklayer) and even here it is very small, although the vice-chair of the union was the secretary of a trade union.[38]

In Dublin, the religious composition of the boards broadly represents the wider community.[39] In contrast, in Belfast – where Catholics made up a quarter of the population in 1911 – only 5 per cent of identified members were Roman Catholic. The average age of the boards was somewhat lower in Dublin (47.6 and 40.0) than in Belfast (52.7). Women made up a small minority of all boards, with eleven in South Dublin, six in Belfast and only two in North Dublin.

36 Only one member of the three boards recorded his occupation as a landlord and it is not clear what the term meant in this context.

37 Perhaps surprisingly, farmers made up a larger proportion of the board in 'industrial' Belfast because of the balance between 'rural' and 'urban' divisions.

38 In their study of local government in Belfast, Budge and O'Leary show that unionists dominated local government taking (in 1911) 87 per cent of council seats: *Belfast: Approach to Crisis*, 186. Unfortunately, the authors shortly dismiss the board of guardians as 'rarely involved in disputatious politics' and do not discuss it in any detail although accepting that politicians such as Joseph Devlin and William Walker 'used an election for poor law guardians as the first step in their political careers' (Ibid. 51).

39 In the North Dublin board six of the forty-six identified members are Church of Ireland, while in South Dublin (out of seventy) there were eight Church of Ireland and two Baptist guardians.

	Belfast	North Dublin	South Dublin
Grocer	6	7	17
Other traders	11	19	24
Professional	7	3	2
Manufacturer	1	1	1
White collar	2	8	7
Manual worker	0	0	5
Farmer	9	2	8
Landlord	0	0	1
None	3	4	6
Not known	16	13	8
Total	55	57	79

Table 9.6 Occupations of Dublin and Belfast guardians, 1910–11
Source: Thom's *Directory* (Dublin); Belfast and Province of Ulster Directory 1912 (Belfast); Census manuscripts 1911.

Thus the boards are much less elitist than in the 1860s and somewhat more representative of the broader community, except in religiously divided Belfast. As in rural areas, grocers and other independent businessmen and, to a lesser extent, farmers dominate the boards. There is a surprising absence of both professional and manufacturing representatives especially if one considers how overrepresented professionals – such as lawyers – were in national politics.[40] The more 'democratic' nature of the boards is, however, severely limited and as has been seen women and working men are involved in very small numbers. As Feingold argued although the transfer of power from landlords to tenants represented, in one sense, a democratisation, it was 'in another sense the replacement of the old landlord elite with a new tenant elite'.[41]

40 See Lyons, *Irish Parliamentary Party*.
41 Feingold, *Tenanty*, 218.

What role did the boards play?

In this section the broader activities of the boards of guardians are considered.

Creating a sense of local government

Firstly, the boards helped to create a sense of local government. As has been seen the establishment of the poor law led to the creation of entirely new political spaces – the poor law unions – with their own (at least partially) elected governments. The weekly meetings of the boards received extensive coverage in the local press. Often they were the most important local government body in the area until the 1898 reforms.

Obviously the boards often took a view on the poor law related issues of the day, such as the debate on union rating (discussed in chapter 4). In addition, and even before the take-over of the boards in the 1880s, the guardians sought to uphold their views as to issues such as the registration of the religion of children (also discussed in chapter 4). More generally, as has been seen, the boards frequently expressed views on broader issues both to do with local development and, increasingly over time, on 'national' issues. In the 1870s one finds the practice of circulating resolutions to boards of guardians on a wide range of broadly political issues. Different boards took different approaches to these issues. For example, the Marquis of Sligo, chair of the Westport board, agreed to sign a petition concerning Sunday closing of public houses.[42] In contrast, the Longford

42 *Mayo Examiner*, 13 January 1877. In the event, the board did not take a position on the issue as the members were not agreed. However, it appears that the board had previously supported a petition on the topic. The board did not have a very consistent attitude to such resolutions. One finds the acting chair Lord John Browne (brother of the Marquis), perhaps with some justification, refusing to entertain a petition opposing clerical abuses legislation before the Italian Parliament: *Mayo Examiner*, 5 May 1877.

board adopted, without dissent, a general resolution refusing to consider any subject foreign to the administration of the poor law.[43] An attempt by the chair of the Ballina board to adopt a similar approach on a memorial on Isaac Butt's Education Bill was, however, overruled by the board which supported the Bill.[44]

One interesting, albeit unusual, example of a broader political resolution is that adopted by the North Dublin union in 1869.[45] The resolution states that

> Absenteeism being a great evil of this country, the board of guardians of this union will call upon the Prime Minister of England to grant a royal residence and a national Parliament, as the only legitimate remedy for the pauperism and widespread dissension which exists…

The resolution was moved by Mr Erson JP and seconded by Captain Brinkley JP and passed with one exception. The North Dublin union subsequently wrote to other unions seeking their support for the resolution 'with a view to united action and hearty co-operation'. The Poor Law Commission took great exception to this resolution and issued a circular to unions objecting to it and trusting that they would decline to entertain the proposal. Erson subsequently complained to the Commission denying that the resolution was introduced for the purposes of agitation and stating that he was motivated by loyal and patriotic motives while Brinkley also argued that the resolution was not political agitation and complained to the Commission that they should confine themselves to administering the laws for the relief of the poor in Ireland. Lord Talbot de Malahide, chair of Balrothery union, subsequently presented this resolution to the House of Lords as a petition emanating from 'a body of gentlemen of the highest

43 *Longford Journal*, 12 January 1878. Proposed interestingly by an active Home Rule supporter.

44 *Mayo Examiner*, 21 April 1877. In January 1878, the Ballina board signed a petition on Sunday closing without debate on the issue of considering non-poor law matters. *Mayo Examiner*, 19 January 1878.

45 NAI CSORP/1870/54. See also the Twenty-third Annual Report of the Poor Law Commissioners 1870, HC 1870 [c.156] xxxvi, 1 at 40.

respectability including landed proprietors and commercial men of all section in politics and belonging to all religions', although noting that he himself opposed repeal of the Union.[46]

A further example of the involvement of boards in broader political issues is the support of Castlebar board for the release of the Fenian 'political prisoners'.[47] In September 1871, Charles O'Malley B.L., acting chair of the board, proposed a motion calling for the release of the Fenian prisoners.[48] This was adopted by the board despite the objections of some members. This motion (or similar motions) were adopted by a number of other boards.[49] It is interesting to note that Gladstone, rather than condemning this activity, wrote to the board rejecting their request as he did not consider the crimes were political but noting the temperate language used in the motion and the loyal feeling evinced.[50]

The support of the Kilmallock board for the reform of land tenure provides another example. As Feingold has reported, the Kilmallock union was the site of one of the earliest battles between tenant farmers and landlords for control of the board. In 1870, William Bolster a wealthy tenant farmer and president of the Limerick, Clare, and Tipperary farmers club won election as the chairman of Kilmallock board of guardians. Having lost office in 1871, Bolster retained the chairmanship in 1872 and retained

46 Hansard, 201, 1–2, 2 May 1870. The guardians surprise at the response may be explained by the fact that the board's earlier resolution on the land question had received a positive response from both Earl Granville and Gladstone: NAI Minute book of the North Dublin Union, 16 October 1869, NAI MFGS 49/104. The North Dublin board had also passed a resolution on the overtaxation of Ireland, NAI Minute book of the North Dublin Union, 4 November 1868, NAI MFGS 49/101.

47 On this issue see D. Thornley, *Isaac Butt and Home Rule*, Macgibbon and Kee, London, 1964, 53–6, 65–8; R.V. Comerford, *The Fenians in Context: Irish Politics and Society 1848–82*, Wolfhound, Dublin, 1985, 170–8.

48 *Mayo Examiner*, 11 and 25 September 1871.

49 The neighbouring Swinford and Newport boards adopted resolutions approving the Castlebar motion. Killadysert and Ballinasloe boards also adopted motions (albeit in the later case after the majority of members had left the meeting); *Nation*, 7 October 1871, Ibid., 8 June 1872.

50 *Mayo Examiner*, 16 October 1871.

it throughout the 1870s.[51] On 14 January 1875 the Kilmallock board met, with Mr Bolster in the chair and W.H. O'Sullivan Home Rule MP for Limerick County and a poor law guardian on the same board in attendance.[52] Following the normal work of the board, a circular was read from the land conference to be held in Dublin later that month requesting a deputation from the board.[53] Bolster argued that the board should be represented but was opposed by Mr Saunders who objected to the introduction of such questions at meetings of the boards of guardians. Saunders and two other board members, including Mr Townsend the former chair,[54] left the meeting and it was subsequently agreed that the board would send a delegation consisting of the chair, vice chair and deputy vice-chair. All three dissenters were justices of the peace and likely to have been ex-officio members.[55] A complaint was made to the chief secretary arguing that such issues should not be debated at board meetings and proposing the prohibition of discussion of issues unconnected with the poor law. However, when the matter was referred to the Local Government Board for its views it argued that the 'disposition to discuss politics is by no means general' at most boards and that Kilmallock was an exception due to local circumstances. The Board argued that no such general rule would be effectual.

A fourth example is the case of a Home Rule motion proposed before the Roscommon board by Alexander O'Connor Eccles, an elected member, co-founder of the Roscommon Home Rule Association, and owner of the *Roscommon Weekly Messenger*.[56] The chairman, Lord Crofton, refused to

51 See Feingold, *Tenantry*, 83–5 and NAI CSORP/1871/9458.

52 *Cork Examiner*, 15 January 1875. See NAI CSORP/1875/2360.

53 On the conference, see Thornley, *Isaac Butt and Home Rule*, 247–50 (which refers to Bolster's involvement).

54 Or 'the nominee of the Tory Landlords' as he was described in a Bolster election poster in 1871, NAI CSORP/1875/2360.

55 Although justices of the peace were entitled to be members ex-officio, in some cases JPs stood for election and served as elected members so it is not necessarily the case that all three were ex-officios: Return of the number of magistrates, elected and ex-officio, on each board of guardians… in Ireland, HC 1843 (347), xlvi, 583.

56 This is discussed in detail in Feingold, *Tenantry*, 3–10. See *Roscommon Journal*, 11, 18, 25 May 1872.

receive a motion of a political nature but sought the views of the board. When the board voted narrowly to receive the motion, Lord Crofton and the vice-chairman resigned. Following a complaint to the Local Government Board, the Board ordered an election for the officer posts which was strongly attended by the ex-offico members. Three ex-offico members were elected to the officer positions but a resolution, proposed by the former vice-chair, barring political discussion at all future board meetings was withdrawn. Feingold reports that eight more years were to pass before the Nationalist guardians were successfully able to challenge the ex-officios for the office of chairman.[57] It appears that a number of other unions adopted similar pro-Home Rule motions.[58] However, as is shown by the comments of the Local Government Board on the Kilmallock case, these cases appear to be exceptions to the general activities of local boards at the time.

In this way the boards both created a sense of a political space to be governed and increasingly played the role of a broader organ of local government reflecting the views of the people on a wide range of issues. As has been seen in chapter 5, the adoption of 'political' resolutions became much more common after the take-over of the boards in the 1880s. The boards undoubtedly became less important after the 1898 Act established a broader system of local government but (as Feingold pointed out) the boards formed an important training ground for future local politicians and, as will be seen below, many board officers went on to play a role in that broader system of local government.

57 Op. cit. p. 85.

58 The *Nation* reports that similar motions were adopted by boards in Dublin, Cork, Drogheda, Galway, Kilkenny, Edenderry, Mullingar, Bailieborough, Kilmallock, Killadysert and Millstreet: 8 June 1872. Feingold states that at least twenty-six boards adopted a Dublin Corporation motion on Home Rule citing the *Roscommon Journal*, 25 May 1872.

Learning politics

As Agulhon has said, 'C'est en votant qu'on apprend à voter, c'est en campagnes (électorales) qu'on apprend "la politique".'[59] The boards played an important role in the political learning of the Irish people through the annual elections. Unfortunately no comprehensive returns of poor law elections in the nineteenth century exist. However, it is clear that relatively few of the annual poor law elections were contested. Evidence to the Select Committee on poor law guardians in 1878 indicates that the number of contested electoral divisions varied from 9.2 per cent in 1876 to 6.9 per cent in 1878.[60] It appears that contests were more frequent in cities.[61] For example, there had been contests in four of the fourteen electoral divisions and wards[62] in the North Dublin union in each of the years 1876 to 1878 while in the South Dublin union there had been three, eight and nine contests respectively in a union with sixteen electoral divisions and wards. In contrast there had been only seven contests in the rural Carrick-on-Shannon union in the last three years (out of twenty-five electoral divisions).[63]

A study of the local newspapers in the period also indicates that there was, in general, little controversy about the re-election of the existing officers. In general the officers were re-elected unanimously and *en bloc*. As has been seen above, analysis of the chairs of the unions indicates a rather low level of turnover. Of the 162 chairmen in 1871 (Millstreet union was dissolved at the time), 109 (or two-thirds) retained their chairmanship in 1876 and a number of the new chairmen appear to have replaced family

59 Maurice Agulhon, 'Présentation', in *La Politisation des Campagnes au XIXe Siècle*, 2000.

60 Report of the Select Committee on poor law guardians etc., HC 1878 (297), xvii, 209, evidence of Benjamin Banks. The figure for 1877 is 7.6 per cent.

61 O'Brien, 'The Establishment of the Poor-Law Unions', 116 makes the same point for the period around 1840.

62 North Dublin Union had nine electoral divisions, of which the large North City division was divided into six wards. Similarly, the large South City division was subdivided into nine wards.

63 Report of the Select Committee on poor law guardians etc., HC 1878 (297), xvii, 209, evidence of Abraham O'Connor, Q. 5863.

members in that position.[64] Almost 40 per cent of chairmen were in office in 1859, 1871 and 1876, indicating a considerable degree of continuity.[65] However, at least by the late 1870s, calls for a fair share of officerships for the elected guardians were becoming more common.[66]

On what basis were elections contested? On this issue very little information is available before the 1880s. Even where local newspapers reported that elections have been contested, they tend not to provide any detailed coverage of the election contests nor do they refer in detail to the reasons behind such contests.[67] The Irish witnesses who gave evidence to the 1878 Select Committee on poor law guardians, which was appointed to enquire into the system of election of local boards in England, Scotland and Ireland as a result of dissatisfaction with the existing systems on the part of many MPs, indicate some difference between the practice in Dublin and the rest of the country in this regard. Witnesses indicated that elections in Dublin were contested on party and religious grounds. For example, John Byrne, clerk of the South Dublin union and a former Conservative guardian, stated that elections were fought 'on party grounds exclusively'.[68] Benjamin Banks, secretary of the Local Government Board, described Dublin elections as 'guided by religious and political feeling to a very large extent' and stated that lists were made up of party candidates.[69]

64 Over half the chairs in 1871 had been in office in 1859.

65 This figure may be slightly inflated in that, in a number of cases, the chairs are held by titled members and it is not readily apparent when a new person succeeds to the title.

66 See, for example, the discussion at the Naas and Mountmellick boards: *Leinster Express*, 31 March and 7 April 1877.

67 See, for example, the reports of a heated contest in the *Limerick Reporter*, 26 and 29 March 1878 which, despite including the victor's speech, leaves the reader no wiser as to the issues involved.

68 Report of the Select Committee on Poor Law Guardians..., HC 1878 (297), xvii, 273.

69 Ibid. at 209 and 215. See also the evidence of Liberal Catholic Thomas Mayne (an unsuccessful candidate for the post of guardian) Q. 4860 et seq.; of the North Dublin union returning officer George Cree at Q. 5805; and of John Byrne (clerk to the South Dublin union) at Q. 6017. For example, the *Freeman's Journal* published a list of the Liberal candidates, urging its readers to vote for them: 18 March 1878.

James Daly, editor of the *Connacht Telegraph* and a member of two boards himself, in contrast indicated that politics were relatively rarely involved in the elections in Mayo. Daly described contests as involving sometimes religious, sometimes political and sometimes private feeling.[70] In contrast, Abraham O'Connor, clerk and returning officer of Carrick-on-Shannon union, stated that the, admittedly rare, contests were mainly on 'religious and political questions'.[71]

In what manner were elections carried on? Elections could, on occasion, be very robustly contested and in a manner which went far beyond what it might be considered legitimate by the standards of the time.[72] For example, in March 1875 there was a contest in the electoral division of Tircahan in the poor law union of Bawnboy, Co Cavan. Four candidates were nominated for the two vacancies: Albert Hutton and William Reynolds, two Protestants, and Patrick McGovern and Francis King, two Roman Catholics. On the night of 19 and 20 March 1875, a party of nine or ten men, some of them who had hay ropes twisted about their necks as a disguise, visited the house of one Francis Maguire and demanded his poor law voting papers. On refusal, the crowd broke down the front and back door of the house on which the voting papers were handed out, defaced by the crowd and returned. The same crowd proceeded to at least another four houses in the area but with only limited success. The constabulary report stated that there had been other similar cases in the area. However, when the petty sessions held a magisterial investigation, all the witnesses said that they did not know any of the attackers. In the event, Hutton lost the election by six votes (forty six votes for McGovern to forty for Hutton) and complained to the Local Government Board alleging intimidation by McGovern. Despite the clear evidence of intimidation, however, the Board replied that the returning officer could not allow defaced papers nor give

70 Ibid., Q. 269.

71 Ibid., Q. 5895.

72 The following discussion needs to be seen in the context of the high level of electoral violence in parliamentary elections at the time (Hoppen, *Elections, Politics and Society in Ireland*, at 388–408) and in the broader context of levels of violence in Irish society.

a second voting paper. The Board did not believe that there were sufficient grounds for an inquiry. Later that year, Hutton's brother wrote to Michael Hicks Beach MP, chief secretary for Ireland, complaining of the refusal of the Local Government Board to investigate. The Board, while accepting such occurrences 'happen too frequently,' argued that its powers under the Poor Law Act did not extend to the investigation of this type of voting irregularity. However, the Attorney General, whose views were sought on the matter, did not agree and felt that they did have the power to inquire. Nonetheless, Dublin Castle, in view of the short period remaining before the next annual election in March 1876, instructed the Local Government Board that no further steps need be taken but suggested that inquiry into the validity of elections would have a salutary effect in discouraging such irregularities in the future and pointing out that it was the Attorney General's view that the Board did have the power to investigate.[73]

This was far from an isolated case. However, as has been seen, the Local Government Board was reluctant to get involved in individual issues. In a case involving the alleged forgery of a vote, the Board stated that 'cases of this kind... are of merely local interest' and that it did not feel that it would be justified in undertaking prosecutions in such cases, even where success was probable, at the charge of the Imperial Exchequer, pointing out that any person could institute a prosecution in such case. The limited extent of the Board's involvement in this area is illustrated by the fact that between 1853 and 1878 it issued only eighty-nine orders to the effect that a person was not duly elected or not entitled to act as a guardian.[74] This amounts to an average of only 3.4 such cases per annum. Although the precise numbers varied from year to year no particular trend is apparent and the very limited numbers contrast sharply with the fifty-one orders issued in the three years between 1883 and 1885, when the Board obviously took a much more active approach.

73 This account is based on the material in NAI CSORP/1878/8595. There is no sign that the Local Government Board acted on this advice.

74 Index of Poor Law Orders, NAI BG2005/57 2 and 3.

The archives include the results of an investigation in 1878 into the extent of intimidation in close elections.[75] The detailed background to the investigation is not known but it presumably arose from concerns in Dublin Castle about the exercise of undue influence. The undersecretary, T.H. Burke, wrote to the local constabulary in twenty eight areas asking them to investigate whether undue influence, coercion or intimidation had occurred at the recent poor law elections. The twenty-eight cases represent 12 per cent of the total electoral contests in 1878. It is noteworthy that most related to 'rural' areas and none were in Dublin, Belfast or Cork city unions. As has been seen the voting papers were distributed to the houses of voters. The main concerns as to undue influence appear to have arisen from the fact that it seems to have been somewhat common practice for those distributing the votes to be followed by the supporters of one or more candidates. However, in only three electoral divisions was undue influence reported. In the Tullamore union it was alleged that the followers entered the voters' houses and used every means short of violence to have the papers signed in favour of their preferred candidate, in some cases filling them in themselves. In Tobercurry it was reported that the parish priest had used all his influence in favour of the Roman Catholic candidate. The priest had, allegedly, led bodies of men armed with sticks to visit the house of voters. It was also alleged that candidates' names had been written and then crossed out. Although the constabulary had investigated the matter they could not get firm evidence. In the Louisburgh electoral division in Westport union, the constable delivering the votes had seen a boy of fifteen following him and entering the houses where the papers had been left. On questioning the youth, he said he had been sent by one of the candidates to fill in the voting papers. The constable investigated one case and found

75 NAI CSORP/1878/8595. On the influence of both landlords and priests in parliamentary elections see Hoppen, *Elections*, 127–51; and 232–56; and J.H. Whyte, 'The Influence of the Catholic Clergy on Elections in Nineteenth-Century Ireland', *Catholic Historical Review*, lxxv, (1960), 239–59 and 'Landlord Influence at Elections in Ireland, 1760–1885', *English Historical Review*, lxxx (1965), 740–60. For a very interesting local study of the role of Catholic priests in rural politicisation, see J. O'Shea, *Priests, Politics and Society in Post-Famine Ireland*, Wolfhound Press, Dublin, 1983.

that the boy had filled in the paper in the name of that candidate although the absent voter had intended to vote for an alternative candidate. In total, clerical involvement was reported in eight cases, although only one of these involved undue influence. It is interesting to note that the dictates of the Roman Catholic clergy were clearly not followed in all cases and in Drumsna (Carrick on Shannon union) it was reported that the Roman Catholic clergy solicited votes but were refused in many instances.[76] Landlord involvement was also reported in two cases.[77] However as no specific questions were asked as to clerical or a landlord involvement, it may well be that such involvement occurred in other instances and, not amounting to undue influence, was not reported by the constabulary. Overall the three cases in which undue influence was recorded amount to only about one per cent of all elections in that year.

The evidence from the survey is broadly supported by the evidence to the 1878 Select Committee. Benjamin Banks was of the opinion that undue influence was more common in rural areas.[78] Although Banks accepted that complaints were 'of every-day occurrence' for about six weeks during the course of elections, he believed that a 'great many' were so frivolous and unfounded as not to raise any concerns.[79] George Cree, returning officer of the North Dublin Union, stated that he had 'no experience of corruption' under the existing electoral system;[80] while John Norwood, a

76 In Balbriggan (Balrothery union), in contrast, the parish priest read a letter from the Archbishop to the effect that the voters should chose the candidates best qualified to act as guardians.

77 Reports of landlord involvement in poor law elections were common. For example, in the 1871 elections, Lord Kingston's bailiff visited electors in the Boyle union with a letter from his Lordship seeking their vote for his land steward a Mr Dickie (who was, however, defeated by the 'popular' candidate): *Roscommon Journal*, 1 April 1871.

78 Report of the Select Committee on Poor Law Guardians…, HC 1878 (297), xvii, 273: Q. 4642 see also Qs. 4770–82. Because the Board took the view that it had 'nothing to do with the motives under which a man voted' such complaints were not separately recorded by the Board (Qs. 4660–1).

79 Qs. 4641, 4772–3.

80 Q. 5783 et seq. Cree's definition of corruption appears to have been rather narrow. John Byrne claimed the Dublin franchise was 'practically pure' and that intimidation had

Conservative, and both vice-chair of the North Dublin union and guardian in South Dublin, stated that he had never in twenty years heard of any cases of intimidation.[81] John Mulligan, a Liberal member of Dublin Corporation, accepted that there was no direct intimidation although he suggested that there was 'indirect' intimidation in that persons (such as shopkeepers) abstained rather than 'incur the displeasure of those who were dealing with them'.[82] Abraham O'Connor (returning officer in Carrick-on-Shannon) ventured that only a 'little' intimidation was practiced 'on both sides'.[83] Thus while it is clear that levels of undue influence existed which would not satisfy contemporary standards, there is little to suggest that, up to 1878, intimidation or corruption in poor law elections rivalled that which existed at the parliamentary level.[84]

Home Rule MPs proposed legislation to introduce voting by secret ballot, introduced for parliamentary elections in 1872, in the House of Commons on a number of occasions in the late 1860s and 70s but without success.[85] In response to one such Bill, in 1874 the Local Government Board asked its officials to report as to whether voting by ballot should be introduced in Dublin. However, they recommended against any change in the existing position as the present approach had worked satisfactorily. They argued that an interest in voting was not generally felt concerning poor law elections and that voting would be reduced if personal attendance was required. This, they stated, especially applied to female voters who made up a considerable portion of the electorate in the two Dublin unions.

'never been heard of' in Dublin; but as the man mainly responsible for organising the Conservative vote, his evidence may be treated with some caution: Qs. 6221, 6288.

81 Q. 6362.

82 Q. 6402.

83 Q. 5899. James Daly gave some examples of intimidation by landlords: Qs. 5951, 5961.

84 Henry Robinson's subsequent claim that 'it was proved clearly before the Committee that sat in 1878, that intimidation and undue influence existed to a very great extent' is not borne out by the evidence to that Committee: Report from the Select Committee of the House of Lords on the Poor Law Guardians (Ireland) Bill…, 1884–5 (297) x, 364. Evidence of Sir Henry Robinson, Q. 34.

85 Bills were proposed annually from 1874 to 1880 and continued into the 1890s.

The officials stated that they were not aware of cases in Dublin of corruption or intimidation; that the expense involved in elections would be much increased by the introduction of the ballot; and that personation would be difficult to control. The Board accepted these recommendations[86] and subsequently argued against the introduction of ballot elections for poor law guardians although accepting that it would reduce the type of abuse frequently complained of.[87] The Select Committee on poor law guardians in 1878 recommended against the introduction of the ballot and, although further Bills were introduced by the Irish Parliamentary Party throughout the 1880s, no change was made in this regard until the 1898 local government reforms.[88]

As has been seen in chapter 5, the late 1870s and 1880s saw a great increase in the level of political contention at poor law elections and the take-over of the boards by Nationalists. By 1885, the evidence to a House of Lords Select Committee was that elections had become 'very numerous'.[89] In 1884, there had been contests in 17 per cent of divisions and wards – roughly double the level of the mid 1870s.[90] Henry Robinson stated that 'political and religious reasons' were a major influence on the voters and that 'intimidation and undue influence [existed] to a very great extent'.[91]

86 It will be recalled that while the report related to Dublin, the main concerns about this type of voting abuse, in fact, related to more rural areas.

87 See NAI CSORP/1878/8595. It is interesting to note that T.H. Burke, the under-secretary, did not agree with the Local Government Board's position and favoured voting by ballot: Ibid., Burke to chief secretary Hicks-Beach, 2 May 1877.

88 Report of the Select Committee on Poor Law Guardians…, HC 1878 (297), xvii, 1.

89 Report from the Select Committee of the House of Lords on the Poor Law Guardians (Ireland) Bill. Evidence of Sir Henry Robinson, Q. 120.

90 Ibid., Q. 121.

91 Ibid., Qs. 34 and 120. Garrett C. Tyrrell, ex-officio guardian of Edenderry union, stated that elections had been fought on political grounds 'within the last three or four years': Q. 982. Henry Smyth, ex-officio (though tenant) guardian in Roscommon union, stated that there was 'a good deal of intimidation at present on the popular side', citing an example of a threatened boycott against electors who voted for a 'land grabber': Qs. 1195 et seq. Henry Ringwood, deputy vice-chair in Gorey said that elections were seen as 'a political matter': Q. 1543. Patrick Meehan, publican, land

Robinson stated that of the 557 elections in 1884, no less than 109 guardians were objected to, of whom twenty-one were unseated on enquiry. Again, however, the Board appears to have confined its investigation to the formalities (such as the nomination procedure) and not to allegations of intimidation. The evidence of those involved in local poor law activities suggests an increase in the degree of competition and, consequently, in intimidation and undue influence. Richard Bagwell, ex-officio guardian in Clonmel and Clogheen, stated that there had been intimidation 'in many ways and from many quarters', acknowledging that the Irish gentry had been 'a little bit' oppressive itself on occasion.[92] There were reports of armed groups threatening to shoot voters or their families;[93] landlords withdrawing turbary rights,[94] threatening to dismiss workers and threatening immediate collection of the 'hanging gale'; and of priests using undue influence on their flocks.[95]

---

leaguer and Nationalist chair of Mountmellick, also cited landlord intimidation, including threatened dismissal from employment and threatened eviction: Q. 2126 et seq. Colonel Carden, however, the former landlord chair of that union, denied that any dismissal had taken place (though not the threat) and alleged, in turn, that undue influence by priests occurred in the area: Q. 2538. However, Ebenezer Molloy, clerk of Naas union (and president of the Union Officers' Association) denied that there was any intimidation in Naas. On Meehan and Carden: see J.W.H. Carter, *The Land War and its Leaders in Queen's County, 1879–82*, Leinster Express Newspapers, Portlaoise, 1994.

92 Ibid., Qs. 939 et seq.

93 Ibid., Q. 941.

94 Harry McCann, Nationalist deputy vice-chair of Longford union accepted that a 'great deal of influence' was used 'on every side': Q. 1794 et seq. McCann cited 'very serious cases of undue influence on the part of landlords' including the deprivation of turbary (i.e. the permissive right to cut turf on a particular area of bog) where tenants voted against the wishes of the landlord. This case (or a similar case) was also raised in Parliament: Hansard, 24 May 1883 vol 279 col 771; 18 February 1884 vol 284 cc1182–3.

95 See, for example, NAI CSORP/1885/8784 where Rev. James Connolly of Edenderry advised his flock to vote for the Nationalist candidate in the poor law elections and not the Orange and freemason candidate. A placard was subsequently published on those who had voted or declined to do so.

Through the politicisation of the poor law elections – as discussed above – the boards helped to create the sense that local government bodies *should* be elected and to teach local activists and voters the practices involved in electoral politics. This would have been particularly important in the early 1880s given the extension of the Parliamentary franchise in 1885 which led to a rise in the Irish electorate from 224,000 to 738,000 (including many small farmers and agricultural labourers). Of course, it was not only the voters who 'learned' politics but also the politicians. Feingold has made the general point that the poor law boards formed a training ground for local politicians long before the 1898 Local Government Act. However, one can also see the role which the boards provided in providing the personnel which made up the post-1899 county councils. Comparing the listings of the 1898 officers of the boards of guardians with the members of the thirty-two county councils first elected in 1899, the officers made up, on average, 11 per cent of the council membership and board officers became the chairs of no less than ten counties.[96] This greatly understates the input of board members as it looks only at board officers in 1898, thus excluding the much more numerous non-officer guardians and those who had been officers and guardians in earlier years.[97] It also looks only at involvement in the county councils and does not take account of participation in urban and rural district councils.[98]

96 These are listed in Thom's directory. In Cork, former board officers made up almost one-quarter of the first Cork county council (including the chair).

97 It is also possible that, in a small number of cases, persons who had served on a board located mainly in one county went on to serve on a council in a neighbouring county.

98 From 1899, the boards of guardians and rural district councils had the same membership (although they normally had different officers). The chairs of the RDCs were ex-officio members of the county council.

Conclusion

In addition to their role in the administration of the poor law, boards of guardian played an important role in the politicisation of Irish society by assisting in the creation of the concept of democratically elected local government and, in conjunction with national elections, providing a training ground for local activists and electors in the mechanisms of electoral politics. Their symbolic importance as a forum of local democracy can, for example, be seen from the efforts (discussed in chapter 8) of boards to grant the use of the boardrooms to the United Irish League.

One of the issues which has been a subject of considerable debate in the French literature is the thesis of 'top-down' politicisation: *la descente de la politique vers la masse*, in Agulhon's famous term.[99] Agulhon argued that the politicisation of the countryside came about through the diffusion of more modern political ideas and practices.[100] The Irish experience throws some interesting light on this debate. First, one must make the point that the 'rules of the game' were imposed on Irish communities by the Imperial Parliament. The poor law unions and their boards reflected English ideas and, albeit recently established, practices. As has been seen the intention of the establishment of (at least partially) elective bodies was to give it a 'popular character' and to make the ratepayers responsible for administration. To this extent, the intentions of Nicholls and the other originators of the Irish poor law system were achieved – if not quite in the manner which they envisaged. However, to what extent was the vibrant politicisation of the Irish boards driven centrally by ideas coming from Dublin or Belfast and to what extent was it developed autonomously at a local level? No doubt, the rapid development of Ireland in the second half of the nineteenth century – including growth in literacy, the growth of the provincial

99 M. Agulhon, *La Republique au Village*, Plon, Paris, 1979.

100 See also Weber, *Peasants into Frenchmen*, for a slightly different approach but one which also sees politicisation as a centre-led phenomenon.

press,[101] and the extension of the railway network – all meant that local people were more aware, and more rapidly aware, of ideas and practices developed centrally. However, when one looks at the detailed politicisation of the local boards – despite the occasional call, perhaps overstated in the literature, from a leading figure for local action on a particular point – when one examines the archives there is very little indication that local action was centrally led or controlled in any specific manner and every indication that local leaders were acting largely on their own initiative in the areas which they saw to be important.[102] So one sees a combination both of an externally-imposed electoral system, ideas and practices diffused from the centre and the prioritisation and implementation of particular ideas and practices seen to be important at the local level.

The findings concerning the importance of farmers and traders on the boards are relevant to the debate between Clark and Feingold as to the relative importance of these classes in the development of Irish Nationalism. Clark argued that town traders (the 'shopkeeper-publican-politician') 'occupied a central position in the network of common interests which the land agitation represented and provide a invaluable link which enabled these interests to be united in a national and associational structure'.[103] Feingold, however, suggested that this thesis required some modification and was, in part, driven by Clark's focus on the west of Ireland where – Feingold accepted – traders did play a leading role in the absence of a strong large farmer class.[104] However, he suggests that in Muster and Leinster where cattle graziers were numerically strong, they formed the leading social class. Of course, the findings as to 1901–11 do not speak directly to what happened in the 1880s. However, the data do show that by 1901–11, traders formed on

101 M.-L. Legg, *Newspapers and Nationalism: the Irish Provincial Press, 1850–1892*, Four Courts, Dublin, 1998.

102 See, for example the surviving minute books of the Timahoe and Mothel braches of the United Irish League which show that they (apparently largely at their own initiative) nominated candidates for the local, poor law elections and, to a greater or lesser extent, took up poor law issues: NL MSs. 33,561 and 34,909.

103 Clark, *Social Origins of the Irish Land War*, 356–7.

104 Feingold, *Tenantry*, 225–6.

average about one-third of board officerships in many areas and up to 50 per cent of board membership in Dublin. Only in Clare does the number fall to (a still sizeable) 20 per cent of officers.[105] Outside urban areas, farmers form a (numerically more important) block constituting from about half to over two-thirds of identified officers in all rural areas.

Kennedy argues that traders were strongly represented both numerically and in terms of their influence in organised political activity and that, in contrast, 'political involvement by the bulk of farmers in formal structures was weak'.[106] He also shows that, at least in some areas of agricultural politics, farmers and traders had contradictory interests and that, perhaps surprisingly, traders appeared to be more influential than farmers. Jackson suggest that in Unionist mid-Armagh key interest were (i) farmers, (2) great landed magnets and (3) wealthy commercial and professional classes such as 'linen barons'. He argues that 'little effort was expended either on recruiting or satisfying other elements of the protestant electorate' including small traders.[107] However, his study does not discuss local government in any detail. Given the importance of traders in Antrim and Down boards, this suggests that the lack of emphasis on local government may have obscured the importance of this class.

Echoing Feingold's findings for the 1880s, one can say that in the earlier twentieth century – at least in rural Ireland – the two key classes were large farmers and town traders. However, in the larger urban areas, traders formed the clearly dominant social class in local government. These findings are similar to those of Kennedy who found that 27 per cent of the chairs

105 Whether this represents an indication of a lower involvement in Munster or is simply an artefact of the data cannot be determined. Given the small numbers involved and levels of non-identification it would be unwise to put too much weight on such variations without further research.

106 L. Kennedy, 'Farmers, Traders and Agricultural Politics in Pre-Independence Ireland', in L. Kennedy, *Colonialism, Religion and Nationalism in Ireland*, IIS, Belfast, 1996, 93.

107 A. Jackson, 'Unionist politics and Protestant Society in Edwardian Ireland', *Historical Journal*, 33, 4 (1990), 839–66, at 851.

and vice-chairs of county councils in 1905 were traders.[108] The current data indicate that farmers were, in fact, strongly represented on boards of guardians. Traders were also strongly represented – particularly in urban areas – but while traders were clearly numerically over-represented they could not (outside the larger cities) hope to control boards without the support of considerable numbers of farmer guardians. In any case, unlike the area of agricultural politics, it is not obvious that these two social groups had considerably different views on key issues of poor law policy. Therefore, the findings of this study tend to refine the work of Feingold, Clark and Kennedy in agreeing that large farmers and town traders were obviously the dominant groups in rural society but suggesting that the question of the relative importance of both classes may miss the points that (i) it was, in general, necessary for the two groups to work together as both frequently shared common interests and neither could achieve long-term political hegemony on its own, and (ii) the influence and interests of the two groups varied both over time and space and in relation to the policy issues involved.

108 L. Kennedy, 'Farmers', 93. Unfortunately, he does not give the comparable figure for farmers.

CHAPTER 10

The End of the Poor Law, 1907–1914

This chapter looks at the poor law in the period to the outbreak of war in 1914. Although the poor law was not abolished (at least in name) in southern Ireland until 1922 and in Northern Ireland until after the Second World War, this is the period in which decisions to introduce old age pensions and unemployment and national health insurance really marked the end of the poor law as the main system of relief, although the poor law and its successors continued (and continue) to play an important role in Irish social policy.

Key poor relief trends

The percentage of the population on poor relief fell over the period. The fall was greater in outdoor relief (36 per cent) than it was for indoor relief (20 per cent), and with outdoor relief the main fall came after 1911.[1] This fall was largely as a result of the introduction of the old age pension with the dropping of the poor relief disqualification in January 1911 leading to the more rapid fall in relief levels. Reflecting the fall in the numbers on relief the total expenditure also fell but by only 8 per cent in the period between 1909 and 1913. The fact that expenditure fell more slowly than the fall in the number of claimants was, at least in part, due the boards (i) *having to* spend more per head (due to rising prices and/or the fact that claimants remaining in the system were the most costly) and/or (ii) *choosing to* spend more – with average per capita expenditure (on indoor relief) rising from 3*s.* 11¼*d.* in 1909 to 4*s.* 3¾*d* by 1913.

1 Annual Reports of the Local Government Board, 1908–14.

Policy issues

The poor law was not a major policy issue in the period. The main developments in this area were elsewhere with the introduction of the old age pension and national insurance legislation. There was continued concern about the rise in the numbers of tramps and vagrants.[2] A number of, mainly northern, unions had adopted strict policies to discourage tramps from entering the workhouse such as giving them cold baths and/or requiring them to break stones.[3] Witnesses to the Viceregal Commission generally favoured rather draconian measures including more police supervision of tramps, compulsory work in workhouses, and placing tramps in labour colonies.[4] The members of the Royal Commission in their tour of Irish workhouses commented very negatively on the accommodation and sanitation provided for vagrants. The members referred to 'primitive sanitary accommodation' and 'stench', while accommodation was variously described as 'dark and dirty', 'black with age and filth', 'filthy' and 'very dirty'.[5]

Conversely there was a more positive attitude to the treatment of children and older people and ongoing concern about boarding out of

2 For example, the Annual Report of the Local Government Board for Ireland for… 1909…, HC 1909 [Cd. 4810] xxx, 1 refers to a rise in the number to an average of 1,000 per day.

3 Minutes of evidence taken before the Vice-Regal Commission on Poor Law Reform in Ireland. Volume III. Minutes of evidence and index, 1906 [Cd. 3204] lii, 1, qs. 7103 (Clones), 8632 (Cavan), 9102 (Lurgan), 12405 (Downpatrick) and 21912 (Borrisokane). Ballymoney also adopted a policy of giving cold baths which was condemned by the Local Government Board as 'cruel and illegal': see the *Irish Weekly Independent*, 5 September 1908 which has a large cartoon criticising the Local Government Board for this view.

4 Minutes of evidence taken before the Vice-Regal Commission on Poor Law Reform in Ireland. Volume III. Minutes of evidence and index, 1906 [Cd. 3204] lii, 1 at 1007.

5 Royal Commission on the Poor Laws and Relief of Distress. Appendix volume XXVIII. Reports of visits to Poor Law and charitable institutions and to meetings of local authorities in the United Kingdom, 1910 [Cd. 4974] liv, 99.

children, or rather the fact that relatively few children were boarded out.[6] The Local Government Board carried out an investigation of the extent to which children were boarded out and reported that of the 7,338 children in workhouses (including 719 in special schools) only 1,566 were legally eligible to be boarded out, but of these 919 were considered unsuitable due to reasons such as age, illness, or physical or mental defects.[7] The reasons given by boards for not boarding out included the difficulty in getting suitable foster parents, although in seven unions the guardians considered that children were better in the workhouse while in a further eight the boarding out system had not been adopted (with no reason given). The Local Government Board suggested that guardians be given the power to board out all children of whom they could legally assume control, as in England.[8]

In general the newspapers give more space to 'colour' stories – such as a 'poetical petition' in Nenagh workhouse[9] and matchmaking in a workhouse[10] – than to substantive policy issues. There were indeed continuing 'political' motions by boards about issues such as Home Rule[11] but by this time the role of the boards as an expression of local opinion had been largely taken over by the county and district councils.

6 The Local Government Board report for 1912 notes a meeting with the Irish Workhouse Association which called for boards to be encouraged to use their powers in this regard: Annual Report of the Local Government Board for Ireland, for the year ended 31st March, 1912, 1912–13 [Cd. 6339] xxxvii, 1, at xvii.

7 Annual Report of the Local Government Board for Ireland, for the year ended 31st March, 1913, 1913 [Cd. 6978] xxxii, 457, at xii et seq.

8 The 1914 report noted that a bill had been introduced in the House of Lords to broaden boards' powers (Annual Report of the Local Government Board for Ireland, for the year ended 31st March, 1914, 1914 [Cd. 7561] xxxix, 595 at xx).

9 *Weekly Freeman's Journal*, 20 June 1908.

10 *Irish Weekly Independent*, 8 February 1908.

11 See, for example, *Weekly Freeman's Journal*, 11 April 1908 (Macroom, Delvin and Killarney).

Relationship between poor law, mental asylums and industrial schools

One of the tendencies of the late nineteenth century was the development of alternative forms of institutional support for specific groups such as the mental asylums and industrial schools. In numerical terms the district mental asylums were the largest alternative provider of institutional care.[12] A public network of lunatic asylums pre-dates the poor law – dating back to 1817. There was a dramatic growth in the number of people in public mental asylums over the period, from about 4,500 in 1861 to over 20,000 by 1911.[13] Thus, by the end of the period, the mental asylums had about half as many people as the total number on indoor relief in poor law workhouses.

Workhouses themselves always included a certain number of 'lunatics' and 'idiots' and this number was rather stable over time. There is little information as to who constituted this group of people although it would appear that they were probably the more 'incurable' and 'harmless' lunatics.[14] Unsurprisingly a considerable number of issues arose as to the relationship between poor law and the asylums, particularly in the later 1800s when the number in asylums increased considerably – a tendency by no means confined to Ireland. There is considerable correspondence in the archives on various issues concerning the asylums, their relationship with workhouses and, in particular, funding issues.[15] There has been only limited study of the reasons behind the considerable rise in the number of people in Irish district asylums in the late 1800s.[16] This is relevant for the present

12 See generally J. Robins, *Fools and Mad: a History of the Insane in Ireland*, IPA, Dublin, 1986; M. Finnane, *Insanity and the Insane in Post-Famine Ireland*, Croom Helm, London, 1981.

13 See generally Finnane, *Insanity and the Insane in Post-Famine Ireland.*

14 See the Viceregal Commission on the Poor Law, *Report*, chapter IX.

15 As seen in chapter 8, Gerald Balfour proposed legislation addressing some of these issues in 1896 although this was not adopted.

16 An 1894 report of the inspectors of lunacy commented on the rise in the number of lunatics and idiots. They suggested that this rise was mainly due to accumulation

study in so far as the asylums may have been used as a functional alternative to the workhouse. Two (interrelated) issues are involved. Firstly, to what extent were persons who might have been admitted to workhouses admitted instead to asylums in the later nineteenth century? Secondly, to what extent were persons transferred from one system to the other?

On the first point, the limited studies indicate that residents of the asylums were considerably younger than those of workhouses and admissions to the former were highest in the 30–9 age range.[17] Malcolm's study of admissions to four Irish asylums is particularly relevant.[18] She suggests that the typical Irish asylum inmate at the turn of the century was fairly representative of the general socio-economic make up of the population. This, she suggests, indicates that the inmates were not marginalised either socially or economically, contrary to Scull's argument that those committed to public asylums in England were 'the awkward and unwanted, the useless and potentially troublesome'.[19] However, given that most persons were committed by their families, it is not clear that the fact that an individual came from a typical labouring or farming background means that that individual was not personally marginalised (or perceived to be so marginalised by other family members).[20] In fact, a number of the case studies which Malcolm subsequently quotes would indeed provide support for Scull's thesis and,

---

rather than a real increase but accepted that there had been some increase in insanity in particular districts which they attributed to heredity, consanguineous marriages, poor dietary and a moderate use of nervous stimulants, and agricultural depression and dislocation: Special Report from Inspectors of Lunatics to Chief Secretary on alleged Increasing Prevalence of Insanity in Ireland, 1894 [C. 7331] xliii, 647. See also Supplement to the Fifty-fourth Report of the Inspectors of Lunatics… Ireland. Being a Special Report on the Alleged Increase of Insanity. 1906 [Cd. 3126] xxxix, 1.

17 Finnane, *Insanity and the Insane*, at 130–1.

18 E. Malcolm, 'The Asylum, Family and Emigration', in E. Malcolm and G. Jones (eds), *Medicine, Disease and the State in Ireland*, Cork University Press, Cork, 1999.

19 A. Scull, *The Most Solitary of Afflictions: Madness and Society in Britain, 1700–1900*, Oxford University Press, Oxford, 1993.

20 See, on the general issue of families and mental illness R.D. Laing and A. Esterson, *Sanity, Madness and the Family*, Penguin, Harmondsworth, 1973. See also M. Finnane 'Asylums, Families and the State', *History Workshop Journal*, xx, (1985), 134–47.

as Malcolm notes, 'family or neighbourhood disputes over livestock, land and money figure in many committal documents'.[21] Malcolm goes on to agree with Finnane's conclusion that many Irish families used the asylum to discipline unruly members, a purpose for which, one might note, the workhouses would not serve in most cases.[22]

On the second point, studies of the asylums indicate that both institutions tried to shift costs to the other. Although legislation (1875) allowed asylums to contract with workhouses for the provision of services for harmless lunatics, Finnane suggests that this was little used and that some asylums instead simply discharged patients who then had to be admitted to workhouses at no cost to the asylum. Conversely, both Finnane and Robins suggest that workhouses got rid of troublesome patients by having them declared dangerous lunatics which meant that they had to be admitted to the local asylum.[23] Robins suggests that the level of transfer of patients to asylums rose significantly after the local authorities took over control of the asylums following the Local Government Act in 1898. The reason for this appears to be that local authorities became responsible for both the poor law and asylums under the Act and exchequer funding towards asylums was more favourable. The Local Government Board also encouraged unions to transfer insane persons to asylums arguing that they could provide more suitable treatment.[24]

On the basis of current knowledge, one can say that to a certain extent the workhouses and asylums were functionally equivalent in relation to at least some groups of poor persons in Ireland.[25] It would appear that

21 Malcolm, 'The Asylum, Family and Emigration', at 183.

22 At 186.

23 Finnane, *Insanity and the Insane*, at 97 and 115; Robins, *Fools and Mad*, at 145.

24 Robins, *Fools and Mad*, at 167–8. Robins points out that 381 inmates were transferred from workhouses to asylums in 1891, rising to over 1,000 by 1904. For the approach of the Board see Thirty-first Annual Report of the Local Government Board for Ireland, for the year ending 31st March, 1903, 1904 [Cd. 2012] xxvii, 1 at vii–viii.

25 The Viceregal Commission, op. cit. (1906) devoted a chapter to lunatics and idiots (chapter IX). The focus is on what should be done with such persons in workhouses in Ireland and whether an extension of auxiliary lunatic asylums was desirable. The Commission found that the condition of lunatics in workhouses was most

some persons could find themselves either in a workhouse or in the district asylums or move from one to the other. It seems likely that many persons admitted to asylums were somewhat better-off than workhouse admissions, i.e. they were admitted for reasons other than destitution. In addition, the indications that persons were often admitted to asylums for 'disciplinary' reasons would also suggest that there were distinctions between asylum and workhouse admissions. Up to the late 1890s, there is nothing to indicate that the rise in the numbers in asylums was solely or a largely due to any 'transfer' of persons from the workhouses. While the number of persons transferred to asylums may have increased somewhat thereafter, the total number of 'lunatics and idiots' in workhouses declined only from 4,125 in 1897 to 2,641 by 1911.[26] Therefore, changes in this area did not have a major impact on the overall numbers on relief.

---

unsatisfactory. Although there was no legal to power to detain lunatics, they were in practice confined. The Commission recommended that 'harmless and chronic' lunatics should be detained instead in auxiliary asylums. It envisaged that a number of workhouses would be converted into auxiliary asylums but it is somewhat unclear from the recommendations how conditions were to be improved – especially given that the Commission expressed its concern about unnecessary improvements in an existing auxiliary asylum (including 'lighting by electricity').

26 The manner in which the Local Government Board provides data changed over the period. The earlier data include 'epileptic lunatics'. In 1911, there were a further 421 epileptics 'not mentally affected'. It may well be that such persons were included in the total of lunatics and idiots in 1897, which would reduce the apparent fall in numbers. See Annual Report of the Local Government Board for Ireland, 1898 [C. 8958] xli, 1 at 18; Annual Report of the Local Government Board for Ireland for… 1912, 1912–13 [Cd. 6339], xxxvii, 1 at xix. In 1897 almost a third of the total number of lunatics in workhouses was in only six unions, with over 10 per cent in Belfast union alone.

Industrial schools

Industrial schools were established in 1868 with the extension of English legislation to Ireland.[27] There was a significant growth in the number of children in these schools from 1,500 in 1871 to about 8,000 by 1911.[28] By the late nineteenth century, there were more children in the industrial schools than in the workhouses.[29] In addition there were significant differences in approach. First, the industrial schools were 'privately' run and managed – normally by religious orders – although being funded and supervised by the state. Children were the only inmates – unlike the workhouses – and were entirely separated from their parents.[30] Unlike the workhouses, children were committed to the schools and could not leave of their own volition. Barnes suggests that the treatment in industrial schools was better than in workhouses but this is hard to verify. Education in industrial schools does seem to have achieved better results but Barnes' book was published before the widespread controversy about ill-treatment of children (sexual and otherwise) in industrial schools in twentieth-century Ireland and it is not known to what extent this existed in nineteenth-century institutions.

These trends suggest two things: first, that the general trend of late nineteenth-century social policy towards specialisation and segregation had advanced in an Irish context, albeit in a somewhat unplanned manner, with the development of separate services for children and lunatics and the workhouses becoming hospitals and old folks homes, although not exclusively so. Second, the rise in both the numbers in lunatic asylums and in the industrial schools suggests a change in attitudes in Irish society and the development of a more 'orderly' society less tolerant of 'eccentrics', 'unruly' family members, child beggars and other 'undesirable' groups. This analysis is also consistent with the apparent growth of concern around the turn of the century about vagrants, although opposition to this group can be seen throughout the nineteenth century.

27 J. Barnes, *Irish Industrial Schools 1868–1908: Origins and Development*, Irish Academic Press, Dublin, 1989.

28 There were also a further number of children in the more penal 'reform schools' but the numbers involved here were always significantly smaller.

29 Barnes, *Irish Industrial Schools*.

30 See Barnes, *Irish Industrial Schools*, at 88–9.

Poor law reform

As discussed above, the publication of the recommendations of the Viceregal Commission on poor law reform received a broad public welcome.[31] However, as the Royal Commission on the poor law had been established by this time, the Liberal government was able to await the findings of that report before taking action. The tone of chief secretary Augustine Birrell's (1907–16) comments suggests that he found the waiting more congenial than the thought of doing anything in the area of poor law. H.A. Robinson, vice-president of the Local Government Board, despite having been a driving figure behind the establishment of the Viceregal Commission was now a member of the Royal Commission[32] and (for this or other reasons) had become less enthusiastic about the Viceregal Commission's report. Despite this lack of interest, it does appear that heads of a Bill were prepared but never introduced (see below).

The Royal Commission itself reported in 1909.[33] In brief, the majority of the Commission favoured a reform of the existing poor law, the involvement of voluntary aid committees, and the establishment of a national system of labour exchanges while the minority (led by Beatrice Webb) favoured breaking up the poor law into discrete services to support children, the sick, the mentally defective, and the aged and infirm. The Irish members of the Commission (Robinson and Denis Kelly, Roman Catholic bishop of Ross),[34] who formed part of the majority, drafted a short report on Ireland which was agreed by the majority. This report largely applied

31 Although it was far from clear that all those welcoming it had a very clear idea what the recommendations were.

32 For reasons which are unclear (Robinson cited pressure of work) he did not act himself on the Viceregal Commission but nominated W.L. Micks.

33 Report of the Royal Commission on the Poor Laws and Relief of Distress, 1909 [Cd. 4499] xxxvii, 1. See A.W. Vincent, 'The Poor Law Reports of 1909 and the Social Theory of the Charity Organisation Society', in D. Gladstone (ed.), *Before Beveridge: Welfare before the Welfare State*, Institute of Economic Affairs, London, 1999, 64–85.

34 The latter had replaced the O'Connor Don on his death.

the recommendations of the main report to the Irish situation.[35] It recommended, in particular, that the guardians (of whom there were 8,200 or an average of fifty-one per board) be abolished and replaced by public assistance authorities (appointed as committees of local authorities); that appointed public assistance committees take over the day-to-day administration of relief; that general workhouses also be abolished and replaced with classification *by* institution (rather than within institutions); and that labour colonies be established for the able-bodied.[36] Given the extent of agricultural self-employment in Ireland, the report found that the system of labour exchanges proposed for England and Wales did not seem adapted to Irish conditions. It also recommended that outdoor relief be renamed as home assistance but shared the Viceregal Commission's reservations and recommended that such assistance only be granted after thorough enquiry. The minority in a brief report praised the approach of the Viceregal Commission and concurred with the main principles of that report. In fact, both majority and minority claimed that their approach was in line with the principles of the earlier Commission;[37] both accused each other of removing relief from democratic control;[38] and both criticised each other's lack of knowledge of Irish conditions and disregard for Irish opinion. Of course, by the time the Royal Commission reported in 1909 old age pensions were in operation and the poor law had been partially reformed by default.[39]

35 Report on Ireland, 1909 [Cd. 4630] xxxviiii, 1. Although the Report on Ireland comments only briefly and somewhat tentatively on the role of voluntary aid in Ireland: ibid, at 43.

36 Report on Ireland, at 81 et seq.

37 Majority at, for example, 48; Minority at 84. While the Minority could point to the Viceregal Commission's advocacy of economic development and its recommendation that hospital services be removed from the poor law, the latter's approach to poor relief was surely more in line with reform based on classification and segregation as recommended by the Majority report.

38 Minority at 84; Majority in a comment by the bishop of Ross and Sir H.A. Robinson at 87.

39 See the interesting exchange of views on the Royal Commission in CAB/37/98/40 (2 March 1909, Asquith) 99/59 (9 June 1909, author unspecified but critical of Asquith and arguing for Minority report proposals).

There were frequent parliamentary questions about the government's response to the recommendations of the Commissions which received somewhat obscure and uninformative responses.[40] Unionist members put down a private members Bill on the topic in 1908 but John Redmond MP (leader of the Irish Parliamentary Party), while expressing considerable sympathy with the intention, found himself unable to vote in favour of the Bill, citing (with some justification) flaws in its construction.[41] The Irish Parliamentary Party abstained, allowing the government to vote the Bill down. Despite the fact that the matter was regularly raised by Irish parliamentarians no government measure appeared and in 1911 the Chancellor of the Exchequer, Lloyd George, stated that the introduction of national insurance had changed the context of poor law reform (although not ruling out the continued need for reform).[42] No action had been taken to implement the reports of either Commission by 1914 and the leading members of the Liberal party were obviously concerned with broader social policy issues, such as the old age pensions, and indeed broader issues generally while, as noted above, there is little sense that the key figures in Ireland (Birrell and Robinson) pushed the issue in any way.[43]

40 See, for example, Hansard, 183, 724, 4 February 1908 (Birrell intends to introduce poor law legislation but not this session); 188, 701, 11 May 1908 (Birrell hopes to introduce legislation next year); 1, 431, 22 February 1909 (Asquith now says that the whole question of poor law reform must await the publication of the Royal Commission's report); 1. 580, 23 February 09 (refers to previous answer); 1 1272, 2 March 1909 (ditto.); 3 612, 1 April 1909 (ditto), 4. 1815, 12 May 1909 (Birrell says preparations being made with a view to legislation but not this session); 10, 537, 1 September 1909 (Birrell says not possible to give a date for reforms); 12, 1980, 4 November 1909 (Irish Attorney General Cherry says heads of a bill prepared but could not say it would be introduced this session); 14, 209. 23 February 1910, (Bill along the lines of the Royal Commission and Viceregal reports under consideration); 16, 2299, 21 April 1910 (refers to previous answer.); 17, 1430, 15 June 1901 (refers to previous answer); 18, 951, 29 June 1910 (Birrell hopes to have legislation some time next year); but by 21. 425, 9 February 1911 (no chance of legislation this session); 25, 1040, 9 May 1911 (refers to previous answer); 30, 714, 31 October 1911 (the heads of a bill are prepared but it is not possible to make any statement as to the prospects of publication).

41 Hansard, 187, 818 et seq, 3 April 1908.

42 Hansard, 25, 431, 3 May 1911.

43 The Irish under-secretary Sir James Dougherty (1908–14) does not appear to have had any involvement with poor law issues.

Old age pensions

The introduction of old age pensions has been discussed extensively in the historiography.[44] However, there has been rather little discussion about Ireland's role in the development of the proposals. This would appear to be, in major part, because it didn't have any. This, in itself, is surprising. As soon as the legislation was adopted, the Irish newspapers showed considerable interest in it and there was extensive discussion about different aspects of its implementation and a rush for application forms when they appeared. When the Act was introduced, the higher levels of poverty in Ireland, the Irish population age structure,[45] combined with the absence of official records of age meant that Ireland had a much higher claim rate for old age pension than other parts of the United Kingdom.[46] This appears to have come as something of a surprise to British policy makers, although H.A. Robinson had predicted precisely these issues in a memo to the then chief secretary Gerald Balfour a decade earlier.[47] Of course that British policy-makers should be profoundly ignorant of Irish conditions is not

44 See generally P. Thane, *Old Age in English History*, Oxford University Press, Oxford, 2000; Id., 'Non contributory versus insurance pensions, 1878–1908' in P. Thane ed. *Origins of British social policy*, Croom Helm, London, 1978; B.B. Gilbert, *The Evolution of National Insurance in Great Britain*, Michael Joseph, London, 1966; J. Macnicol, *The Politics of Retirement in Britain, 1878–1948*, Cambridge University Press, Cambridge, 1988; E.P. Hennock, *The Origin of the Welfare State in England And Germany, 1850–1914. Social Policies Compared*, Oxford University Press, Oxford, 2007.

45 Although Ireland had only 11 per cent of the United Kingdom population, it had an estimated 15 per cent of the population over seventy.

46 See T.W. Guinnane, 'The Poor Law and Pensions in Ireland', *Journal of Interdisciplinary History*, 24(2) (1993), 271–91 and C. Ó Gráda, '"The Greatest Blessing of All": The Old Age Pension in Ireland', *Past and Present*, 175 (2002), 124–61. By 1911 persons resident in Ireland received 22 per cent of all pensioners, and Guinnane states that about 69 per cent of potential Irish pensions (those over seventy) received the pension compared to 63 per cent in England.

47 Memorandum on old age pension scheme, 22 November 1899, NA, PRO 30/60/28.

in itself unusual.[48] However, given the impact that the pensions legislation did have and given that this could have been predicted by Robinson, a man of no more than usual insight, one might have expected that the implications of the pensions legislation for Ireland would have occurred to somebody.

As is well known, even leaving aside the rapid aging caused by the introduction of the pensions, Ireland had (what would now be known as) a higher old age ratio (ratio of older people: working population) due to the massive post-Famine emigration. In addition, the standard rate of pension meant that the pension was worth much more in Ireland.[49] Finally, the fact that Ireland was poorer meant that a higher percentage of older people would benefit from the pension. All of these – rather obvious – points meant that the pension was going to be a major boon to Ireland. In principle such an approach might be adopted (a) because British policy-makers wanted to adopt a 'United Kingdom standard' approach; (b) for some 'Irish' policy reason such as a Liberal variant on 'killing Home Rule with kindness' and/or building links with the Irish Parliamentary Party; or (c) more or less by default because policy makers gave insufficient attention to the issue or thought it was too much trouble to devise an alternative. There is no evidence in the historiography or in the cabinet papers for a United Kingdom standard approach.[50] Policy-makers rarely averred to anywhere except England[51] and there is little, if any, indication that most

48 It is interesting to read the various official commissions on 'social policy' questions in the late nineteenth and early twentieth centuries (e.g. the various pension commissions). Although not so confined in their terms of reference, they all focus (some exclusively) on conditions in England. Witnesses are mainly English and research is mainly carried out on English conditions. Ireland is very largely ignored, Scotland slightly less so (Wales apparently does not exist).

49 The average weekly wage for an Irish agricultural labourer in 1902 was 10*s*. 9*d*, compared to an average wage of 17*s*. 5*d*. in England.

50 See, for example, NA CAB/37/85/96, 88/44 and 89/81.

51 Interestingly, A.J. Balfour (who had been both secretary for Scotland and chief secretary for Ireland) proposed a regional approach in the late 1890s ('Pensions and Poor Law Reform' 15 November 1899, NA PRO/30/60/28, also CAB/37/51/87; and 12 December 1899 'Pensions and Deserving Poor', ibid, and CAB/37/51/95); and the

gave any thought to the impact in Ireland of the approach adopted, let alone intended it. A standard United Kingdom approach was not adopted in other policy areas, such as lunacy/mental health, at the time.

Nor is there any evidence that Irish policy reasons had any impact. Ó Gráda shares this assessment, stating that 'Ireland hardly featured in the pre-1908 policy debates about the pension.'[52] As just mentioned, on the United Kingdom side, there is no indication that policy makers gave any thought to Irish issues at all. More surprisingly, there is no indication in the archives examined, parliamentary debates or newspapers that Irish MPs gave any attention whatsoever to the pensions issue until the legislation was adopted.[53] It received a surprisingly lukewarm welcome.[54] Irish Parliamentary Party MPs generally voted with the Liberals on the passage of the Bill but there was little sign of enthusiastic support and most of the

---

Report of the Departmental Committee on Old Age Pensions (1898 [C. 8911] xlv, 465] provided separate costings for Ireland based, in part, on data provided by the Local Government Board (see NA PRO/30/60/23).

52 Ó Gráda, 'The Greatest Blessing', at 126.

53 John Redmond's extensive papers have now been catalogued and there is no reference at all in the listings to old age pensions (nor national health nor – with the exception of superannuation for officials – to any poor law matters). Nor do the John Dillon papers appear to contain any such material. The archives of key British figures at the time (insofar as these are catalogued) do not appear to contain any correspondence with Redmond or Dillon in the relevant time period which might refer to pensions issues. Of the 600 witnesses to the Viceregal Commission in 1906–7, only a small handful made any reference to old age pensions.

54 J.C. Flynn, Irish Parliamentary Party MP said in the House that the bill had been 'generally approved of' in Ireland citing a Trade Union Congress resolution in its support (though seeking a lower age limit): Hansard, 190, 750 et seq., 15 June 1908. However, in reporting Asquith's 1908 announcement, the *Freeman's Journal* welcomed it but suggested that an Irish government might better devote the resources involved to industrial development (17 June 1908) while the *Weekly Freeman's Journal* welcomed the proposals but would have wished for a 'bolder trial'; and argued that they needed 'vast improvement' (16 May 1908). The *Irish Weekly Independent* was similarly lukewarm, 20 June 1908. The council of the United Irish League (in effect the local organisation of the Irish Party) discussed the bill and generally welcomed it but gave no indication that they had been aware of – let alone had any input into – the proposals: *Freeman's Journal*, 14 May 1908.

key Irish Parliamentary Party figures had nothing at all to say about the Bill. It was only after its introduction that Joe Devlin (Irish Parliamentary Party MP for West Belfast) described it as 'one of the greatest proofs of humanitarian statesmanship' in the last fifty years.[55] Even then, John Redmond remained very unenthusiastic. In 1909 on the debate on Lloyd George's Budget, Redmond, while accepting that pensions were valued in Ireland, argued that

> To spend £2½ millions a year on old age pensions is an extravagance and an extravagance that would not have been indulged in by an Irish Parliament manned by Irishmen responsible to the country and knowing its conditions.[56]

This again supports the view that the Irish Nationalist politicians did not have a particularly positive view of 'social policy' issues. Interestingly, in the discussions of the financial aspects of Home Rule, it was agreed that the Imperial exchequer would meet the cost of old age pensions payable at the time of Home Rule but it appears that this was simply because the sum involved was of the right size rather than for any policy reasons to do with pensions. This decision was based on the recommendations of the Committee on Irish Finance.[57] The Committee argued that if the government had had to construct a scheme of pensions specifically for Ireland it would have devised a 'much less costly' one and doubted that an Irish Parliament would have followed the British example (referring to unspecified statements to this effect by leading Irish politicians presumably including Redmond). All of which leads to the conclusions that the 'United King-

55 Hansard, 4, 2052–4, 13 May 1909. Interestingly, a cartoon in the pro-Irish Parliamentary Party *Irish Weekly Independent* in August 1908 shows Redmond 'bringing home the work of the session' which includes the Irish Universities Bill and Evicted Tenants' legislation but *not* the Pensions Act (which had just received Royal Assent): 8 August 1908.

56 *Irish Independent*, 10 June 1909.

57 See NA CAB/37/108/132. The Committee attributed the pension's 'unchanged and unadapted' application to Ireland as being 'in consequence of the political connection' (p. 10 of the report).

dom' approach was adopted more by default than design and that an Irish Parliament would have been unlikely to adopt a similar approach.

The impact on the poor law[58]

The impact of the old age pension on poor relief has been examined in detail by Guinnane.[59] He found that the pension removed large numbers of older people from the poor law, allowed unions to reduce the poor rate,[60] and to increase support for persons below pension age. However, this did not affect any fundamental change in poor relief practices in the short term. He also found (drawing on a sample of manuscript census data for rural Ireland) that the pension appeared to have increased household co-residence, presumably on the basis that the pension both allowed older people to remain in the community and made them more attractive co-residents. Multiple families (using the Laslett classification)[61] containing an older person rose from about 2 per cent of the total households containing an older person in 1901 to 6 per cent in 1911.

Given the importance of the introduction of the old age pension, its impact on the Irish poor law has been re-examined. The research looked at the changes for all unions in total expenditure, the numbers on indoor and

58 The focus here is on the impact on the poor law. For a broader account of the introduction of OAP see Ó Gráda, 'The Greatest Blessing of All', op cit.

59 T.W. Guinnane, 'The Poor Law and Pensions', *Journal of Interdisciplinary History*, xxiv: 2 (1993), 271–91. See also Annual Report of the Local Government Board for Ireland..., 1912, 1912–13 [Cd. 6339] xxxvii, 1 at xvii which reports a fall of 15,700 in indoor relief and 2,200 in outdoor relief due to the introduction of OAP. It appears that these figures relate to the number of people who left the poor law as a result of OAP rather than the overall impact of the measure, i.e. taking account of the reduced inflows to poor relief because of the existence of OAP.

60 Particularly in poorer unions, Guinnane found that expenditure on outdoor relief per pauper was reduced but expenditure on indoor relief was increased.

61 P. Laslett and R. Wall, eds, *Household and Family in Past Time*, Cambridge University Press, Cambridge, 1971.

outdoor relief, costs per head and rates over the period from 1907, prior to the announcement of the old age pension, to 1911, when it came fully into effect with the abolition of the disqualification of those previously in receipt of poor relief. It also examined regional differences. In order to identify the specific impact of the pension, age-related data were also analysed.

As might be expected, there was a significant fall overall in both indoor and – to a greater extent – outdoor relief (per 100 population) by about 13 per cent and 37 per cent respectively.[62] The different impact as between indoor and outdoor relief has already been highlighted by Guinnane. Persons over seventy outside the workhouse could be expected to become entitled to the old age pension. However, persons in workhouses may have had nowhere to go or to be unable to leave the workhouse. There was some regional variation in these falls with the northern unions, despite paying much lower relief to begin with, managing to reduce their level of relief by about the average. The reasons for this appears to have been that the relatively small proportion of people on outdoor relief in the northern unions were more likely to have been old whereas the southern unions had a more mixed clientele. The peripheral unions saw even greater falls but, as will be seen below, this was balanced by a rise in the per capita cost of indoor relief. Urban unions saw less change with indoor relief falling by about 10 per cent and out relief by only 17 per cent.

The combination of falling numbers on relief and a rise in the per capita cost of indoor relief (of about 12 per cent on average) meant that overall expenditure fell by less than 5 per cent. The (already low spending) northern unions reduced their expenditure by the highest percentage (8 per cent), while peripheral unions (despite the sharp drop in numbers) saw only a marginal fall in expenditure. On average, urban unions saw expenditure fall by about 5 per cent, but this conceals a considerable variation. This led to a fall in rates in most unions. Again rates fell most in the northern unions – although only marginally ahead of the southern unions – while the peripheral unions saw only a minor fall.

So far, the overall change in poor relief patterns over the period of the introduction of the old age pension has been examined. The assumption has

62 Fuller details are reported in Cousins, 'Poor Relief in Ireland', 2010, chapter 10.

been that the pension has been responsible for much of the change. However, it is necessary to look more closely at age-related patterns to establish if this has been the case. Detailed age related data are available for 1906 as a result of the enquiries of the Royal Commission on the Poor Laws.[63] For 1911, one can draw on the 1911 census which provides details as to the age of persons in workhouses. This is only available at a county level but this does not greatly affect the ability to analyse regional changes (except that it is not possible to disaggregate results for the peripheral group of unions). It is also possible to isolate results for Belfast and Dublin (taking the two Dublin unions together). Similar data are not available for outdoor relief but examination of a number of sources indicates that, after 1911, few persons over seventy were granted outdoor relief.[64]

63 Royal Commission on the Poor Laws and Relief of Distress. Appendix volume XXXI. Statistics relating to Ireland, 1910 [Cd. 5244] liv, 763.

64 See the examination of the Banbridge and Newtownards outdoor relief applications discussed in chapter 2. In Newtownards there was only one claimant over seventy. In Banbridge there were eight such claimants mainly where the person was disqualified for pension due to absence from the United Kingdom (one was simply continued on relief until the pension was put into payment, one was in respect of attendance during illness only, and one involved a person who had been disqualified for pension due to a conviction for fraud relating to his claim for the same pension). The Ballinrobe outdoor relief register shows that while in 1908 and 1909, half of all applications for outdoor relief came from persons shown as aged seventy or over, this fell to 11–13 per cent in 1909 and 1910. The percentage rose to 23 per cent in 1911, but most were at or just over seventy, which may indicate that their claims for pension had not been accepted on age grounds. In subsequent years the percentage of claims by persons aged seventy or over fell to below 10 per cent. In Lismore (County Waterford) out of over 200 claims (including some repeat claims) in the period March 1911 to March 1914, only three were from persons over seventy (and one of these was refused because the claimant was already in receipt of old age pension): NAI BG111/EB1. There is, of course, a strong possibility that anybody shown as aged seventy in an outdoor relief register in 1911 was, chronologically speaking, somewhat younger.

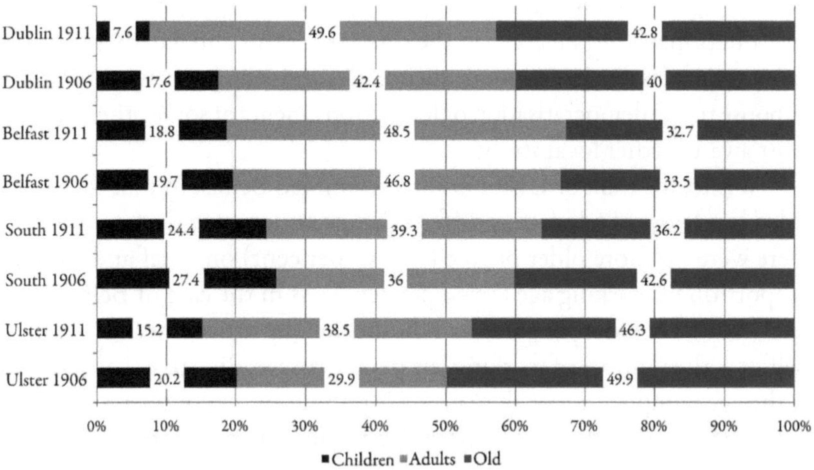

Figure 10.1 Age composition by region, 1906–1911
Source: Database of poor law statistics. Note that Ulster excludes Belfast and South excludes Dublin in Figure 10.5.

As can be seen, the age composition was both different by region and changed somewhat over the period.[65] Belfast stands out as having a higher percentage (almost 50 per cent) of the workhouse population of working age (fifteen or sixteen to sixty), while in 1906 only a third were old (over sixty), and this fell marginally by 1911. When it is recalled that Belfast had a relatively low proportion of the population on relief at all times, this indicates that it provided relatively little support to older people. The number of older people in the Belfast workhouse fell by 23 per cent between 1906 and 1911 while the number of (presumably younger) people on out relief rose by 70 per cent (1907–11). Thus Belfast used the resources available from the reduction in older people supported to increase support to the

65 Unfortunately the age data runs from 0–16 in the 1906 data and from 0–15 in 1911, so that some fall (about 6 per cent) in the proportion of children in the workhouses would be expected.

working age group on outdoor relief.[66] However, it seems unlikely that the introduction of the pension was the catalyst for this and whether this rise in out relief was due to economic difficulties and/or a (somewhat belated) response to the democratisation of local government (or some other reason) must await further local study.

While, the bulk of Ulster unions resembled Belfast in that they provided low levels of relief, they differed in age structure in that, on average, there were far more older people (46–50 per cent) on relief and a lower proportion of working age (30–9 per cent). As in the case of Belfast, the total number of older people in workhouses fell (by 18 per cent) but – unlike Belfast – the number of working age people rose leading to a sharper shift in the age composition of the 'rural' Ulster unions. In contrast to Belfast, the numbers on outdoor relief *fell* so that while Belfast appears to have used available resources to support more working age people on outdoor relief, the other Ulster unions combined a mixture of lower costs and increased numbers of working age people on *indoor* relief.

The Dublin unions had an unusually low proportion of younger people and this fell considerably in the period (perhaps due to the availability of other services).[67] The number of older people in Dublin workhouses fell by 20 per cent in the period but the slower decline in working age people and the rapid drop in children saw the proportion of older people rise from 42 per cent to half of all inmates. As has been seen, the Dublin unions had relatively high levels of people on relief so this meant that support to older people was high in Dublin. Finally, the southern unions (excluding Dublin) had a somewhat different age-composition again. In these unions children constituted about a quarter of the population.[68] The number of

66 There was also a significant fall in the number of working age people in Belfast workhouse so there appears to have been a general shift from indoor to out door relief in the union (although out relief remains very low in comparative terms).

67 The Annual Reports of the Local Government Board show some rise in the number of children boarded out in this period (although not sufficient to account for the significant fall in workhouse numbers).

68 The apparent fall in the period 1906–11 is probably due simply to the slightly different age groupings.

older people fell by 24 per cent, bringing their proportion of the population down to 36 per cent (from 43 per cent in 1906). The working age group fell only marginally, seeing their proportion rise somewhat from 36 per cent to 39 per cent.

In conclusion it can be seen that – as highlighted by historians such as Guinnane and Ó Gráda – the introduction of old age pensions did have a significant effect on the poor law and led, in particular, to sharp falls in the number of people of outdoor relief and to somewhat lesser falls in the numbers on indoor relief. However, given the scale of the new pension, it is perhaps surprising that the impact was not even greater. The regional differences in the provision of relief can again be seen and there is little indication that the introduction of the pension narrowed these differences – showing again the extent to which the implementation of poor relief was a matter of local discretion. No clear 'urban' pattern can be seen and there are sharp distinctions between relief practices in the southern and northern cities. While the impact of the pension was perhaps the most important factor in the period, it was not the only one and other issues, such as the fall in the number of children in Dublin and the rise in outdoor relief in Belfast, were also important.

National insurance

As in the case of old age pensions there is no indication that Irish issues were given any particular attention in the formulation of the national health insurance[69] or unemployment insurance proposals. The unemployment insurance proposals, in particular, were less relevant to many parts of Ireland given the limited initial scope of the scheme and the extent of

69 See for example NA CAB/37/106/40 and Braithwaite's account (*Lloyd George's Ambulance Wagon*, Methuen, London, 1957.).

agricultural employment in Ireland.[70] This meant that in many areas, at least in the initial years of the national insurance scheme, poor relief remained an important source of support for many unemployed and sick workers. In addition the insurance proposals were less of a clear benefit than the pensions scheme, given that they were, in part, funded directly by employer and employee contribution. Although Joe Devlin supported the proposals and a range of related policies,[71] the Irish Parliamentary Party as a whole did not express any clear view on national insurance in advance of publication. When introduced, Redmond welcomed them in principle but wisely put down a caveat as to their applicability to Ireland.[72] There was immediate opposition to the proposals in Ireland from a range of bodies as being unsuited to Irish conditions[73] but the Irish Parliamentary Party seems to have taken a tactical approach of consulting widely as to the amendments required[74] which, in effect, meant that it would support the legislation subject to whatever amendments it could wring out of Lloyd George.[75]

70 In addition to Gilbert's *Evolution* and Hennock's recent *Origin of the Welfare State* op. cit.: see J. Harris, *Unemployment and Politics: a Study in English Social Policy 1886–1914*, Oxford University Press, Oxford, 1972; and Braithwaite, *Lloyd George's Ambulance Wagon*.

71 See, for example, Devlin at Hansard, 31, 249, 14 November 1911. See also *Weekly Freeman's Journal*, 1 February 1908 (on social conditions in Belfast).

72 Hansard, 25, 651–4, 4 May 1911. See also 26, 1234, 1 June 1911.

73 Including the General Council of county councils (*Weekly Freeman's*, 27 May 1911); and the Council of Agriculture (Ibid. 3 June 1911). The General Council recognised the need for the Bill in Britain but argued that Ireland already had a medical service, that only a small proportion of workers would benefit from sickness benefits and pointed out that few trades were covered for unemployment insurance. It called for a new bill to address Irish conditions.

74 See *Weekly Freeman's Journal*, 24 June, which reports a number of Irish Parliamentary Party MPs speaking in their constituencies either supporting the bill and/or outlining the ongoing consultations about it. Interestingly, however, while the party itself did not take a strong proactive approach, the Devlin-controlled Ancient Order of Hibernians was sending officials to local branches to explain the merits of the bill: *Weekly Freeman's Journal*, 10 June 1911.

75 There was strong parliamentary opposition to the bill from some Irish MPs but this related more to faction fighting between the Irish Parliamentary Party and sometime members led by William O'Brien and Tim Healy.

Ultimately the legislation was applied to Ireland with the exception of medical benefit. The issues have been discussed by Barrington who tends to portray the Irish Parliamentary Party as trying to balance the interests of various groups including conflicting views within the Irish medical profession, and the Irish Roman Catholic hierarchy which issued a statement of opposition to the legislation.[76] Key figures in the party appeared to be more concerned however, with the mechanism through which the scheme would operate than the content of the scheme. Two of the key MPs (Joe Devlin and James Lardner) involved in negotiations were presidents of the Ancient Order of Hibernians and the Irish National Foresters which became two of the six largest approved societies.[77] This suggests that the Irish Parliamentary Party was using the national insurance legislation, as it did most policy issues, as another opportunity for strategic incorporation of interests under the Party banner.[78]

Conclusion

In summary, it appears that there were few important policy developments in the poor law itself in this period. However, this was not because nothing happened but rather because so much happened elsewhere as the poor law became less important in the provision of relief and, more generally, social services. In the late nineteenth century, there had been a significant growth

76 R. Barrington, *Health, Medicine and Politics in Ireland, 1900–1970*, op. cit.

77 The major approved societies operating in Ireland were the Ancient Order of Hibernians (130,000 members resident in Ireland), the Orange and Protestant Friendly Society (61,750), the Prudential (35,000), the National Amalgamated (32,000), the Irish National Foresters (30,630) and the Presbyterian Health Insurance Society (24,000): Hansard, 46, 2255, 16 January 1913. As can be seen, at least four were in principle or practice likely to be confined to the members of one religion.

78 See M. Cousins, 'The Creation of Association: the National Insurance Act 1911 and Approved Societies in Ireland', in J. Kelly and R.V. Comerford (eds), *Associational Culture in Ireland and Abroad*, Irish Academic Press, Dublin, 2010.

of alternative institutional services for specific groups of people (lunatics, the insane and disadvantaged children). Although their impact on the poor law is difficult to quantify, these developments must have led to some reduction in the numbers relying on the poor law and, more importantly, indicate both a trend towards the provision of more specialised services and (arguably) an increasing intolerance for 'unruly' members of society.

The turn of the century and the advent of New Liberalism saw a more 'modern' policy turn, with the introduction of national welfare systems such as the old age pension and national insurance. The pension, in particular, had an important impact on the poor law and led to a considerable fall in the numbers on relief, particularly on outdoor relief. The national insurance scheme had a less direct impact on those in receipt of poor relief. Interestingly, however, the pension does not seem to have led to much convergence in policy between the different regions, highlighting again the extent to which the details of poor relief policy were locally determined.

Conclusion

Objectives and key conclusions

As set out in the introductory chapter, this study aimed to establish the empirical basis of the provision of poor relief in the period; to chart and explain regional variations in poor relief; to examine issues which highlight political and social class struggles; and to consider the broader role of the poor law and the boards of guardians in local politics and community. As discussed in the introduction, there has been only limited study of poor relief in the period from 1850 to 1914. This study, therefore, breaks new ground: first, in providing a detailed analysis of trends in poor relief and, second, echoing the UK historiography, in highlighting the regional variations which occurred in Ireland. This allows an analysis of the factors going to explain different levels of poor relief. Third, developing on the work of authors such as Feingold and Crossman, this study examines the relevance of political and social class struggle to the provision of poor relief. The research strongly supports Feingold's thesis as to the take-over of the poor law boards by Nationalist guardians in the period from the late 1870s-early 1880s. However, it emphasises the point that poor law boards were rarely (if ever) simply administrators of poor relief and that broader political and social questions were seldom absent from the minds of the boards of guardians. It also questions the assumption that the take-over of power by Nationalist guardians led to significant changes in poor law policy, arguing both that there was a strong element of continuity in poor law policy in terms of regional patterns and overall levels of relief (as a proportion of national income) and that changes which did occur – such as a shift to outdoor relief – were driven by factors other than the purely political composition of the boards. Finally, drawing on largely French social theory, the study argues that any apparent inconsistency between the fact that Nationalists attached sufficient importance to the poor law boards to struggle for their control but did not implement major reform of poor relief can be explained by the fact that the boards were important, not just for their actual role in the provision of poor relief and other services, but for the fact that, for much of the nineteenth century, they were the main embodiment of local democracy in many parts of Ireland. These points are engaged with and expanded on in this concluding chapter.

Developments in poor relief policy

In chapter 1 it was seen that, despite the considerable changes in Irish society over the period from the Famine to the eve of the First World War, there was a surprising degree of stability in the provision of poor relief. The total amount of spending remained broadly stable over the period as a proportion of national income. There was indeed a significant shift from indoor to outdoor relief. However in a broader United Kingdom and European perspective, even by the early 1900s Ireland still had a rather low level of outdoor relief.[1] In chapter 3 it was seen that in the mid-Victorian period indoor relief was provided (at least in times of crisis) to quite a broad range of family and household types. However, by the early twentieth century, those in workhouses were predominantly old, sick or from 'incomplete' households (such as unmarried mothers with children or children without parents) while 'vagrants' formed a considerable proportion of the daily admittances. The research suggests, however, that the shift to outdoor relief contributed to this change in role for indoor relief as out relief was provided to a much wider range of households.

1 For a comparison with the United Kingdom see table 1.2. For a broader comparison see P. Lindert, 'Poor Relief before the Welfare State: Britain versus the Continent, 1780–1880', *European Review of Economic History*, 1998, 101–40.

We also saw (in Chapter 1) that if one included other 'social' services such as lunatic asylums, industrial schools and poor law-related services such as labourers' cottages, there was a marked growth in social spending (as a proportion of national income) over the period examined. This, first, highlights the fact that the system of poor relief itself became gradually less important in the overall social services provided by the state. Second, the growth of separate services for children and 'lunatics' indicates that, albeit in a somewhat unplanned manner, a degree of specialisation and segregation developed in the provision of Irish 'social' services. Third, the development of such specialist services and the increase in 'incarceration' in lunatic asylums and industrial schools, suggests a change in attitudes in Irish society and the development of a more 'orderly' society less tolerant of 'eccentrics', 'unruly' family members, child beggars and other 'undesirable' groups.

Regional variations

This research indicates considerable regional variations in the provision of poor relief. Three clear groupings of unions can be identified over the period from the 1850s to the 1900s. These are:

1) northern unions (consisting of most Ulster unions) which were of average wealth but provided rather low relief (and generally very little outdoor relief);
2) peripheral western unions (mainly along the western coastline) which were very poor and where the level of relief provided was constrained by a lack of resources; and
3) southern unions (controlled from the 1880s by Nationalist guardians) which provided higher levels of relief but which had a high level of variation in terms of wealth and relief.

This again emphasises a degree of stability over the period as the groupings change only marginally in their precise composition over the sixty years covered by this study.

Social and political change

However, if continuity in the provision of relief has been emphasised,[2] the major change in the composition of the guardians who ruled the poor law at a local level has also been highlighted (following Feingold). As discussed in chapter 9, the composition of the board officers changed dramatically from the pre-Land War period when they were overwhelmingly landowners, frequently extensive and titled landowners, to the early twentieth century by which time the boards were dominated by the rising classes of farmers and traders. This change, of course, reflects the broader change in power in Irish society over the period in question. This research shows a broadly similar change for the full boards of the Belfast and Dublin unions. In the 1860s, these boards were dominated by large landowners and merchants whereas by 1911 traders had become the dominant group. Even after the democratisation of the boards in 1898, there are only a small number of labourers on the boards and relatively few in officer positions.

While the study finds strong support for Feingold's general argument concerning the take-over of control,[3] the study does not, in general,

2 An important issue which it has not been possible to study here in any depth and which deserves further research is the experience of individuals claiming relief. Brandes, for example, suggests that indoor relief had become a much more benign experience by the twentieth century than that portrayed by the image of the Victorian workhouses: I. Brandes, '"Odious, degrading and foreign" institutions? Analysing Irish workhouses in the nineteenth and twentieth centuries' in A. Gestrich, S. King and L. Raphael (eds), *Being Poor in Modern Europe: Historical Perspectives 1800–1940*, Peter Lang, 2006, 199–228.

3 Although one of the questions which it asks is what 'control' means, again distinguishing the symbolic from the administrative.

find that Nationalist boards acted significantly differently in terms of the provision of poor relief to landlord controlled boards either on 'national' grounds or more generally.[4] In relation to outdoor relief (as discussed in chapter 6) it is argued that the rise in outdoor relief was largely related not to 'national' political issues but to the presence or absence of agricultural labourers.[5] A detailed local study of the response of boards to the plan of campaign (1886–91) finds little indication of any strategic approach by Nationalist guardians to the use of the poor law as part of the plan of campaign (chapter 7).

This research challenges Crossman's conclusion that 'granting relief to evicted tenants enabled poor law guardians to make a substantive contribution to the land campaign by shifting the balance of power in land disputes away from landlords and towards tenants'.[6] The detailed studies outlined in chapters 6 and 7 indicate that Crossman understates the extent to which boards which pursued this approach (a) were exceptional and (b) failed to achieve their objectives. It also modifies her conclusion that the increasing influence of elected poor law guardians 'encouraged a more populist approach to poor law administration, most evident in the provision of labourers cottages and outdoor relief'.[7] As we have seen, there was, in fact, little change in the overall level of poor relief spending despite the take-over of the boards by elected guardians and although the democratisation of the local government franchise in 1898 does appear to have contributed to a rise in the building of cottages, there was little change in the provision of outdoor relief which was lower both in total and as a percentage of the population in 1901 compared to 1891.

4 Although, as discussed below, it is clear that Ulster boards (which were generally 'landlord' controlled) formed a distinct group in terms of levels of relief and of rates.

5 See G.R. Boyer, *An Economic History of the English Poor Law, 1750–1850*, Cambridge University Press, Cambridge, 1990 for a related argument concerning the pre-1834 English poor law.

6 *Politics, Pauperism and Power*, 99.

7 Ibid., 217. The author does not define what a more 'populist' approach might involve.

Consideration of these issues leads to discussion of the role of Nationalism and social class in shaping the Irish poor law. Superficially one can argue that as Nationalism came to dominate the poor law boards, so the administration of the poor law became less draconian than in the early post-Famine period and developed a greater emphasis on outdoor relief. However, if one looks at almost any European country, one can see a similar development over the nineteenth century as democratisation led to a softening in approach to the provision of welfare.[8] In this area one can argue that Irish Nationalism was simply the chosen expression of popular democracy and one needs to ask whether and how Nationalism led to any different outcome than democratisation generally. In fact, as has been seen in chapters 6 and 7, there is very limited evidence that Irish Nationalists used poor relief to advance specific Nationalist causes in any strategic manner nor that tenant controlled boards were more likely to provide outdoor relief than landlord controlled boards in the 1880s.[9] Admittedly southern boards did provide more relief and more outdoor relief than northern boards. In part, it will be argued, this was due to the fact that agricultural labourers were less important in the northern labour force. In addition, the difference in approach was determined not by the fact that northern boards were controlled by 'conservative' (in Feingold's terms) guardians but by the fact that they were controlled by *sectarian* conservative guardians and, in Belfast and Londonderry, by sectarian boards concerned to control the impact of in-migration on the poor rates.[10]

8 Even if in England and Wales this was by no means linear with a hardening of attitudes with the initial new Poor Law in 1834 and again in the 1870s with the crusade against out relief recently discussed by Elizabeth Hurren in *Protesting About Pauperism: Poverty, Politics and Poor Relief in Late-Victorian England, c. 1870–1914*, Boydell and Brewer, Woodbridge, 2007. For France see A. Gueslin, *Gens Pauvres, Pauvres Gens sans la France du XIXe Siècle*, Aubier, Paris, 1998.

9 By the 1900s (after the local government reforms of 1899) almost all southern boards were 'Nationalist' controlled making such comparison much more difficult.

10 I use the term 'sectarian' in the negative sense of bigotry, discrimination, intolerance or hatred arising from attaching importance to perceived differences between subdivisions within a group, such as between different denominations of a religion.

In terms of social class, the study focuses on the role played in the management of the poor law after the take-over of the boards by large farmers and shopkeepers/businessmen (often both), a factor already identified by Feingold. It highlights that the take-over of the boards was not by Nationalism or by the tenantry but by a group of large farmers and businessmen with strong Nationalist views. However, these men (and they were almost always men) operated in a, more or less, democratic environment and had to take account of the views of other members of the community. The study also suggests the need for further study of the role of (largely) landless labourers in the post-Famine period. Agricultural labourers have been depicted generally as a disappearing and marginal class in Irish society.[11] There can be no doubt that this class did ultimately lose out but as late as the early 1900s they still constituted a large proportion of the rural population, particularly in the south-east, and this study suggests that the boards of guardians were considerably influenced in their policy as regards both outdoor relief and labourers' cottages by the presence of this group for both economic and political reasons.[12]

Poor law and politicisation

This contrast between a dramatic change in the composition of the boards and a certain stability in their provision of relief points to one of the key conclusions of this study: that the importance of the boards of guardians

11 D. Fitzpatrick, 'The Disappearance of the Agricultural Labourer, 1841–1912,' *Irish Economic and Social History* 7 (1980) 66–92; J.W. Boyle, 'A Marginal Figure: The Irish Rural Laborer', in S. Clark and J.S. Donnelly (eds), *Irish Peasants: Violence and Political Unrest, 1780–1914*, University of Wisconsin Press, Madison, 1983.

12 For a similar 'rehabilitation' of the role of agricultural labourers see F. Lane, 'Rural Labourers, Social Change and Politics in late Nineteenth-Century Ireland', in D. Ó Drisceoil and F. Lane, (eds), *Politics and the Irish Working Class, 1830–1945*, Palgrave Macmillan, Basingstoke, 2005.

lay not only in the provision of relief but also in their broader role in the politicisation of Irish society. As shown in chapter 9, the system of local government though boards of guardians played an important role both in creating a sense of local government and in the 'learning' of politics by both electors and politicians. The importance of the boards can be seen in terms of their prominence in the local newspapers; their role in the distribution of patronage; as a symbol of local democracy, e.g. as a forum for expressing views on broadly political issues; in the movement to 'take-over' the boards in the late 1870s and 1880s; and as a training ground for the local authorities introduced under the 1898 legislation.

Even before the 1880s take-over, boards fought to establish their (Catholic and Nationalist) identity in a number of important areas.[13] The emphasis on the more 'symbolic', but no less real, function of the boards helps to explain the apparent anomaly that Nationalists tenants took-over control and then made limited use of it in terms of poor relief policies.[14] In symbolic terms the change of control made a very significant difference with, for example, strongly Nationalist resolutions replacing resolutions on the Prince of Wales' birthday, a 'wearing away' of the political and social authority of local (often titled) landlords, the use of union boardrooms by the United Irish League;[15] and a campaign by several boards to favour Nationalist traders.[16]

13 In the period before disestablishment in 1871, this often took the form of disputes about religious issues: see M. Cousins, 'Registration of the religion of children under the Irish poor law, 1838–70', *Journal of Ecclesiastical History* (2010) 61(1), 107–24.

14 The division between symbolic and administrative is nicely captured by the actions of the (strongly Nationalist) Youghal board which, in the middle of one of the most viciously fought struggles of the plan of campaign, was surcharged not for assisting evicted tenants (which with very limited exceptions it did not do) but for buying a bust of Nationalist leader William O'Brien.

15 With, by this time, a significant overlap between the officerships of the Nationalist boards and the United Irish League (UIL). The fact that local UIL leaders wanted to use the boardrooms as a symbol of authority highlights the extent to which boards were seen as symbols of local power as does the statement by one guardian (in a debate as to the use of the boardrooms) that 'We are the people now!'.

16 Although the Irish Government adopted a (partially successful) legal strategy in relation to the latter two activities. No doubt the UIL preference was another example of mixing politics with business.

A complex framework of governance

The boards of guardians formed just one part of the complex system of poor law government. At the apex of control (at least in theory) sat the Imperial government and Parliament. However, as has been seen, there were relatively few important legal changes in poor relief over the period and although poor law issues frequently arose in Parliament (particularly in parliamentary questions and in debates on local government estimates) the United Kingdom government rarely displayed any great interest in the operation of the Irish poor law. The Irish chief secretary was a de jure member of the Poor Law Commission and (later) the Local Government Board. It is clear from the archives that at least some chief secretaries and under-secretaries paid considerable attention to poor law issues. However, even in the case of those who clearly did play an active role in poor law administration such as T.A. Larcom, and A.J. and Gerald Balfour, this tended to be in response either to specific economic crises or as part of an overall response to land agitation (as discussed in chapters 5 and 8). The Irish government tended to have limited interest in the administration of poor relief per se as shown by the long period of inaction on the union rating issue in the 1860s and 1870s and the (lack of) response to the recommendations of the 1906 Viceregal Commission despite the apparent broad support for its proposals. Perhaps the major reform of the period – the Local Government Act, 1898 which democratised the governance of the poor law and introduced union rating – was introduced for reasons almost entirely unrelated to the poor law itself.

The Poor Law Commission/Local Government Board (which is referred to here as the Board) was a key body in the development and implementation of poor relief policy. The Board had more extensive powers than its English equivalent being entitled to dissolve boards of guardians and it clearly did intervene in micro-issues of poor law management. On the other hand, the regional variations in poor relief and the details of the many struggles recounted in this study show that the Board was by no means an omnipotent body. Rather than the exercise of power being one way, the governance of the poor law involved, in a Foucauldian sense, a continuous relationship of power between the Board and the local boards of guardians.[17] While the Board in the 1880s, driven by the energy of A.J. Balfour, was able to check the illegal provision of support to evicted tenants, it was unable to check the rise in out relief in the 1870s and 1880s and had difficulty in insisting on specific measures such as the provision of appropriate religious services, the appointment of qualified nurses, and the adoption of adequate dietaries. In some cases, it can be seen that having initially opposed an initiative, such as the employment of nuns in workhouses, the Board came to see the advantages of this measure and, at least on occasion, encouraged it.[18] On occasion, as in the case of the religious registration of children, it adopted the view that administrative discretion was the better part of valour and sought to change what it felt was an unimplementable law. This study emphasises the extent to which the exercise of the Board's power was a negotiated process. While Sir H.A. Robinson's memoirs may give the impression of a pompous, unimaginative and somewhat remote figure, the Board was clearly successful in maintaining a close and not disrespectful (albeit sometimes fractious) relationship with the local boards.[19]

17 See, for example, M. Foucault, 'The Subject and Power', in H.L. Dreyfus and P. Rabinow, *Michel Foucault: Beyond Structuralism and Hermeneutics*, University of Chicago, 1982.

18 B. Althammer, I. Brandes and K. Marx-Jaskulski, 'Religiously motivated charitable work in modern times. Catholic congregations in the Rhineland and Ireland' in A. Gestrich, L. Raphael, and H. Uerlings (eds), *Strangers and Poor People: Changing Patterns of Inclusion and Exclusion in Europe and the Mediterranean World from Classical Antiquity to the Present Day*, Peter Lang, 2009, 371–414.

19 H.A.R. Robinson, *Memories: Wise and Otherwise*, Cassell & Co, London, 1924. Although it falls after the period of this study, it is worth noting that the local boards – taken over by Sinn Féin in 1920 – only reluctantly broke with the Local Government Board later that year and then only because the British government foolishly gave them little option: A. Mitchell, *Revolutionary Government in Ireland: Dáil Éireann 1919–1922*, 1995, Gill & Macmillan, Dublin, 1995.

The Irish poor law in a United Kingdom context

The United Kingdom context of the Irish poor law highlights a number of important points and raises questions for broader comparative studies of European systems of poor relief. Clearly the poor law was imposed on Ireland largely for English reasons and it seems unlikely that an Irish Parliament of whatever political complexion would have enacted such a system.[20] Indeed it is England and Wales which is unusual in a European context in having such a national poor law system. Thus the Irish case allows one to examine how an 'imperial' poor law operated in a 'colonial' context and where the majority religion in the colony was different to that of the metropole. In the initial years of the poor law the members of the Poor Law Commission were almost all English and clearly brought their ideas about the administration of poor relief to an Irish context. Over time, however, Irish (albeit Protestant and Anglo-Irish in many cases) men took up leadership positions in the Local Government Board and the influence of purely English ideas appeared to wane.[21] As has been seen few English political leaders took much interest in the Irish poor law. Key developments in the later English poor law such as the development of specialist services and related building of new workhouses,[22] or the 'crusade' against out door relief[23] are largely absent from the history of Irish poor relief. After disestablishment in 1869, the issue of religion became less salient in poor law policy generally although, as we have seen, religious divisions remained prominent particularly in northern unions.

20 Gray argues, convincingly, that the form of the poor law was, to a certin extent, 'negoiated' between the Liberal government and aspects of Irish public opinion: P. Gray, *Making of the Irish Poor Law*, 8. This does not make it any less an Imperial imposition.

21 The archives show little indication of close contact between the English and Irish boards in the period: NA MH 19/53.

22 F. Driver, *Power and Pauperism: the Workhouse System, 1834–1884*, Cambridge University Press, Cambridge, 1993.

23 K. Williams, *From Pauperism to Poverty*, Routledge and Kegan Paul, London, 1981; E. Hurren, *Protesting about Pauperism: Poverty, Politics and Poor Relief in Late-Victorian England, 1870–1900*, Royal Historical Society, Woodbridge, 2007.

The political take-over of the boards also followed quite a different trajectory occurring earlier in Ireland and representing a change from the old to the new bourgeoisie with little indication of any substantial challenge from labour interests.[24] In contrast, in England, although a national study has not yet been carried out, the 1894 local government reforms (which, as far as the poor law goes, were similar to those later enacted in Ireland) appear to have led to a greater representation by the working classes which led to a challenge to restrictive outdoor relief policies (at least in some unions).[25] The apparent convergence of the levels of poor relief (shown in table 1.2) appears to have arisen from independent trends in both countries with the Irish system, which had begun with no out relief, switching over time to a higher level of outdoor relief and the English system, which had historically a heavy reliance on outdoor relief, moving in the opposite direction.[26] Thus while the Irish poor law remains very much a British creation, the precise form which it took was 'negotiated' both by an increasingly Irish leadership in the Local Government Board and by the local boards of guardians.

24 Although the then under-secretary Sir David Harrell estimated that, after the 1898 reforms, labour representatives controlled one-sixth of urban seats (quoted in Crossman, *Politics, Pauperism and Power*, 165) and 'labour' candidates were elected as vice and deputy vice chairs in Thomastown in 1911: M. Silverman, *An Irish Working Class: Explorations in Political Economy and Hegemony, 1900–1950*, University of Toronto Press, Toronto, 2001, 231–2. Clearly the extent and meaning of labour representation at local government (including poor law boards) requires further study.

25 See Hurren, *Protesting about Pauperism: Poverty*, for Brixworth union. More generally see A. Brundage, *The English Poor Laws, 1700–1930*, Palgrave, Basingstoke, 2002, 126–7, 134–5.

26 As Lindert notes the 'convergence of poor relief methods between England-Wales and Ireland is more noteworthy for the convergence that didn't happen than for the convergence that did': op. cit. at 120.

Explaining levels of relief

In conclusion, this study suggests that the explanation for different levels of relief both regionally and over time cannot be found in any one factor alone. The wealth of a local union was obviously important and, in broad terms, levels of relief are positively correlated with the wealth of a union. In particular poor peripheral unions were constrained in what they could spend by the poverty of the union and the lack of an adequate taxation base. However, the link between wealth and relief only goes part of the way to explain these patterns and the wealthiest unions did not spend most on relief. The employment context also counts. It was argued in chapter 6 that the payment of outdoor relief and (unsurprisingly) the building of labourers' cottages was closely linked to the presence of agricultural labourers in the local labour force. This both met the political demands of the labouring population and subsidised the labour costs of the farmers, many of whom were of course represented on the boards of guardians, who employed the labourers. For reasons which require further study it appears that industrial employers did not adopt a similar strategy. As has been argued, there is little indication that labourers themselves were able to exert significant control on boards (in terms of board membership) but clearly they were able to influence in a positive manner some aspects of poor relief policy such as the building of cottages.[27]

This study suggests that there is little evidence that Nationalist control of the boards in itself made a considerable difference in terms of poor relief policy. It has been argued that changes in poor relief patterns broadly reflect wider European trends and that Nationalism was important, not because it had any distinctive view of poor relief, but simply because it was the form in which democracy was expressed in (much of) Ireland. The separate north-south pattern of poor relief can be seen before the 1880

27 In contrast, although one routinely finds delegations of labourers calling for out relief in times of crisis, there is nothing like a sustained campaign for such relief in contrast to the popular demand for labourers' cottages.

take-over of the boards and while the rise in outdoor relief did occur in areas where Nationalists took control, as discussed in chapter 6, there is only limited evidence that the two factors were causally linked. It would appear that Nationalist guardians may have been somewhat more inclined that their Conservative colleagues to build labourers' cottages (allowing for other factors) but the issue of labourers' cottages deserves a study in its own right. Lindert has argued that (at least in an English context) 'redistribution to the poor depends on who has political voice, and on their selfinterested perceptions of the likelihood that the poor might revolt or exit from labour supply'.[28] The hegemony of the farmer-trader classes in Irish society and the limited challenge from the working class (including agricultural labourers) appears to have led to limited change in Irish poor relief patterns despite the expansion of the franchise.[29]

The different patterns in much of Ulster can, in part, be explained by the factors discussed above. Most of the northern unions were not particularly wealthy and agricultural labourers made up a smaller proportion of the workforce. However, these factors cannot fully explain the striking difference in poor relief patterns. It is argued that northern guardians had, from the establishment of the poor law, a different approach to the provision of relief and that sectarian attitudes prevalent in Ulster society affected poor relief patterns. Guardians were mainly Protestant while Catholics were overrepresented amongst the poor. In a society divided on religious grounds this created an incentive to minimise payment of relief (particularly to Catholics). In addition, unlike most southern cities, Belfast and Londonderry grew rapidly and guardians used low levels of poor relief as a tool to discourage unwanted in-migration.

Finally, policy legacies are important in explaining poor relief patterns. A striking degree of policy continuity has been shown in chapters 1 and 2 despite the changes in governance. This suggests that policies adopted for specific reasons remained in place under new management.[30]

28 P. Lindert, 'Poor Relief before the Welfare State', 135.

29 As noted, the expansion of labourers' cottages may be a limited exception to this.

30 The classic example of the impact of policy legacies is the resilience of outdoor relief in England despite the repeated attempts to reduce it.

APPENDIX I

Poor Law Unions, 1851–1907

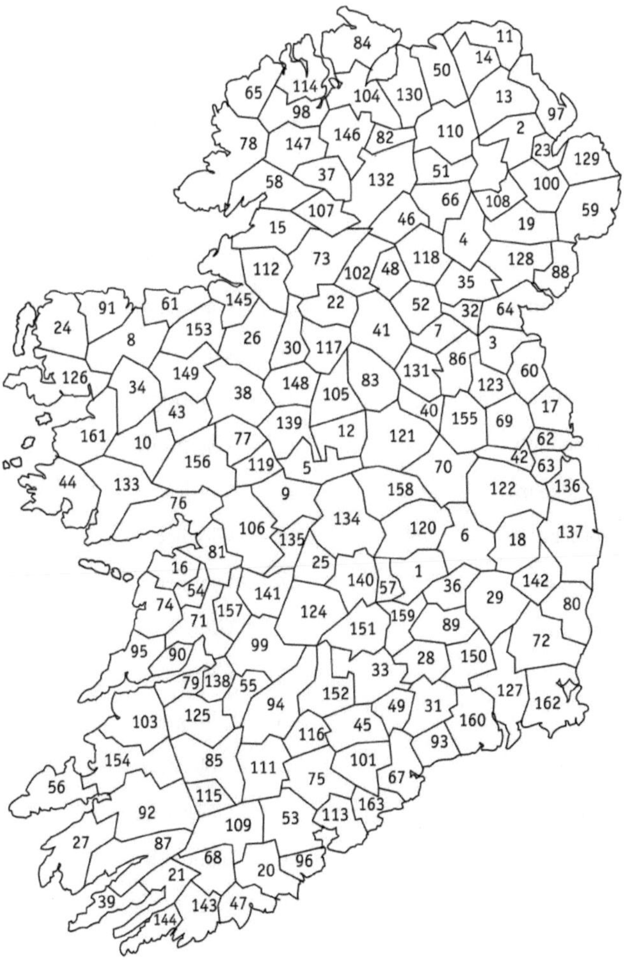

Map A1 Poor Law Unions, 1851–1907

1. Abbeyleix
2. Antrim
3. Ardee
4. Armagh
5. Athlone
6. Athy
7. Bailieborough
8. Ballina
9. Ballinalsoe
10. Ballinrobe
11. Ballycastle
12. Ballymahon
13. Ballymena
14. Ballymoney
15. Ballyshannon
16. Ballyvaughan
17. Balrothery
18. Baltinglass
19. Banbridge
20. Bandon
21. Bantry
22. Bawnboy
23. Belfast
24. Belmullet
25. Borrisokane
26. Boyle
27. Cahirciveen
28. Callan
29. Carlow
30. Carrick-on-Shannon
31. Carrick-on-Suir
32. Carrickmacross
33. Cashel
34. Castlebar
35. Castleblaney
36. Castlecomer
37. Castlederg
38. Castlerea
39. Castletown
40. Castletowndelvin
41. Cavan
42. Celbridge
43. Claremorris
44. Clifden
45. Clogheen
46. Clogher
47. Clonakilty
48. Clones
49. Clonmel
50. Coleraine
51. Cookstown
52. Cootehill
53. Cork
54. Corofin
55. Croom
56. Dingle

57. Donaghmore (amalgamated with neighbouring unions in 1886)
58. Donegal
59. Downpatrick
60. Drogheda
61. Dromore West
62. Dublin North
63. Dublin South
64. Dundalk
65. Dunfanaghy
66. Dungannon
67. Dungarvan
68. Dunmanaway
69. Dunshaughlin
70. Edenderry
71. Ennis
72. Enniscorthy
73. Enniskillen
74. Ennistymon
75. Fermoy
76. Galway
77. Glenamaddy
78. Glenties
79. Glin (amalgamated with neighbouring unions in 1894)
80. Gorey
81. Gort
82. Gortin (amalgamated with Omagh in 1870)
83 Granard
84. Inishowen
85. Kanturk
86. Kells
87. Kenmare
88. Kilkeel
89. Kilkenny
90. Killadysert
91. Killala
92. Killarney
93. Killmacthomas
94. Kilmallock
95. Kilrush
96. Kinsale
97. Larne
98. Letterkenny
99. Limerick
100. Lisburn
101. Lismore
102. Lisnaskea
103. Listowel
104. Londonderry
105. Longford
106. Loughrea
107. Lowtherstown (later known as Irvinestown)
108. Lurgan
109. Macroom

110. Magherafelt
111. Mallow
112. Manorhamilton
113. Middleton
114. Milford
115. Milstreet
116. Mitchelstown
117. Mohill
118. Monaghan
119. Mountbellew
120. Mountmellick
121. Mullingar
122. Naas
123. Navan
124. Nenagh
125. Newcastle
126. Newport (amalgamated with Westport in 1885)
127. New Ross
128. Newry
129. Newtownards
130. Newtownlimavady
131. Oldcastle
132. Omagh
133. Oughterard
134. Parsonstown (later known as Birr)
135. Portumna
136. Rathdown
137 Rathdrum
138 Rathkeale
139. Roscommon
140. Roscrea
141. Scarrif
142. Shillelagh
143. Skibbereen
144. Skull
145. Sligo
146. Strabane
147. Stranolar
148. Strokestown
149. Swineford
150. Thomastown
151. Thurles
152. Tipperary
153. Tobbercurry
154. Tralee
155. Trim
156. Tuam
157. Tulla (amalgamated with Scarriff in 1908)
158. Tullamore
159. Urlingford
160. Waterford
161. Westport
162. Wexford
163. Youghal

APPENDIX 2

Databases of Poor Law Statistics and of Board of Guardians Officers

1. Poor law statistics

For the purposes of this study, the author compiled a database of poor law related statistics drawing on the annual reports of the Poor Law Commission and Local Government Board and on special returns for the 1906 Viceregal Commission and 1909 Royal Commission on the poor laws.[1]

Geographical unit

The unit of collection was the union, so data was collected for the total number of unions existing at the relevant time (up to 163 at the maximum).

Point in time

The data was collected primarily for four points in time which marked significant points in the periodisation of the history of poor relief in nineteenth- and early twentieth-century Ireland. These were:

1 Appendix to the Report of the Vice-Regal Commission on Poor Law Reform in Ireland. Volume II, 1906 [Cd. 3203] li, 441; Royal Commission on the Poor Laws and Relief of Distress. Appendix volume XXXI. Statistics relating to Ireland, 1910 [Cd. 5244] liv, 763.

i) 1859 – when the lowest number of people were on poor relief in the period and when the poor law perhaps best corresponded to the original vision of George Nicholls (albeit in an Ireland radically different to that of the 1830s);
ii) 1877 – just before the start of the Land War and related agricultural depression and after a period of growth in outdoor relief;
iii) 1892 – at the effective end of the first period of land agitation, after a very significant rise in outdoor relief and the initial phase of the take-over of the boards of guardians by nationalists; and
iv) 1907 – the last year of the poor law before the introduction of the old age pension which resulted in a significant reduction in the number of older people on indoor and (more particularly) outdoor relief.

However, data was also collected for other periods as discussed in different chapters of this study.

Data content

The data which was collected focussed primarily on:

i) The extent of both indoor and outdoor relief. Both the average daily numbers on relief (per 100 population) and expenditure per head on relief was collected but as both were closely correlated only the former data has been reported here at union level.
ii) The wealth of unions. *A priori* it seemed likely that the wealth of a union and its ability to fund relief would have an impact on levels of relief. In order to assess this, the wealth of each union was measured based on its rateable valuation per head of population. The rateable valuation of land was intended to represent the value of land in the union and was used as a basis for assessing rates payable by individual landholders. There are, of course, a number of difficulties in using valuation as a measure of wealth. The relationship of valuation to, for example, the rent of land varied both over time and space. However, it would seem to provide the best available indicator of wealth.
iii) The level of rates paid.

Again, however, a range of more specific data was collected in relation to specific issues. For example, age-related data was collected for the period 1906–11 in order to look at the impact of the introduction of old age pensions (discussed in chapter 10).

2. Boards of guardians officers

As discussed by Feingold, there is no comprehensive published record of the membership of boards of guardians. However, the three officers (chairman, vice chairman and deputy vice chairman) of each union are recorded on an annual basis in *Thom's Directory*.

Data on the membership of the boards was complied for a series of years in order to assess issues such as:

i) the 'longevity' of the chairs of boards, i.e. the extent to which there was a change in the chairmen;
ii) the extent to which chairs were titled or members of parliament; and
iii) the extent to which board officers went on to become members of the county councils established under the Local Government Act 1898.

In order to assess changes in the social composition of board officers, the study drew on Feingold's existing analysis (based on land holding) for 1877, and carried out new research by matching boards officers for selected unions in 1901–11 to data from the Census manuscripts for those years.

In addition, the study also examined the composition of the full Dublin and Belfast boards (for whom data is available in commercial directories) for the years 1865–6 and 1910–11 (as discussed in chapter 9).

List of Sources Consulted

National Archives of Ireland (NAI)

Chief Secretary's Office Registered Papers (CSORP) (1851–1914)
Chief Secretary's Office Official Papers (1851–1914)
Index of Poor Law Orders
Relief of Distress papers 1891
Balrothery union minute books
Lismore union outdoor relief papers
North Dublin Union minute books
South Dublin union minute books
South Dublin union indoor relief register

National Library of Ireland (NLI)

Thomas Bradley papers (minute books of Timahoe branch of Irish National League)
W.E. Forster papers
Tim Harrington papers
T.A. Larcom papers
Earl of Mayo (Lord Naas) papers
Minute books of Mothel branch of INL

Trinity College Archives

John Dillon papers (including minute books of Irish Parliamentary Party)

Public Record Office of Northern Ireland

Duke of Abercorn papers
Belfast union minute books

British Library

Althorp (Earl Spencer) papers
Gladstone papers

National Archives (United Kingdom)

Arthur Balfour papers
Gerald Balfour papers
Cabinet papers (1880–1914)
Correspondence between Poor Law Commission/Local Government Board (E&W) and PLC/Local Government Board (Irl) [MH 19/53]

Cork City and County Archives

Cork union minute books
Youghal union minute books

Galway County Archives

Galway union minute books
Loughrea union minute books
Mount Bellew union minute books

Louth County Archives

Ardee union minute books
Drogheda union minute books
Dundalk union minute books

Mayo County Archives

Ballinrobe union outdoor relief records

Offaly County Archives

Parsonstown union minute books
Tullamore union application and report book, 1862–3
Tullamore union minute books

Westmeath County Archives

Mullingar union minute books
Mullingar union weekly relief list 1879

Newspapers consulted

National

Daily Express
Dublin Evening Mail
Dublin Evening Packet
Dublin Evening Post
Freeman's Journal
Irish Independent
Irish Times
Irish Weekly Independent
Nation
United Ireland
Weekly Freeman's Journal

Local/regional

Anglo-Celt
Ballinrobe Chronicle
Ballymena Observer
Banbridge Chronicle
Belfast Newsletter
Carlow Nationalist
Clareman
Clonmel Chronicle
Connacht Patriot

Connaught People
Connaught Telegraph
Cork Examiner
Cork Constitution
Down Recorder
Drogheda Argus
Drogheda Conservative
Drogheda Independent
Galway Express
Galway Press
Galway Vindicator
Gorey Correspondent
Kildare Observer
King's County Chronicle
Leinster Express
Leinster Leader
Leinster Reporter and Tipperary Vindicator
Leitrim Advertiser
Limerick Chronicle
Limerick Reporter
Longford Journal
Mayo Constitution
Mayo Examiner
Meath Chronicle
Meath Herald
Meath Reporter
Midland Reporter
Munster Express
Munster News
Nenagh Guardian
Newry Telegraph
Newtownards Spectator
Northern Whig
Roscommon Journal
Roscommon Messenger
Tipperary Free Press
Tuam Herald
Waterford Mail
Waterford News

Western People
Westmeath Examiner
Westmeath Guardian
Westmeath Nationalist
Wexford Independent

Bibliography

Parliamentary papers

Report of the Poor Law Commissioners, on medical charities, Ireland…, HC 1841 session 1 [324] xi, 1

Return of the number of Magistrates, Elected and Ex-Officio, on each Board of Guardians… in Ireland, HC 1843 (347), xlvi, 583

Report of the Select Committee of the House of Lords on the Laws relating to the Relief of the Destitute Poor… in Ireland, HL 1846 [694], xxiv, 1

Report by Captain Spark relative to charges of proselytism in workhouse of Dingle Union, 1851 (427) xlix, 173

Second Annual Report of the Commissioners for Administering the Laws for Relief of the Poor in Ireland…, HC 1854 [1759] xx, 219

Eight Annual Report of the Commissioners for Administering the Laws for Relief of the Poor in Ireland, HC 1854–5 [1945] xxiv, 523

Twelfth Annual Report of the Commissioners for Administering the Laws for Relief of the Poor in Ireland, HC 1859 Session 2 [2546] xi, 317

Return of Number of Attendances at Board of Commissioners for Administering Laws for Relief of Poor in Ireland, 1847–59, HC 1869 p147] lviii, 871

Thirteenth Annual Report of the Commissioners for Administering the Laws for Relief of the Poor in Ireland, HC 1860 [2546] xxxvii, 327

Report from the Select Committee on Poor Relief (Ireland), HC 1861 (408), x, 1

Sixteenth Annual Report of the Commissioners for Administering the Laws for Relief of the Poor in Ireland, HC 1863 [3135] xxii, 341

Twenty-first Annual Report of the Commissioners for Administering the Laws for Relief of the Poor in Ireland, HC 1867–8 [4042] xxxiii, 413

Twenty-second Annual Report of the Commissioners for Administering the Laws for Relief of the Poor in Ireland, HC 1868–9 [4166] xxviii, 339

Return of Number of Attendances at Board of Coms. for Administering Laws for Relief of Poor in Ireland, 1847–59, HC 1869 [147] lviii, 871

Law of Rating (Ireland): Report from the Select Committee…, HC 1871 (423), x, 1

Law of rating (Ireland): Report from the Select Committee…, HC 1872 (361), xi, 1

Return from each Poor Law Union in Ireland, of the number of Persons entitled to Vote in each such Union for Poor Law Guardians…, HC 1874, (253), lvi, 1

Return of Number of Persons Born in England and Wales Receiving Relief in Ireland, HC 1876 [206] lxiii, 85
Return of Owners of Land of one acre and upwards..., HC 1876, [C. 1492] lxxx, 61
Annual Report of the Local Government Board for Ireland..., HC 1877 [c. 1761] xxxviii, 1
Report of the Select Committee on Poor Law Guardians... HC 1878 (297), xvii, 263
Fifth Annual Report of the Local Government Board for Ireland, HC 1878 [c.1761] xxxviii, 1
Report of the Select Committee on Poor Removal, HC 1878–9 [282] xii, 561
Emigration Statistics for Ireland for the year 1878, HC 1878–9 [C. 2221] lxxv, 703
Poor Law Union and Lunacy Inquiry (Ireland) Report, HC 1878–9 [c.2239] xxxi, 1
Return of Cases of Evictions in Ireland..., HC, 1881 (2) lxxvii, 727
Return of Outrages reported to the Royal Irish Constabulary..., HC, 1881 [c.2756] lxxvii, 907–9
Annual Report of the Local Government Board for Ireland..., HC 1883 [C. 3581] xxix, 1
Return of the number of Attendances of Poor Law Guardians at the Board Meetings of each Poor Law Union in Ireland in the year ended 25 March 1884, HC 1884 (335) lxviii, 55
Emigration Statistics for Ireland for the year 1883, HC 1884 [C. 3899] lxxxv, 493
Report from the Select Committee of the House of Lords on the Poor Law Guardians (Ireland) Bill, HL 1884–5(297) x, 364
Poor Relief (Ireland) Inquiry Commission. Report and Evidence,... HC 1887 [C.5043] xxxviii, 1
Annual Report of the Local Government Board for Ireland, being the Sixteenth Report under the Local Government Board (Ireland) Act, HC 1888 [C.5455] l, 1
Annual Report of the Local Government Board for Ireland, HC 1889 [C. 5769] xxxvi, 695
Return showing... the number of Persons of each Sex of 65 years and upwards..., HC 1892 [360] lxviii, 995
Annual Report of the Local Government Board for Ireland..., 1892 [C. 6801] xxxix, 1
Report of the Evicted Tenants Commission, HC, 1893–4 [C. 6935] xxxi
Forty-second report... of the inspectors of lunatics (Ireland), 1893–4 [C.7125] xlvi, 369
Special Report from Inspectors of Lunatics to Chief Secretary on alleged Increasing Prevalence of Insanity in Ireland, 1894 [C. 7331] xliii, 647
Twenty-second Annual Report of the Local Government Board for Ireland, 1894 [C. 7454] xli, 1
Report of the Departmental Committee on Old Age Pensions, 1898 [C. 8911] xlv, 465

Annual Report of the Local Government Board for Ireland, 1898 [C. 8958] xli, 1
Return respecting Local Government Electoral Areas, showing... the Number of... Local Government Board Electors..., 1901 [2] lxiv, 413
Annual Report of the Local Government Board for Ireland, for the year ended 31st March, 1901, 1902 [Cd. 1259] xxxvii, 1
Return showing the Number of Workhouse Infirmaries in Ireland in which Nuns are employed in any capacity, showing for each Infirmary the Number of Nuns so employed and the amount paid to them by way of salaries within the last financial year, 1903 [115] liv, 497
Thirty-first Annual Report of the Local Government Board for Ireland, for the year ending 31st March, 1903, 1904 [Cd. 2012]
Thirty-fourth annual report of the Local Government Board for Ireland, for the year ended 31st March, 1906, 1906 [Cd. 3102] xxxvi, 495
Supplement to the fifty-fourth Report of the Inspectors of Lunatics... Ireland. Being a Special Report on the alleged Increase of Insanity. 1906 [Cd. 3126] xxxix, 1
Report of the Vice-Regal Commission on Poor Law Reform in Ireland. Volume I, 1906 [Cd. 3202] li, 349
Appendix to the Report of the Vice-Regal Commission on Poor Law Reform in Ireland. Volume II, 1906 [Cd. 3203] li, 441
Minutes of evidence taken before the Vice-Regal Commission on Poor Law Reform in Ireland. Volume III. Minutes of evidence and index, 1906 [Cd. 3204] lii, 1
Fifty-sixth Report... of the Inspectors of Lunatics (Ireland), for the year ending 31st December, 1906, 1908 [Cd. 3745] xxxiii, 575
Report of the Royal Commission on the Poor Laws and Relief of Distress, 1909 [Cd. 4499] xxxvii, 1
Annual Report of the Local Government Board for Ireland for the year ended 31 March 1909, HC 1909 [Cd. 4810] xxx, 1
Royal Commission on the Poor Laws and Relief of Distress. Appendix volume XXVIII. Reports of visits to Poor Law and charitable institutions and to meetings of local authorities in the United Kingdom, 1910 [Cd. 4974] liv, 99
Report on Ireland, 1909 [Cd. 4630] xxxviii, 1
Royal Commission on the Poor Laws and Relief of Distress. Appendix volume XXXI. Statistics relating to Ireland, 1910 [Cd. 5244] liv, 763
Annual Report of the Local Government Board for Ireland, for the year ended 31st March, 1912, 1912–13 [Cd. 6339] xxxvii, 1
Annual Report of the Local Government Board for Ireland, for the year ended 31st March, 1913, 1913 [Cd. 6978] xxxii, 457
Annual Report of the Local Government Board for Ireland, for the year ended 31st March, 1914, 1914 [Cd. 7561] xxxix, 595

Books and articles

Books

M. Agulhon, *La Republique au Village*, Plon, Paris, 1979

M. Augulhon et al., *La Politisation des Campagnes au XIXe Siecle*, Ecole Française de Rome Editions, Rome, 2000

J. Barnes, *Irish Industrial Schools, 1868–1908: Origins and Development*, Irish Academic Press, Dublin, 1989

R. Barrington, *Health, Medicine and Politics in Ireland 1900–1970*, IPA, Dublin, 1987

P.M.H. Bell, *Disestablishment in Ireland and Wales*, SPCK, London, 1969

P. Bew, *Land and the National Question in Ireland 1858–82*; Gill & Macmillan, Dublin, 1979

P. Bew, *Conflict and Conciliation in Ireland, 1890–1910*, Clarendon Press, Oxford, 1987

G.R. Boyer, *An Economic History of the English Poor Law, 1750–1850*, Cambridge University Press, Cambridge, 1990

W.J. Braithwaite, *Lloyd George's Ambulance Wagon*, Methuen, London, 1957

I. Brandes and K. Marx-Jaskulski (eds), *Poor Relief and Charity: Rural Societies in Europe, 1850–1930*, Peter Lang, Bern, 2008

C. Breathnach, *The Congested Districts Board, 1891–1923*, Four Courts, Dublin, 2005

I. Budge and C O'Leary, *Belfast: Approach to Crisis – a Study of Belfast politics, 1613–1970*, Macmillan, London, 1973

A. Brundage, *The English Poor Laws, 1700–1930*, Palgrave, Basingstoke, 2002

P. Bull, *Land, Politics and Nationalism: a Study of the Irish Land Question*, Gill and Macmillan, Dublin, 1996

H. Burke, *The People and the Poor Law in Nineteenth Century Ireland*, WEB, Dublin, 1987

J.W.H. Carter, *The Land War and its Leaders in Queen's County, 1879–82*, Leinster Express Newspapers, Portlaoise, 1994

R.D. Cassell, *Medical Charities, Medical politics: The Irish Dispensary System and the Poor Law, 1836–72*, Royal Historical Society, Woodbridge, 1997

S. Clark, *Social Origins of the Irish Land War*, Princeton University Press, New Jersey, 1979

L.A. Clarkson and E.M. Crawford, *Feast and Famine: A history of food and nutrition in Ireland 1500–1920*, Oxford University Press, Oxford, 2001

R.V. Comerford, *The Fenians in Context: Irish Politics and Society 1848–82*, Wolfhound Press, Dublin, 1985

M. Cousins, *The Birth of Social Welfare in Ireland, 1922–1952*, Four Courts, Dublin, 2003

M. Cousins, *European Welfare States: Comparative Perspectives*, Sage, London, 2005

V. Crossman,, *Local Government in Nineteenth Century Ireland*, IIS, Belfast, 1994

V. Crossman, *Politics, Pauperism and Power in the late Nineteenth-Century Ireland*, Manchester University Press, Manchester, 2006

V. Crossman, *The Poor Law in Ireland 1838–1948*, IESHS, Dundalk, 2005

L.P. Curtis, *Coercion and Conciliation in Ireland, 1880–92: A Study in Conservative Unionism*, Princeton University Press, New Jersey, 1963

P. Devlin, *Yes we have no bananas: Outdoor Relief in Belfast, 1920–39*, Blackstaff Press, Belfats, 1981

F. Driver, *Power and Pauperism: the Workhouse System, 1834–1884*, Cambridge University Press, Cambridge, 1993

P. Durnin, *Derry and the Irish Poor Law: a History of the Derry Workhouse*, Derry, Waterside Community Local History Group, 1991

G. Esping Andersen, *Three Worlds of Welfare Capitalism*, Princeton University Press, New Jersey, 1990

M. Farrell, *The Poor Law and the Workhouse in Belfast 1838–1948*, PRONI, Belfast, 1978

W. Feingold, *The Revolt of the Tenantry. The Transformation of Local Government in Ireland 1872–1886,* Northwestern University Press, Boston, 1984

M. Finnane, *Insanity and the Insane in Post-Famine Ireland*, Croom Helm, London, 1981

M. Fraser, *John Bull's Other Homes*: *State Housing and British Policy in Ireland, 1883–1922*, Liverpool University Press, Liverpool, 1996

N. Gash, *Politics in the Age of Peel: A Study in the Technique of Parliamentary Representation 1830–1850*, Longmans, London, 1953

A. Gailey, *Ireland and the Death of Kindness: The Experience of Constructive Unionism, 1890–1905*, Cork University Press, Cork, 1987

L.M. Geary, *The Plan of Campaign, 1886–1891*, Cork University Press, Cork, 1986

L.M. Geary, *Medicine and Charity in Ireland, 1718–1851*, University College Dublin, Dublin, 2004

P. Gibbon, *The Origins of Ulster Unionism*, Manchester University Press, Manchester, 1975

B.B. Gilbert, *The Evolution of National Insurance in Great Britain*, Michael Joseph, London, 1966

P. Gordon, ed., *The Red Earl: The Papers of the Fifth Earl Spencer, 1835–1910. Volume 1, 1835–1885*, Northamptonshire Record Society, Northampton, 1982

A. Gramsci, *Prison Notebooks, Volume 3*, Columbia University Press, New York, 2007

P. Gray, *Famine, Land and Politics: British Government and Irish Society, 1843–50*, Irish Academic Press, Dublin, 1999

P. Gray, *The Making of the Irish Poor Law, 1815–43*, Manchester University Press, Manchester, 2009

A. Gueslin, *Gens Pauvres, Pauvres Gens dans la France du XiXe Siècle*, Aubier, Paris, 1998

T. Guinnane, *The Vanishing Irish: Households, Migration and the Rural Economy in Ireland*, 1850–1914, Princeton University Press, New Jersey, 1997

G.A. Hall, *Ulster Liberalism, 1778–1876: The Middle Path*, Four Courts, Dublin, 2010

S. Halperin, *War and Social Change in Modern Europe*, Cambridge University Press, Cambridge, 2004

J. Harris, *Unemployment and Politics: a Study in English Social Policy 1886–1914*, Oxford University Press, Oxford, 1972

E.P. Hennock, *The Origin of the Welfare State in England and Germany, 1850–1914. Social Policies Compared*, Cambridge University Press, Cambridge, 2007

A.C. Hepburn, *A Past Apart: Studies in the History of Catholic Belfast, 1850–1950*, UHF, Belfast, 1996

T.W. Heyck, *The Dimensions of British Radicalism: The Case of Ireland, 1874–1895*, University of Illinois Press, Urbana, 1974

K.T. Hoppen, *Elections, Politics and Society in Ireland, 1832–1885*, Clarendon, Oxford, 1984

E. Hurren, *Protesting About Pauperism: Poverty, Politics and Poor Relief in Late-Victorian England, c. 1870–1914*, Boydell and Brewer, Woodbridge, 2007

L. Kennedy, P.S. Ell, E.M. Crawford and L.A. Clarkson, *Mapping the Great Irish* Famine, Four Courts, Dublin, 1999

C. Kinealy, *The Great Irish Famine: Impact, Ideology and Rebellion*, Palgrave, Basingstoke 2002

C. Kinealy and G. MacAtasney, *Hidden Famine: Hunger, Poverty and Sectarianism in Belfast*, 1840–50, Pluto, London, 2000

S.A. King, *Poverty and Welfare in England 1700–1850: A Regional Perspective*, Manchester University Press, Manchester, 2000

S.A. King, *Women, Welfare and Local Politics, 1880–1920*, Sussex Academic Press, Brighton, 2006

S.A. King and J.W. Stewart (eds), *Welfare Peripheries: the Development of Welfare States in Nineteenth and Twentieth Century Europe*, Peter Lang, Bern, 2007

A. Jordan, *Who Cared?: Charity in Victorian and Edwardian Belfast*, IIS, Belfast, 1993

R.D. Laing and A. Esterson, *Sanity, Madness and the Family*, Penguin, Harmondsworth, 1964

E. Larkin, *The Making of the Roman Catholic Church in Ireland, 1850–1860*, University of North Carolina Press, Chapel Hill, 1980

P. Laslett and R. Wall (eds), *Household and Family in Past Time*, Cambridge University Press, Cambridge, 1971

D. Lawlor, *Divine Right? The Parnell Split in Meath*, Cork University Press, Cork, 2007

M.-L. Legg, *Newspapers and Nationalism: the Irish Provincial Press, 1850–1892*, Four Courts, Dublin, 1998

D.S. Lucey, *The Irish National League in the Dingle Poor Law Union, 1885–91*, Four Courts, Dublin, 2003

F.S.L. Lyons, *The Irish Parliamentary Party, 1890–1910*, Faber & Faber, London, 1951

J. Macnicol, *The Politics of Retirement in Britain, 1878–1948*, Cambridge University Press, Cambridge, 1988

A. Mitchell, *Revolutionary Government in Ireland: Dáil Éireann 1919–1922*, Gill & Macmillan, Dublin, 1995

J. Mokyr, *Why Ireland Starved: a Quantitative and Analytical History of the Irish Economy, 1800–1850*, Harper Collins, London, 1985

T.A. Mooney, *Compendium of the Irish Poor Laws; and general manual for the Poor Law Guardians and their officers*, Thom, Dublin, 1887

G. Moran, *A Radical Priest in Mayo: Fr Patrick Lavelle*, Four Courts Dublin, 1994

G. Moran, *Sending out Ireland's Poor: Assisted Emigration to North America in the Nineteenth Century*, Four Courts, Dublin, 2004

J. Newsinger, *Fenianism in mid-Victorian Britain*, Pluto, London, 1994

G. Nicholls, *A History of the Irish Poor Law*, Murray, London, 1856

C.C. O'Brien, *Parnell and his party, 1880–90*, Oxford University Press, Oxford, 1957

M. O'Callaghan, *British High Politics and Nationalist Ireland: Criminality, Land and the Law under Forster and Balfour*, Cork University Press, Cork, 1994

A. O'Day, *Irish Home Rule, 1867–1921*, Manchester University Press, Manchester, 1998

C. Ó Gráda, *Ireland: a New Economic History*, Oxford University Press, Oxford, 1994

C. O'Mahony, *Cork's Poor Law Palace: Workhouse Life 1838–1890*, Rosmathún Press, Cork, 2005

K.H. O'Rourke and J.G. Williamson, *Globalization and History: the Evolution of a nineteenth-Century Atlantic Economy*, MIT, Cambridge, 1999

J. O'Shea, *Priests, Politics and Society in Post-Famine Ireland*, Wolfhound Press, Dublin, 1983

M. Potter, *William Monsell of Tervoe, 1812–1894*, Irish Academic Press, Dublin, 2009

A. Power, *A Paper on Out-door Relief in Ireland*, Knight, London, 1875

J. Prest, *Lord John Russell*, University of South Carolina Press, Columbia, 1972

J. Robins, *Fools and Mad: a History of the Insane in Ireland*, IPA, Dublin, 1986

H.A.R. Robinson, *Memories: Wise and Otherwise*, Cassell & Co, London, 1924

A. Scull, *The Most Solitary of Afflictions: Madness and Society in Britain, 1700–1900*, Yale University Press, New Haven, 1993

A. Shields, *Irish Conservative Party, 1852–1868: Land, Politics and Religion*, Irish Academic Press, Dublin, 2007

M. Silverman, *An Irish Working Class: Explorations in Political Economy and Hegemony, 1900–1950*, University of Toronto Press, Toronto, 2001

E.D. Steele, *Irish Land and British Politics: Tenant-Right and Nationality 1865–1870*, Cambridge University Press, Cambridge, 1974

P. Thane, *Old Age in English History: Part Experiences, Present Issues*, Oxford University Press, Cambridge, 2000

D. Thornley, *Isaac Butt and Home Rule*, Macgibbon and Kee, London, 1964

P. Travers, *Settlements and Divisions: Ireland, 1870–1922*, Helicon, Dublin, 1988

M. Turner, *After the Famine: Irish agriculture 1850–1914*, Cambridge University Press, Cambridge, 1996

D. Urquhart, *Women in Ulster Politics, 1890–1940*, Irish Academic Press, Dublin, 2000

K. van Kersbergen and P. Manow, eds, *Religion, Class Coalitions, and Welfare States*, Cambridge University Press, Cambridge, 2009

W.E. Vaughan and A.J. Fitzpatrick, *Irish Historical Statistics: Population*, Royal Irish Academy, Dublin, 1978

B.M. Walker, *Parliamentary election results in Ireland, 1801–1922*, Royal Irish Academy, Dublin, 1978

E. Weber, *Peasants into Frenchmen: The Modernization of Rural France 1870–1914*, Stanford University Press, Stanford, 1976

M. Wheatley, *Nationalism and the Irish Party: Provincial Ireland 1910–16*, Oxford University Press, Oxford, 2005

J.H. Whyte, *The Independent Irish Party, 1850–9*, Oxford University Press, Oxford, 1958

K. Williams, *From Pauperism to Poverty*, Routledge and Kegan Paul, London, 1981

Woodford Heritage Group, *A Forgotten Campaign*, Woodford Heritage Group, Woodford, 1986

Woodford Heritage Group, *Clanricarde Country and the Land Campaign*, Woodford Heritage Group, Woodford, 1987

Articles and chapters

A. Alesina, E. Glaeser and B. Sacerdote, 'Why Doesn't the United States Have a European-Style Welfare State?', *Brookings Papers on Economic Activity*, 32, (2001), 187–278

B. Althammer, I. Brandes and K. Marx-Jaskulski, 'Religiously motivated charitable work in modern times. Catholic congregations in the Rhineland and Ireland', in A. Gestrich, L. Raphael, and H. Uerlings (eds), *Strangers and Poor People: Changing Patterns of Inclusion and Exclusion in Europe and the Mediterranean World from Classical Antiquity to the Present Day*, Peter Lang, Bern, 2009, 371–414

W. Arts and J. Gelissen, 'Welfare States, Solidarity and Justice Principles: Does the Type Really Matter?', *Acta Sociologica*, 44(4), (2001), 283–99

A. Blaikie, 'Nuclear Hardship or Variant Dependency? Households and the Scottish Poor Law', *Continuity and Change*, 17, (2002), 253–80

G.R. Boyer, 'The Old Poor Law and the Agricultural Labour Market in Southern England: an Empirical Analysis', *Journal of Economic History*, xlvi, (1986), 113–36

G.R. Boyer, 'The Poor Law, Migration, and Economic Growth', *Journal of Economic History*, 46(2), (1986), 419–30

G.R. Boyer, 'Malthus was right after all: Poor Relief and Birth Rates in South-Eastern England', *Journal of Political Economy*, 97, (1989), 93–114

J.W. Boyle, 'A Marginal Figure: The Irish Rural Laborer', in S. Clark and J.S. Donnelly (eds), *Irish Peasants: Violence and Political Unrest, 1780–1914*, University of Wisconsin Press, Madison, 1983

I. Brandes, '"Odious, degrading and foreign" institutions? Analysing Irish Workhouses in the Nineteenth and Twentieth Centuries', in A. Gestrich, S. King and L. Raphael (eds), *Being Poor in Modern Europe: Historical Perspectives 1800–1940*, Peter Lang, Bern, 2006, 199–228

N.P. Canny, 'Fusion and Faction in Modern Ireland: a Review Article', *Comparative Studies in Society and History*, 26(2), (1984), 352–65

M. Caplan, 'The New Poor Law and the Struggle for Union Chargeability,' *International Review of Social History*, 23(2), (1978), 267–300

G. Clark and M. Page, 'Is there Profit in Reforming the Poor? The English Poor Law 1830–1842', Department of Economics UC-Davis, Davis, 2000

M. Cohen, 'Religion and Inequality in Ireland', *Journal of Interdisciplinary History*, xxv(1), (1994), 1–21

R.V. Comerford, 'Ireland 1850–70: Post-Famine and Mid-Victorian', in W.E. Vaughan (ed.), *A New History of Ireland*, volume V, Oxford University Press, Oxford, 1989

M. Cousins, 'Poor Law Politics and Elections in Post-Famine Ireland' *History Studies*, 6, (2005) 34–47

M. Cousins, 'Registration of the Religion of Children under the Irish Poor Law, 1838–70', *Journal of Ecclesiastical History*, 61(1), (2010), 107–24

M. Cousins, 'Charity, philanthropy and poverty in Ireland, 1850–1914' in I. Brandes and K. Marx-Jaskulski (eds), *Poor relief and charity: rural societies in Europe, 1850–1930*, Peter Lang, Bern, 2008

M. Cousins, 'The Creation of Association: the National Insurance Act 1911 and Approved Societies in Ireland', in J. Kelly and R.V. Comerford (eds), *Associational Culture in Ireland and Abraod*, Irish Academic Press, Dublin, 2010

M. Cousins, 'Collective Action and the Poor Law: The Political Mobilisation of the Irish Poor, 1851–1878', in W. Sheehan and M. Cronin (eds), *Riotous Assemblies: Riots, Rebels, & Revolts*, Mercier Press, Cork, 2011, 110–26

V. Crossman, 'The New Ross Workhouse Riot of 1887: Nationalism, Class and the Irish Poor Laws', *Past and Present*, 179, (2003), 135–58

V. Crossman, '"With the experience of 1846 and 1847 before them": The Politics of Emergency Relief 1879–84', in P. Gray (ed.), *Victoria's Ireland: Irishness and Britishness, 1837–1901*, Four Courts Press, Dublin, 2004, 167–82

V. Crossman, 'The Charm of Allowing People to Manage Their Own Affairs: Political Perspectives on Emergency Relief in Late Nineteenth-Century Ireland', in D.G. Boyce and A. O'Day (eds), *Ireland in Transition 1867–1921*, Routledge, London, 2004, 193–208

V. Crossman, 'The humanization of the Irish Poor Laws: Reassessing developments in social welfare in post-Famine Ireland', in A. Gestrich, S. King and L. Raphael (eds), *Being Poor in Modern Europe: Historical Perspectives 1800–1940*, Peter Lang, Bern, 2006, 229–50

V. Crossman, 'Welfare and Nationality: The poor laws in nineteenth-century Ireland', in S. King and J.W.S. Stewart (eds), *Welfare Peripheries: The Development of Welfare States in Nineteenth and Twentieth Century Europe*, Peter Lang, Bern, 2007, 67–96

V. Crossman, 'Cribbed, Contained and Confined? The Care of Children under the Irish Poor Law', *Éire – Ireland*, 44(1–2), (2009), 37–61

V. Crossman, 'Facts Notorious to the Whole Country': The Political Battle over Irish Poor Law Reform in the 1860s, *Transactions Of The RHS*, 20, (2010), 157–69

L.P. Curtis, 'Landlord Responses to the Irish Land War, 1879–1887,' *Éire-Ireland*, 38(3–4), (2003), 134–88

R. Dingwall, J.M. Eekelaar, T. Murray, 'Childhood as a Social Problem: A Survey of the History of Legal Regulation', *Journal of Law and Society*, 11(2), (1984), 207–32

P. Durnin, 'Aspects of Poor Law Administration and the Workhouse in Derry 1838–1948', in G. O'Brien (ed.), *Derry and Londonderry: History and Society*, Geography Press, Dublin, 1991

M. Finnane, 'Asylums, Families and the State', *History Workshop Journal*, 20, (1985), 134–48

D. Fitzpatrick, 'The Disappearance of the Agricultural Labourer, 1841–1912', *Irish Economic and Social History*, 7 (1980), 66–92

D. Fitzpatrick, 'Irish Farming Families before the First World War', *Comparative Studies in Society and History*, 25, (1983), 339–74

M.W. Flynn, 'Medical Services under the New Poor Law' in D. Fraser (ed.), *The New Poor Law in the Nineteenth Century*, Macmillan, London, 1976

C. Ford, 'Tradition in the Politicisation of Rural France during the Nineteenth Century', in *La Politisation des Campagnes au XIXe Siècle, France, Italie, Espagne, Portugal*, École française de Rome, Rome, 2000

M. Foucault, 'The Subject and Power', in H.L. Dreyfus and P. Rabinow, *Michel Foucault: Beyond Structuralism and Hermeneutics*, University of Chicago, Chicago, 1982

F. Geary and T. Stark, 'Examining Ireland's Post-Famine Economic Performance: the Distribution of Gross Domestic Product between the Countries of the United Kingdom, 1861–1911', ESRI working paper 71, Dublin, 1996

P. Gibbon and C. Curtin, 'The Stem Family in Ireland', *Comparative Studies in Society and History*, 20 (1979), 429–53

T.W. Guinnane, 'The Poor Law and Pensions in Ireland', *Journal of Interdisciplinary History*, 24(2), (1993), 271–91

T.J. Hatton and J.G. Williamson, 'After the Famine: Emigration from Ireland 1850–1913', *Journal of Economic History*, 53, (1993), 575–600

J.P. Huzel, 'Malthus, the Poor Law, and Population in Early Nineteenth-Century England', xxii, (1969), *Economic History Review*, 430–52

J.P. Huzel, 'The Demographic Impact of the Old Poor Law: More Reflexions on Malthus', xxxiii (1980), *Economic History Review*, 367–81

A. Jackson, 'Unionist Politics and Protestant Society in Edwardian Ireland', *Historical Journal*, 33(4), (1990), 839–66

S. Kahl, 'The Religious Roots of Modern Poverty Policy: Catholic, Lutheran, and Reformed Protestant Traditions Compared', *Archives Européennes de Sociologie*, xlvi(1), (2005), 91–126

K.A. Kennedy, 'Irish National Accounts for the Nineteenth and Twentieth Century' ESRI memorandum series 197, Dublin, 1994

L. Kennedy, 'Farmers, Traders and Agricultural Politics in Pre-Independence Ireland', in L. Kennedy, *Colonialism, Religion and Nationalism in Ireland*, IIS, Belfast, 1996

L. Kennedy, 'The Cost of Living in Ireland, 1698–1998', in D. Dickson, and C. Ó Gráda (eds), *Refiguring Ireland: Essays in honour of L.M. Cullen*, Lilliput Press, Dublin, 2003, 249–76

L. Kiesling, 'Institutional Choice Matters: The Poor Law and Implicit Labor Contracts in Victorian Lancashire' *Explorations in Economic History*, 33(1), (1996), 65–85

S.A. King, 'Poor Relief and English Economic Development Reappraised', *Economic History Review*, l, (1997) 2, 360–8

S.A. King, 'Pauvreté et Assistance. La Politique Locale de la Mortalité dans l'Angleterre des XVIIIe et XIXe Siècles', *Annales*, 61(1), (2006), 31–62

A. Jackson, 'Unionist Politics and Protestant Society in Edwardian Ireland', *Historical Journal*, 33(4),(1990), 839–66

D. Jordan, 'The Irish National League and the "unwritten law": Rural protest and Nation-Building in Ireland 1882–1890', *Past and Present*, 158, (1998), 146–71

F. Lane, 'P.F. Johnson, Nationalism and Irish Rural Labourers, 1869–82', *Irish Historical Studies*, xxxiii, (2002), 191–208

F. Lane, 'Rural Labourers, Social Change and Politics in late Nineteenth-Century Ireland', in D. Ó Drisceoil and F. Lane, (eds), *Politics and the Irish Working Class, 1830–1945*, Palgrave Macmillan, Basingstoke, 2005

L. Le Gall, 'Des Processus de Politisation dans les Campagnes Françaises (1830–1914): Esquisse pour un État des Lieux', in J.-C. Caron, F. Chauvaud (eds) *Les Campagnes dans les Sociétés Européennes (1830–1930)*, PUR, Reims, 2005

M. Levine-Clark, 'The Gendered Economy of Family Liability: Intergenerational Relationships and Poor Law Relief in England's Black Country, 1871–1911', *Journal of British Studies* 45, (2006), 72–89

P. Lindert, 'Poor Relief before the Welfare State: Britain versus the Continent, 1780–1880', *European Review of Economic History*, (1998), 101–40

P.M. McPhee, 'Contours Nationaux et Regionaux de L'Associationnisme Politique en France (1830–1880)' in *La politisation des campagnes au XIXe siècle, France, Italie, Espagne, Portugal.* Rome, École française de Rome, Rome, 2000

E. Malcolm, 'The Asylum, Family and Emigration', in E. Malcolm and G. Jones (eds), *Medicine, Disease and the State in Ireland*, Cork University Press, 1999

T. Margadant, 'Comment on Charles Tilly's "Social Movements"', *Theory and Society*, 27, (1998), 481–8

F. Neal, 'The English Poor Law, the Irish Migrant and the Laws of Settlement and Removal, 1819–1879', in D.G. Boyce and R. Swift, (eds), *Problems and Perspectives in Irish History since 1800,* Four Courts, Dublin, 2004

G. O'Brien, 'The Establishment of Poor-Law Unions in Ireland, 1838–43', *Irish Historical Studies*, xxiii(90), (1982), 97–120

C. Ó Gráda, '"The Greatest Blessing of All": The Old Age Pension in Ireland', *Past and Present*, 175: 124–61

T.P. O'Neill, 'The Catholic Church and Relief of the Poor, 1815–45', *Archivium Hibernicum* 31, (1973,) 132–45

K.H. O'Rourke, 'Monetary Data and Proxy GDP estimates: Ireland 1840–1921', *Irish Economic and Social History*, 25, (1998), 22–51

A.W. Orridge, 'Who Supported the Land War?: an Aggregate-Data Analysis of Irish Agrarian Discontent, 1879–1882', *Economic and Social Review*, 12, (1981), 203–33

L. Rothfield, 'Medical', in H.F. Tucker (ed.), *A Companion to Victorian Literature and Culture*, Blackwell, London, 1998

I. Scherder, 'Galway Workhouses in the Nineteenth and Twentieth centuries: Function and Strategy', in A. Gestrich, S. King and L. Raphael (eds), *Being Poor in Modern Europe: Historical Perspectives 1800–1940*, Peter Lang, Bern, 2006, 181–99

C. Shannon, 'The Ulster Liberal Unionists and Local Government Reform, 1885–1898', in *Reactions to Irish Nationalism, 1865–1914*, Gill and Macmillan, Dublin, 1987

M. Silverman and P.H. Gulliver, '"Common sense" and "governmentality": local government in southeastern Ireland, 1850–1922', *Journal of the Royal Anthropological Institute*, 12 (2006), 109–27

P. Solar, 'Poor Relief and English Economic Development before the Industrial Revolution', *Economic History Review*, xlviii, (1995), 11–22

P. Solar, 'Poor Relief and English Economic Development: a Renewed Plea for Comparative History', *Economic History Review*, l, (1997), 369–74

G. Steinmetz, 'The Local Welfare State: Two Strategies for Social Domination in urban Imperial Germany', *American Sociological Review*, 55, (1990), 891–911

P. Thane, 'Non Contributory versus Insurance Pensions, 1878–1908', in P. Thane (ed.), *Origins of British Social Policy*, Croom Helm, London, 1978

C. Tilly, 'Social Movements and (all sorts of) other Political Interactions – Local, National and International – including Identities', *Theory and Society*, 27, (1998), 453–80

J. Underhill Hannon, 'Poverty in the Antebellum Northeast: the view from New York State's Poor Relief Rolls', *Journal of Economic History*, xliv(4), (1984), 1007–32

A.W. Vincent, 'The Poor Law Reports of 1909 and the Social Theory of the Charity Organisation Society', in D. Gladstone, (ed.), *Before Beveridge: Welfare before the Welfare State*, Institute of Economic Affairs Health and Welfare Unit, London, 1999, 64–85

E. Weber, 'Comment La Politique Vint aux Paysans: A Second Look at Peasant Politicization', *American Historical Review*, 87, (1982), 357–89

I. Whelan, 'The Stigma of Souperism' in C. Pórtéir (ed.), *The Great Irish Famine*, Mercier, Dublin, 1995

J.H. Whyte, 'The Influence of the Catholic Clergy on Elections in Nineteenth-Century Ireland', *Catholic Historical Review*, lxxv (1960), 239–59

J.H. Whyte, 'Landlord Influence at Elections in Ireland, 1760–1885', *English Historical Review*, lxxx (1965), 740–60

Unpublished works

M. Cousins, 'The Voting Behaviour of the Irish Parliamentary Party on Social Issues, 1881–90', paper to the Irish Historical Society, November, 2007

M. Cousins, 'Poor Relief in Ireland, 1851–1914', PhD, Glasgow Caledonian University, 2010

A. Schüle, 'Outdoor Relief in Milford Union, County Donegal, Ireland from 1859 to 1922', Thesis, University of Trier, 2006

Index